K

*Nathan Mayer Rothschild
and the Creation of a Dynasty*

Nathan Mayer Rothschild and the Creation of a Dynasty

THE CRITICAL YEARS
1806–1816

Herbert H. Kaplan

STANFORD UNIVERSITY PRESS

STANFORD, CALIFORNIA

2006

Stanford University Press
Stanford, California

Printed in the United States of America on acid-free, archival-quality paper

Library of Congress Cataloging-in-Publication Data

Kaplan, Herbert H.
 Nathan Mayer Rothschild and the creation of a dynasty : the critical years 1806-1816 / Herbert H. Kaplan.
  p. cm.
 Includes bibliographical references and index.
 ISBN 0-8047-5165-x (cloth : alk. paper)
 1. Rothschild, Nathan Meyer, 1777-1836. 2. Bankers—England—London—Biography.
3. Jewish capitalists and financiers—England—London—Biography. 4. Banks and banking—England—London—History—19th century. 5. Banks and banking—Europe—History—19th century. 6. Napoleonic Wars, 1800-1815—Participation, British. 7. Rothschild family. I. Title.
 HG1552.R83K37 2006
 332.1'092—dc22   2005012306

Original Printing 2005

Last figure below indicates year of this printing:
13   12   11   10   09   08   07   06   05

Typeset by Classic Typography in 11/14 Adobe Garamond

For Judee

In Memory
Jacob Gerstein
1902–1995
Janus Ewens Singer
1901–1996
Barbara Polan Kaplan
1939–1997
Frances Kaplan Malet
1918–2003
Leonard Greenspan
1920–2004

Contents

Figures and Tables

Abbreviations

AH	Abraham Hertz
Ams.	Amsterdam
And.	R. J. Anderson. Deputy Commissary-General
B	Earl Bathurst. Secretary-at-War
BB	Braunsberg & Co. Amsterdam
BC	Benjamin Cohen
Ber.	Berlin
BL	British Library
BLAddMss.	British Library Additional Manuscripts
BP	*Bathurst Papers*. Loan 57. The British Library Manuscript Collections. London
Buist	Buist, Marten G. *At Spes Non Fracta. Hope & Co. 1770–1815. Merchant Bankers and Diplomats at Work*. Hague: Bank Mees & Hope NV, 1974.
Burg	Sir George Burgmann. Commissary-General. Amsterdam
Bru.	Brussels
C	Viscount Castlereagh. Foreign Secretary
CMR	Carl Mayer Rothschild
Correspondence	*Correspondence, Despatches, and Other Papers of Viscount Castlereagh, Second Marquess of Londonderry*. Edited by His Brother, Charles William Vane, Marquess of Londonderry. Third Series. Military and Diplomatic. London. John Murray, 1853. Vol. IX.
Corti	Corti, Count Egon Caesar. *The Rise of the House of Rothschild*. Translated from the German by Brian and Beatrix Lunn. New York: Cosmopolitan Book Corporation, 1928.

Craig	Craig, Sir John. *The Mint. A History of the London Mint from A.D. 287 to 1948.* Cambridge: Cambridge University Press, 1953.
Crom	D. Crommelin & Sn. Amsterdam
Dun.	Dunkerque
Dyer	Dyer, G. P. "The Royal Mint and the Striking of Louis d'Or, 1815," *Seaby. Coin & Medal Bulletin* (Dec. 1977).
ER	Ewart, Rutson & Co. Liverpool
Faber	Frederick Faber & Co. Paris. & Richard Faber & Co. Dunkerque
Ferguson	Ferguson, Niall. *The House of Rothschild. Money's Prophets 1798–1848.* New York: Viking Penguin, 1998.
Fft.	Frankfurt
GAA	Gemeentearchief, Amsterdam
Gash	*Wellington. Studies in the Military and Political Career of the First Duke of Wellington.* Edited by Norman Gash. Manchester: Manchester University Press, 1990.
GH	George Harrison. Assistant-Secretary to the Treasury
Gos.	Gosport
Got.	Gothenburg
Gray & Aspey	*The Life and Times of N M Rothschild 1777–1836.* Edited by Victor Gray and Melanie Aspey. London: N M Rothschild & Sons, 1998.
H	John Charles Herries. Commissary-in-Chief
Ham.	Hamburg
Har	Harman & Co. London
Harw.	Harwich
HC	Hunt Cullen
Hel.	Hellevoetsluis
H. *Mem.*	Herries, Edward. *Memoir of the Public Life of the Right Hon. JOHN CHARLES HERRIES in the Reigns of George III, George IV, William IV, and Victoria.* 2 vols. London: John Murray, 1880.
HP	*Herries Papers*, British Library
HW	Henry Wellesley
JB	Joseph Barber
JC	Joseph Cohen

JF	John Fox
JmD	James Drummond. Office of Commissary-in-Chief
JMR	James Mayer Rothschild
Jonker	Joost Jonker. *Merchants, Bankers, Middlemen. The Amsterdam Money Market During the First Half of the 19th Century.* Amsterdam: NEHA, 1996.
JR	John Roworth
Kelly	Kelly, E. M. *Spanish Dollars and Silver Tokens. An Account of the Issues of the Bank of England 1797–1816.* London: Spink & Son Ltd., 1976.
L	Earl of Liverpool. Prime Minister
LP	*Liverpool Papers.* British Library
Lis.	Lisbon
Liv.	Liverpool
LJ	*London Journals.* RAL
Lon.	London
Man.	Manchester
MAR	Mayer Amschel Rothschild
M & B	Meyer & Bruxner. St. Petersburg
MD	Mayer Davidson
Morel	Veuve Dominique Morel & Frères Dunkerque, Paris & Gravelines

MPG & S: 1810–1811   An ACCOUNT Of the Market Prices of Standard GOLD in Bars; Foreign (i. e. Portugal) GOLD in Coin; Standard SILVER in Bars; and Spanish DOLLARS; or Pillar Pieces of EIGHT: with The Courses of EXCHANGE with Hamburgh, Lisbon, and Paris:—From the 3d of January 1718, to the 3d of December 1736; and from the 3d of January 1746, to the 1st of March 1811 inclusive. Great Britain. Parliament. House of Commons. X, printed 30, penciled 227. Ordered, by The House of Commons, to be printed, 4 March 1811.

MPG & S: 1811–1813   An ACCOUNT Of the MARKET PRICES of Standard GOLD in Bars, Portugal GOLD in Coin, Standard SILVER in Bars, and Spanish DOLLARS: with The Courses of Exchange with Hamburgh, Lisbon, and Paris; from the 1st of March 1811 to 1st of February 1813 inclusive. Great Britain. Parliament. House of Commons. XIII, 131–135. Ordered, by The House of Commons, to be printed, 6 April 1813.

MPG & S: 1813–1814   An ACCOUNT of the MARKET PRICES of Standard
GOLD in Bars, Portugal GOLD in Coin; Standard SILVER in
Bars, and Spanish Dollars or Pillar Pieces-of-Eight:—with the
COURSES of EXCHANGE with Hamburgh, Lisbon, and
Paris:—From the 1st of February 1813, to the 1st of March 1814.
Great Britain. Parliament. House of Commons. XII, 115–117.
Ordered, by The House of Commons, to be printed, 5 April 1814.

MPG & S: 1814–1815   An ACCOUNT of the MARKET PRICES of Standard
GOLD in Bars, Portugal GOLD in Coin; Standard SILVER in
Bars, and Spanish Dollars or Pillar Pieces-of-Eight; with the
COURSES of EXCHANGE with Hamburgh, Lisbon, and
Paris:—From the 1st of March 1814, to the 9th of February 1815.
Great Britain. Parliament. House of Commons. X, 231–233.
Ordered, by The House of Commons, to be Printed, 13
February 1815.

MPG & S: 1815–1816   An ACCOUNT of the MARKET PRICES of Standard
GOLD in Bars, Portugal GOLD in Coin; Standard SILVER in
Bars, and Spanish Dollars or Pillar Pieces-of-Eight; with the
COURSES of EXCHANGE with Hamburgh, Lisbon, and
Paris:—From the 9th of February 1815 to the 26th of April 1816
inclusive. Great Britain. Parliament. House of Commons. XIII,
288. Ordered, by The House of Commons, to be Printed, 1
May 1816.

MPG & S: 1816   An ACCOUNT of the MARKET PRICES of Standard GOLD
in Bars, Portugal GOLD in Coin; Standard SILVER in Bars,
and Spanish Dollars or Pillar Pieces-of-Eight; with the COURSE
of EXCHANGE with Hamburgh, Lisbon, and Paris:—From
the 1st of January 1816 to the 1st of January 1817. Great Britain.
Parliament. House of Commons. XVII, 71. Ordered, by The
House of Commons, to be Printed, 25 February 1817.

MPG & S: 1817   An ACCOUNT of the MARKET PRICES of Standard GOLD
in Bars, Portugal GOLD in Coin; Standard SILVER in Bars,
and Spanish Dollars or Pillar Pieces-of-Eight; with the COURSE
of EXCHANGE with Hamburgh, Lisbon, and Paris:—From
the 1st of January 1817 to the 3rd of February 1818. Great
Britain. Parliament. House of Commons. XIV, 30. Ordered, by
The House of Commons, to be Printed, 13 February 1818.

Muir   Muir, Rory. *Britain and the Defeat of Napoleon, 1807–1815*. New
Haven: Yale University Press, 1996.

NMR   Nathan Mayer Rothschild

Orbell   Orbell, John. *Baring Brothers & Co., Limited. A History to 1939.*
London: Baring Brothers & Co. Limited, 1985.

PF	Peter Fawcett
P. P. Gold Bullion, 1810	Great Britain. Parliament. House of Commons. "Report together with Minutes of Evidence, and Accounts, from the Select Committee on the High Price of Gold Bullion." Ordered, by The House of Commons, to be printed, 8 June 1810.
PRO	The Public Record Office at Kew
PRO AO	The Public Record Office at Kew. Account Office
PROB	The Public Record Office, The Family Records Centre. London
PRO MINT	The Public Record Office at Kew. Mint Papers
PROT	The Public Record Office at Kew. Treasury Papers
RAL	The Rothschild Archive. London
Report	*Report on the Manuscripts of Earl Bathurst, Preserved at Cirencester Park*. London: Historical Manuscripts Commission, 1923.
RL	Rothschild Ledgers: 1809–1810
Rot.	Rotterdam
SC	Solomon/Selig Cohen
Sherwig	Sherwig, John M. *Guineas and Gunpowder. British Foreign Aid in the Wars with France. 1793–1815*. Cambridge: Harvard University Press, 1969.
StP.	St. Petersburg
TD	Thomas Dunmore. Commissary-General. Brussels & Amsterdam
TJHSE	*Transactions. The Jewish Historical Society of England*
Thompson	Thompson, Neville. *Earl Bathurst and The British Empire, 1762–1834*. Barnsley, South Yorkshire, Great Britain: Leo Cooper, 1999.
V	Nicholas Vansittart. Chancellor of Exchequer
VP	*Vansittart Papers. Correspondence of Lord Bexley*. British Library
W	Sir Arthur Wellesley, the Duke of Wellington
WD	*The Dispatches of Field Marshal The Duke of Wellington, During His Various Campaigns in India, Denmark, Portugal, Spain, The Low Countries, and France, from 1799 to 1818*. Compiled from Official and Authentic Documents, by Lieut. Colonel Gurwood. London: John Murray, 1838. Vols. IX–XI.
WF	William Fawcett
WH	William Hamilton. Foreign Office

Will. LBC *Will of Levy Barent Cohen.* PROB 11/1480, under 464, ff. 372–374, filed 14 April 1807/17 June 1808.

WP *Wellington Papers.* Archives and Manuscripts. University of Southampton Library, Southampton, UK.

WSD Wellington, 2nd. Duke of, ed., *Supplementary Despatches, Correspondence, and Memoranda of Field Marshal Arthur, Duke of Wellington, K. G.* London: John Murray, 1858–1872. Vols. VII–VIII.

Weights and Measures

£	=	English pound Sterling = 20 shillings
cf	=	Current [market value of] Dutch florin/guilder
Dollar	=	Spanish-American silver coin
Doubloon	=	Spanish-American gold coin
Ducat	=	Gold coin
Dutch florin/guilder	=	Dutch silver coin = 28 stuivers
English guinea	=	English gold coin = 21 shillings
English shilling	=	12 pence
Friedrich d'Or	=	Prussian gold coin = pistole = 5 thaler
George d'Or	=	Hanoverian gold coin = pistole = 5 thaler
Louis d'Or	=	French 20 franc gold coin
Napoléon d'Or	=	French 20 franc gold coin struck from 1805 to 1815
Port	=	Portuguese-Brazilian gold coin

Troy Weight:

dwt	=	denarius/denarii
	=	1. a Roman silver coin of varying intrinsic value
	=	2. in English monetary reckoning, a penny
24 grains	=	1 dwt
1 dwt	=	1 pennyweight
20 pennyweights	=	1 ounce
12 ounces	=	1 pound

By Way of a Preface

It was coincidence that led me to research and write about the creation of the Rothschild financial dynasty. Just prior to the 200th anniversary of the arrival in England in 1798 of Nathan Mayer Rothschild (1777–1836) from the Jewish ghetto in Frankfurt, I arrived at The Rothschild Archive in London in search of sources relating to the long-established mercantile firm of Levy Barent Cohen (1747–1808), who had been London's leading international diamond trader and who happened to be Nathan Rothschild's father-in-law. Soon after I began my research on Cohen, I was surprised to learn that there were still important questions regarding Nathan that remained unanswered relating to how he made his money and how much he had made. I could not resist the challenge of seeking the answers to those questions.

The challenge was not a simple one. I discovered that, while the history of the Rothschilds has been a well-plowed field, it has not been plowed well. All accounts, including the most recent and the most notable, contain errors of fact and repeated myths, for example, that Nathan Rothschild profited from receiving early news of Napoleon's defeat at Waterloo. I was persuaded that a study based on extant contemporary sources should be written to explain when and how Nathan unexpectedly catapulted into the leadership of Europe's merchant-banking elite, and how, within a generation, Nathan and his four brothers created a financial dynasty the likes of which were unknown in modern times.

For many years, these questions could not possibly have been answered authoritatively. I was reminded of this by David S. Landes, Harvard University Professor Emeritus of History and Economics, when he presented the Inaugural Rothschild Archive Lecture on 30 May 2000.[1] Landes quoted Joseph Wechsberg's declarative statement from his 1966 book *The Merchant Bankers*:

"The Rothschild legend has long ago outrun the facts. This is the Rothschilds' own fault. They are even more reticent and aloof than other merchant bankers when family matters are concerned. They developed the technique of absolute discretion to perfection. Their family labyrinths are complex. . . . Significantly, no Rothschild-approved history of the family has yet appeared. A whole library of books exists about the Rothschilds. All were written without their blessing, often against their wishes, mostly without their co-operation, and sometimes they have protested in court against them.

No one has ever gone through all the family archives. Perhaps once a Rothschild will be permitted but certainly not an outsider. The family has produced many diversified talents in the past two hundred years. Someday there will be a historian named Rothschild and he will write *the* book."[2]

In 1982, Lord Rothschild published *The Shadow of a Great Man*[3] but it is not what Wechsberg had in mind in 1966. *The Shadow of a Great Man* has merit but it is not a full-length study based on an exhaustive investigation of the Rothschild archival manuscripts.

The book that I have written is such a study. But it is not a biography of Nathan Rothschild nor is it a history of the Rothschild family. The available contemporary sources simply do not contain the kind of information that would make those possible. The details for which are almost wholly absent from the multivolume collections of archival sources at The Rothschild Archive and The British Library Manuscripts Collections, two repositories central to this study. Nathan left no philosophical tracts, diaries, memoirs, or other writings that would have provided insight into his character or personality. The bulk of the manuscripts above his name concern his business transactions and reveal that he was a tough negotiator. His autograph appears rarely. John Charles Herries, the British Commissary-in-Chief, who met with him almost daily from 1814 to 1816, rarely remarked about Nathan the man. The richest source for understanding Nathan's personality and character remains the family correspondence which, while primarily focusing on business transactions, is laced with personal commentary and acrimonious exchanges.

This study is a narrative that traces the development of Nathan's early career as merchant, arbitrager, and banker and how he and his brothers exploited circumstance and opportunity during the Napoleonic wars. Subsequently, they created one of the more extraordinarily wealthy and powerful financial institutions in the world during the nineteenth century.

Many of the archival sources used for this study have never before been researched. The greatest number of these are deposited in three archives:

The Rothschild Archive in London [RAL], The Public Record Office at Kew Gardens [PRO], and The British Library in London [BL]. Additional essential sources are in the Hope & Co. collection at the Gemeentearchief, Amsterdam [GAA], in The Wellington Papers at the University of Southampton Library, Southampton, UK [WP], in the Northbrook Papers at the Baring Archive, ING Group NV, London, and the Public Record Office, The Family Records Centre, London [PROB].

The manuscripts in The Rothschild Archive in London comprise several different categories of value for this study but the correspondence of the five Rothschild brothers is indispensable. The Rothschilds wrote in several languages: English, French, German, and Judendeutsch, which was the spoken German of Frankfurt during the first two decades of the nineteenth century and which was written in Hebrew script. Judendeutsch is one of the more difficult languages to translate into intelligible English, not only because the original letters are devoid of punctuation but also because their authors presumably wrote in as unsophisticated a manner as they spoke. Following the Second World War, a team of "translators" undertook to summarize into English a voluminous number of the Judendeutsch correspondence, which now comprises the T-files at RAL, but these translations are untrustworthy. About fifteen years ago, the archival administration undertook to translate anew these letters in a team-organized project that still is in progress. Each of the Judendeutsch letters is translated into oral German and taped, and that tape is subsequently transcribed into a German text and translated into English. I have used this set of Judendeutsch letters as translated into English. From time to time, I have consulted Mr. Mordichae Zucker and Dr. Rainer Liedtke (members of the translation team) about letters I have considered problematic and I have acknowledged their assistance in notes. Nevertheless, I am solely responsible for use of the Judendeutsch letters in English translation.

The multivolume collection of the John Charles Herries Papers at the British Library [HP] was as indispensable for this study as the manuscripts at RAL. As Commissary-in-Chief, Herries not only held an extraordinarily important position in the British government and was charged with supplying money to the British Military Chest on the Continent and paying subsidies to British allies who fought against Napoleon, but he also was the only British official who supervised and met with Nathan Rothschild almost daily for the purpose of executing these responsibilities. From time to time, Herries corresponded with Nathan's brothers and worked with them when he visited Amsterdam, Frankfurt, and Paris. Moreover, while RAL contains many important manuscripts and accounts associated directly or indirectly with Herries, the Herries Papers contain several volumes of manuscripts and accounts associated directly or indirectly with Nathan Rothschild and his brothers.

The archives of The Royal Mint are currently deposited at the PRO and they contain information relating to the British government's minting of foreign gold coins—namely, the Hanoverian George d'Or and the French Louis d'Or, which Herries and the Rothschilds deposited into the Military Chest and also used to pay subsidies to Great Britain's allies. These sources and those at the BL and RAL are crucial to an understanding of how the Royal Mint was used to effect British policy during the later years of the war against Napoleon.

The multibox collection of Treasury Papers at the PRO provide a detailed contemporary account of the Treasury's responsibilities and actions regarding money flows into the Military Chest and subsidies paid to Great Britain's allies. It contains numerous communications to and from Nathan Rothschild, John Charles Herries, and Commissary Generals. However, it is a difficult collection to work with because the materials are not catalogued in a straightforward manner. The reports and correspondence addressing a particular affair of state are clustered together, with each report or correspondence folded one into the other and with the business of each sometimes covering a period of several years. The only way to research these papers effectively is to go through each piece in every box from the later months of 1813 through March 1816.

Notes

1. "Research Is the Art of Encounter: The Sources of Business History," *The Rothschild Archive. Review of the Year April 1999–March 2000* (London: The Rothschild Archive Trust), p. 7.

2. Ibid., citing Wechsberg, Joseph. *The Merchant Bankers* (paperback ed.). New York: Pocket Books, by arrangement with Little, Brown, pp. 263–64.

3. London: New Court, St. Swithin's Lane.

Acknowledgments

I wish to thank the Trustees of The Rothschild Archive, London, for providing me access to its repository of manuscripts. I am exceedingly grateful to Mr. Victor Gray, Director, Ms. Melanie Aspey, Archivist, Ms. Elaine Penn, Assistant Archivist, Mr. Mordichae Zucker and Dr. Rainer Liedtke (members of the translation team), and other members of the staff who not only facilitated but also encouraged my research activities over several years. Hardly a day passed when I did not burden them with a question, a request, or a conversation about my work. Special mention is due to Melanie Aspey, who from the moment she greeted me on my first day at the Archive, was a continuing source of inspiration and erudition.

I am indebted to the staffs of the British Library, the Public Record Office at Kew, the Public Record Office, The Family Records Centre, London, the University of Southampton Library, Southampton, UK, and Gemeentearchief, Amsterdam for their assistance. Lou J. Malcomb, Head, Government Information, Microforms and Statistical Services, made available to me the excellent library resources of Indiana University in Bloomington. I am thankful to Dr. John Orbell and Jane Waller, archivists of The Baring Archive, ING Group NV, London, for my introduction to The Rothschild Archive and for permission to reference Baring Brothers archival manuscripts.

I wish to thank friends and colleagues for their constructive comments while I was researching and writing this book. Several of them also read drafts of the manuscript.

For several years, Dr. Joost Jonker of Amsterdam shared with me his considerable knowledge of the financial and commercial markets of The Netherlands. He also provided me with an extensive critique of the manuscript. Dr. Augustus Veenendaal of Amsterdam, who read the manuscript for the Stanford University Press, made several valuable suggestions for the improvement of the manuscript. Mordichae Zucker and Dr. Rainer Liedtke verified the accuracy and context of the Judendeutsch translations I used for this study. Professor Steven M. Lowenstein consulted with me on the usage of Yiddish and graciously allowed me to read his unpublished scholarship. Professor Neville Thompson shared with me his knowledge of Wellington manuscript sources. G. P. Dyer, Librarian & Curator of the Royal Mint, traveled to London to discuss with me my findings about the Mint and also provided me with offprints of several of his scholarly studies. John Kleeberg, sometime Curator of Modern Coins and Currency, The American Numismatic Society, not only provided me with several offprints of his scholarly studies but also a greater understanding to the coins referenced in archival manuscript sources. Blanche and Albert Schlessinger read an early draft of the manuscript and offered suggestions regarding readership. Professor Jeremy Black, Professor Donna Guy, Gary Kramer and Dr. Thomas Waldman offered suggestions for placing the manuscript.

Two old and dear friends—Joseph Breu and Professor Aron Rodrigue—deserve special mention and thanks. Known for his excellent close line-editing, Joe read numerous drafts of the manuscript. He challenged every word and sentence I wrote and disputed every idea and interpretation I professed. Because of him, this is a better book. From the beginning, Aron understood the value of the book I was researching and writing. His patience, wisdom and faith in me and what I was doing were critical to the making of this book. Without their supportive involvement, I could not have completed this study and published this book.

Even before Judee became my wife, she also became as knowledgeable as anyone would want to be about Nathan Mayer Rothschild. Invariably, she would politely ask about the progress I was making in my research and writing, and I, invariably, would tell her everything I learned that day. She even listened patiently to my recitation of each chapter, one by one, and read drafts of the manuscript. She asked some of the best questions and questioned some of my best interpretations. Because of her, this is a better book.

Finally, I was constantly comforted by the companionship of Baby, Fluffie, Tortie, and Kokopelli. However, I am solely responsible for the book and its errors.

*Nathan Mayer Rothschild
and the Creation of a Dynasty*

PART ONE

The Cohens and the Rothschilds

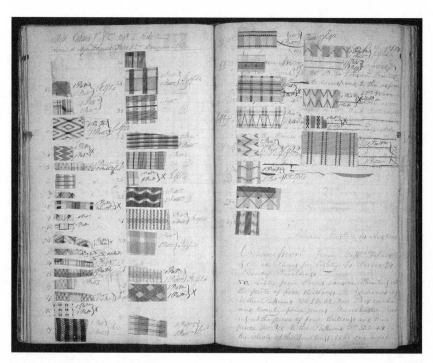

"The Cotton Book," 1801–1804. Reproduced with the permission of The Rothschild Archive.

ONE

A Marriage of Merchants

I have learnt with pleasure that the Arrangements of
your connection with the family of Mr. L. B. Cohen are
in the hands of the Attornies [*sic*] which I hope will
now be duly arranged.

I beg you to send me without delay a Copie [*sic*] of
all what you and Mr. Cohen agreed together.

—MAYER AMSCHEL ROTHSCHILD *to*
NATHAN MAYER ROTHSCHILD.
10 January 1806.[1]

In the late eighteenth century, Frankfurt am Main had become a significant trade and financial center in northern Europe, owing to external political events and "from a creative entrepreneurial achievement," to which Mayer Amschel Rothschild contributed.[2]

Mayer Amschel Rothschild (1743–1812) was a well-known wealthy Jewish general merchant, dealer in coins, and aspiring banker, who lived most of his adult life in Frankfurt, although he traveled frequently throughout northern Germany to recruit and serve clients. In 1769, the year before his marriage to Gutle, the daughter of Wolf Salomon Schnapper, the Saxony-Meiningen court factor, Rothschild became the court agent [*Hoffaktor*] to Crown Prince Wilhelm of Hesse-Hanau, the future Elector Wilhelm IX of Hesse-Kassel, who became his most lucrative and illustrious client.[3] The Rothschilds had ten children: five daughters, all of whom made good marriages, and five sons, who together made history.[4]

The most famous was Nathan Mayer Rothschild, the third son, who was born in 1777 in the Judengasse, the Jewish ghetto of Frankfurt.[5] Nothing is known about Nathan's early years in Frankfurt. There are no existing records relating to his rearing, education, or business activities that he may have undertaken with his father. All that is known is that in 1798 he traveled to England and in 1799 he established a mercantile firm in Manchester where he also acted as agent for his father's mercantile house in Frankfurt.[6]

And, during his early years in Manchester, not much is known about Nathan and his business activities. Nathan's "Manchester days between 1799 and 1809 are perhaps the least documented of any phase of his life," according to Bill Williams, an authority on the Jews of Manchester: "Letter and account books provide some evidence of his economic activities as a major cotton merchant on the Manchester Exchange, but apart from a few chance references in the local press little is known of his relationship either to what was then the world's most rapidly expanding industrial city or to its nascent Jewish community."[7]

The most important quality for a merchant to possess in the eighteenth and nineteenth centuries was "character." It meant that he was honest, punctual, responsible, and ethical. It also meant that he could be trusted to make the best, the right, or the most appropriate decision, when confronted with an unexpected circumstance in his business affairs. The evidence is both explicit and implicit that Nathan was not a merchant of character.

The surviving correspondence between Nathan and his father makes it stridently clear that their business methods and ethics were strikingly different. It might be argued that, during those early years, Nathan was disadvantaged because he was not skilled in the English language, the sine qua non for doing business. But clients, friends, and especially his father repeatedly criticized him not simply for his inadequacy in English, which they believed could be remedied by self-education and the employment of a native Englishman, but also for his brusque personal style, his irresponsible bookkeeping practices, and his lack of ethics. Merchants viewed Nathan as a sharp practitioner and did not like dealing with him.

It must have been embarrassing for Mayer Amschel Rothschild to learn that Harman & Co., a distinguished London merchant-banking house with worldwide connections that rivaled Baring Brothers & Co. (London) and Hope & Co. (Amsterdam),[8] would not extend his credit because payment on his account was in arrears owing to his son's laxity. Nathan had regular business dealings with Harman & Co. and from time to time he mixed his father's account with his own. When Nathan failed to balance his father's account with Harman & Co., his father was forced to sell the British securities he had with the firm to pay off his account.[9]

To protect his son and his business investments, Mayer Amschel Rothschild frequently interceded with clients who complained that Nathan had not marked cargo chests/cases correctly;[10] had not sent invoices promptly;[11] had shipped goods not ordered;[12] had sent poor quality merchandise;[13] and had not informed them about when and where they could expect delivery of their orders.[14] The elder Rothschild repeatedly cautioned his son: "all of your correspondents complain, dear Nathan, that you are so disorderly,"[15] and "I beg *you* in the *future* to take *better* notice *& care* to serve your customer [*sic*], *lest you may lose them all.*"[16]

When clients balked at his practices, Nathan frequently responded as the aggrieved party and accused them of unfair treatment. His relationship with Lyon de Symons, a well-known London general merchant and international diamond trader, who accepted bills of exchange and arranged insurance for his clients, was never smooth. They frequently exchanged testy letters about receipts, bills, and even more serious concerns. De Symons was taken aback when Nathan accused him of speculating in the exchange and for showing "so little confidence" in Nathan by giving him "a credit for £3000 *only*."[17] On another occasion, Nathan charged that de Symons's Account Current with him had errors. De Symons angrily replied that he would adjust the account only "when You favor me with the particulars," something that was *de rigueur* in such matters. De Symons declared that, henceforth, he would only carry Rothschild accounts provided: "your good Father & Yourself will mutually guarantee each other's Transactions with me."[18]

Nathan did a fair amount of business with Behrens Brothers & Co. of Hamburg. But, when he accused the firm of treating him harshly, B. L. Behrens retorted that his firm's conduct was induced by Nathan's behavior: "You would like to make me believe you, as virtuous as Cato, and as rigid in being as good as your Word as Regulus . . . which I have neither humour nor Leisure to investigate. . . . I don't like to quarrel with a Man, whom I once thought my friend. . . . I can't find any thing that could possibly induce you to such an ill timed Allusion, is it a fit of ill humour or the Spleen that does betake you sometimes?"[19] The bickering continued until Mayer Amschel Rothschild interceded, prompting B. L. Behrens to write Nathan: "Your father is here; he made me the pleasure to visit me a few times. He is a very honest man and he loves you very very much."[20]

Frankfurt merchant Israel E. Reiss complained to the Rothschilds that he never would do business with Nathan.[21] In November 1805, Reiss ordered goods from him but never received information about the intended shipment.

In March 1806, he still had not received delivery and the fair already had opened. Reiss stood to lose income and customers, who would go elsewhere for their needs. He also told Nathan's older brother, Salomon, that he had the previous year asked Nathan to arrange insurance for a shipment with the London firm of Aron Goldsmid Son & D. Eliason but Nathan charged him two-thirds more than Goldsmid's rate. "I can assure you," Salomon wrote Nathan: "I have done all in my power to pacify him but I am myself aware of the justice of his complaints."[22]

The large number of complaints by clients about overcharging and book-keeping irregularities suggest that there was something fundamentally amiss at Nathan's Manchester establishment. Although he employed Joseph Barber to keep his books, Nathan was ultimately responsible for all transactions. N. L. Hanau, another Frankfurt merchant, was "quite astonished" by the Account Current "which I did not expect of such a good & regular Book Keeper as Mr. Barber." In returning it, he stated "I am resolved not to accept any drawft [sic] from you, before we have settled the present Account, as I think, Exactness and Regularity, is [sic] the chief object in business."[23] Part of the problem may have originated because Nathan did not distinguish that firm from that of Hanau Junior in Amsterdam, to whom he regularly sent poor quality merchandise and confused billings.[24] In late 1805, the firm of Hanau Junior suspended payments and in effect went bankrupt.[25]

Why did Nathan Rothschild act as he did? We do not know the answer to this question. The quantity of his letters, either written by himself or written for him, which have survived is quite meager, and they provide lit-tle explanation for his motivations, except for the obvious raison d'etre of a merchant to conclude another deal and to make more money.

In 1805–1806 there occurred an event that was to be of utmost impor-tance to Nathan's life, not only personally, but in the development of his mercantile career. It was his betrothal and marriage to Hannah Cohen, the third daughter of Levy Barent Cohen (1747–1808), a well-known wealthy London general merchant and an international dealer in diamonds.

Until recently, little had been known about Cohen and his family. He was born into a large extended mercantile family[26] and departed his native Amsterdam for London, arriving there about 1770. During the next thirty-eight years, he witnessed and participated in London's ascendancy in inter-national commerce and in the international diamond trade.

Cohen married twice. When Fanny/Fania, his first wife, died in or before 1780, he married her sister, Lydia/Lida. Fanny and Lydia were daughters of

Joseph Diamantschleifer of Amsterdam.[27] Together, they gave birth to eleven children who lived to their maturity.[28]

Similarly, little had been known until recently about Cohen's mercantile activities.[29] There is not one scholarly article that details how he made his money or how much he made. There are no ledgers, Account Currents, or data that would permit an estimate of his firm's worth. His *Will* at the Public Record Office and the manuscripts at The Rothschild Archive comprise virtually all the archival sources in London. The *Will* is the most important and informative source about Cohen, his family, and his firm. It is the only extant document that provides his approximate personal wealth and gives its disposition to his wife, his children, his staff, and his charities.[30] It does not, however, state the wealth of his firm, L. B. Cohen & Co., and, therefore, only the minimum value of his assets can be estimated. Yet, by any contemporary standard of measure, the *Will* testifies that Cohen was an exceedingly wealthy and generous man, judging only from his bequest of more than £50,000 in cash and stock. He was also a man of significant property.[31]

As a general merchant firm, L. B. Cohen & Co. traded in commodities and textiles at home and abroad. Surprisingly, there is no evidence in the London archival sources that he had been a diamond trader. This "private" activity is well documented in the archival collection of Hope & Co., the premier Amsterdam merchant banking establishment during the second half of the eighteenth century. In the tradition of a small number of English and Dutch Jewish diamond merchants, Cohen consigned his diamonds to Hope & Co. for sale through its vast network of clients in Europe and Russia. It is not known from whom and at what price he purchased his diamonds, but they most likely were Brazilian diamonds, which dominated the market at that time. Although his gross income can be estimated, his profits cannot be determined; but there are numerous records attesting to the quantity and value of his consignments and the names of Hope & Co.'s clients who purchased his diamonds. Cohen was London's leading international diamond trader from 1781 through 1794 with transactions of more than an average of 12,000 carats and £15,000 per annum.[32] His name appears subsequently only once, when Hope & Co. and Baring Brothers & Co. were deprived in 1802 of a major purchase of Brazilian diamonds in Paris. A group of London Jewish diamonds merchants, led by a Goldsmid, a Gompertz, and a Cohen, outbid these two most powerful merchant banking institutions.[33] On his death, Cohen apparently took with him whatever talent, skill, and clientele he had amassed in the diamond business because there is no evidence that his sons continued in the trade.

The stewardship of the Cohen family mercantile establishment comprised Levy Barent Cohen, the founder of L. B. Cohen & Co.; son Joseph, who as early as 1805 established the firm of Joseph Cohen & Co.; and son Solomon, who managed L. B. Cohen & Co. The younger Cohen sons also contributed their services to the business but much less is known about them during this early period. Benjamin's and Isaac's signatures appear frequently on routine business correspondence. Barent worked actively for his father and there is one extant lengthy and informative letter he wrote to his father from Madeira, in which he describes his business contacts, but no more is known about him and it is presumed that he died shortly thereafter at the age of twenty-seven.[34] Abraham Hertz, the principal clerk, represented the Cohens in business transactions and occasionally held a modest share on his own account in their ventures. He communicated frequently with Nathan Rothschild, who on occasion also permitted Hertz a modest share in his ventures. Hertz devoted himself to the Cohens and he considered himself a "member" of the family: he zealously protected their interests and he worshiped Hannah.[35]

Levy Barent Cohen was a good and profitable businessman owing to his keen appreciation of the value of the merchandise he traded and a trust in the trueness of the merchants with whom he did business. The Cohens had acculturated themselves to the dominant gentile business community: they learned its language and its civility, and they conducted their business in a responsible and accountable manner. Cohen lived his life as a religious Jew and he wanted to be remembered that way. But he is remembered more for the social dynasty he founded than for his religiosity or any business achievement during his sixty-one years. It is impossible to read the story of the most prominent members of the English Jewish community during the nineteenth and twentieth centuries without seeing at least a brief mention of his name and, occasionally, his philanthropy.[36]

What is puzzling is why such a man as Levy Barent Cohen would entrust his educated and cultured daughter to someone so different from himself and his sons, someone who had the reputation of being an unsavory person with questionable business practices. Had Cohen divined in Nathan a special quality that others had failed to discern? No one knows the answer to those questions. Nor do we know what sparked the marriage, whether it was for love or money or some other motivation.[37]

The earliest known bona fide indication about the marriage is buried in an English letter from Mayer Amschel Rothschild to Nathan, dated 20

December 1805, to which Carl, Nathan's younger brother, wrote a postscript: "C[arl] M[ayer] Rothschild most respect to Messrs Barber, Rey & Fox and congratulate you, to my dear Brothers [*sic*] promise with Miss Cohn [*sic*]."[38] This letter was followed by another on 10 January 1806 in which Mayer Amschel Rothschild asks about the terms of Nathan's marriage contract with Levy Barent Cohen.[39] In February, Hannah Cohen and her friends gathered to celebrate her forthcoming marriage, causing one admirer to comment to Nathan: "I had the pleasure of seeing your worthy fiancée yesterday on the occasion of the reception [*kallah chevrah*]. You have good taste. I am completely enamored of her [*ich bin von ihr ganz eingenommen*]."[40] In August, members of the Rothschild family extended their best wishes to both Nathan and Hannah with regrets that they could not attend their wedding.[41]

On 21 October, 1806, Levy Barent Cohen contracted a "Settlement" for the benefit of his daughter, and the "Solemnization" of the marriage between the twenty-nine-year-old Nathan Mayer Rothschild and the twenty-three-year-old Hannah Cohen took place, according to Jewish Ceremony, the following day, 22 October 1806. By the "Settlement," Levy Barent Cohen agreed to transfer for Hannah the sum of £3,248.14.06 in 3 percent Consolidated Bank Annuities [3 percent Consols][42] into the names of Joseph and Solomon Cohen and Samuel Moses Samuel, who married his daughter Esther (1803). Subsequent to the "Solemnization" of the marriage, the trustees were to pay Hannah the "Dividends, interest and annual produce" from the 3 percent Consols "for her own sole and separate use and benefit for and during the term of her natural life *independent* of the said Nathan Mayer Rothschild . . . *or any part thereof may in no case be or become subject or liable to the Debts* . . . of the said Nathan Mayer Rothschild." Immediately after she died, if Nathan survived her, the trustees were to pay him the above-mentioned sums and on his death to pay the same to their children survivors.[43]

Moreover, the "Settlement" required that Nathan also make a monetary provision for Hannah, should she survive him. Within six calendar months after Nathan's death, the executors of his heirs were to pay Hannah "the full Sum of Three thousand pounds of lawful money of Great Britain with interest." After his death, she was immediately to have "the full and absolute dominion and control" over all her wearing apparel and jewels "of every kind and description and shall and may use and enjoy the same as her own absolute property in such manner as she may think proper."[44]

The "Settlement" demonstrates that Cohen was a generous, caring, and protective father. From the point of view of historiography, it also dispels some old and new myths associated with Nathan. The "Settlement" was an "Indenture" in three parts; a *trust*, involving Levy Barent Cohen, Nathan Mayer Rothschild, Joseph Cohen, Solomon Cohen, and Samuel Moses Samuel. It was not a *dowry*, as it was incorrectly identified by Niall Ferguson in his book, *The House of Rothschild: Money's Prophets 1798–1848*. It is wrong to contend as Ferguson did that it added to Nathan Rothschild's capital. The money was intended for Hannah's use and there is no evidence that it was used by Nathan Rothschild.[45]

Following the marriage, Hannah joined Nathan in Manchester, and Nathan continued his business relationship with the Cohens in London. Marriage had no effect on Nathan's business practices; he treated the Cohens in the same unpleasant and unorthodox way he treated his father and other clients. Abraham Hertz's business letters reflected the attitude of the Cohen establishment and his personal, professional, and proprietary relationship with the Cohens often caused him to upbraid Nathan:

> having sent you a Box by the Coach, and you don't mention the Receipt, I beg you will let me Know in Return of Post if you have receivd [*sic*] it or not. I think you are very neglectful in answering Letters, Mr. Jos Cohen sent you a Bill on Friday last, and has receivd [*sic*] no answer, he is indeed very uneasy, such a letter might be lost, but if not you should mention the Receipt. . . . I don't think that you attend to your Business as usual, and I am afraid I shall be oblig'd to write to Mrs. Rothschild, to correct you a Little.
> Mr. [L. B.] Cohen spoke [to] me at the Exchange, complains likewise of having no answer to his Letters, what is all this? [U]pon my life I don't comprehend. [Y]ou have not so much to do at the present.[46]

Hertz was proud of his bookkeeping and management practices and was baffled by Nathan's claim that he did not understand his Account Current with L. B. Cohen & Co.; he was "astonished" that Nathan wrote Joseph Cohen claiming that he had not received letters with the samples which he himself had packed and sent him; and he was especially miffed that "Miss J[udith] Cohen told me that Mrs. Rothschild wrote, you are surprised [*sic*] we should send Samples without a Single line, I cannot comprehend."[47]

Solomon Cohen was more sophisticated in his dealings with Nathan. Solomon considered himself an entrepreneur, who possessed superior business acumen, greater command of mercantile and maritime regulations, and more common sense than his brother-in-law, only one year his junior. An excellent example of their different temperaments and business practices is found in a rare correspondence, one of the few extant sources describing the intricacies of a smuggling operation. The correspondence depicts Nathan as inexperienced in planning and executing a dangerous overseas mercantile venture, as a risk-taker or as reckless, and Solomon as a cautious, decisive man focused on detail.

Smuggling was not only risky but also tricky. British merchant smugglers who wanted to sell their goods on the Continent focused on the Amsterdam market. Despite the French expansion and occupation of The Netherlands, the Amsterdam trade accelerated significantly in 1802–1803 after the precarious Peace of Lunéville (1801) and Peace of Amiens (1802).[48] But after Napoleon inaugurated the Continental Blockade (1806) and Great Britain's Orders in Council (1807) prohibited neutral ships from carrying trade between enemy ports and between enemy countries and their colonies, the Amsterdam overseas trade traffic tightened considerably.[49]

Nevertheless, in the fall of 1807, Nathan and Solomon joined with Ewart, Rutson & Co., Humble & Holland & Co., and William Fawcett of Liverpool to smuggle West Indian coffee and sugar to Amsterdam via Gothenburg on an American neutral vessel, the *Laura*. Nathan sent his clerk, John Fox, to Liverpool to supervise the operation and to chaperon the cargo to Amsterdam where it would be sold.[50]

The preparations Nathan made worried Solomon. On 19 October Solomon wrote the first of a series of letters that not only document his concern but show how he took the direction of the operation away from his brother-in-law. "I should have preferred another flag as I am afraid" an American ship from Gothenburg "is not usual . . . and therefore I am decidedly of the opinion that Mr. Fox ought not to proceed to Amsterdam, as there are many Persons who know Mr. Fox, the whole Transaction will not only be discovered immediately but information may be laid against him as an Englishman, and his employers made known, he would endanger the whole Cargo Consigned."[51]

It was late in the shipping season and Solomon believed that there were too many details to be completed before the *Laura* could hope to sail. The cost of insurance was staggering because "the underwriters are afraid of Holland," he wrote Nathan, "there being now so many Ships detained, without hope of release."[52] He, therefore, had to pay 6 percent on the first £3,000 and 12 percent on the next £8,000 of insurance.[53] Ewart, Rutson & Co. encountered difficulties in assembling the cargo, as previously agreed on, and asked Nathan for permission to "select Jamaican Coffee of qualities -

resembling St. Domingo which may be done on more reasonable terms."[54] Solomon warned Nathan: "You ought to Know and to be quite sure of those friends who put goods on Board along with ours, as in the Eye of the Law this is Considered a Joint Concern, and all the Partners are liable one for another."[55]

Early in November, rumors of a new war breaking out heightened everyone's anxiety.[56] Cohen criticized the management of the operation to Fox and argued that the *Laura* should proceed to Christiansand, Norway, where it might find a safe haven.[57] In Liverpool, the contrariness of the weather—"it blows a perfect hurricane"—and the mails frustrated Fox, who had successfully loaded the *Laura* but had not received an invoice and a counterfeit certificate of American citizenship.[58] He grew angry with both Nathan and Cohen because they had not written to him and he did not know if he should sail to Christiansand.[59] Cohen vented his displeasure to Nathan when, finally, the invoice materialized. The cargo and insurance costs totaled £12,267. Even though the Liverpool investors' share came to one-fourth, Ewart, Rutson & Co. drew the entire amount on L. B. Cohen & Co. Cohen, in turn, debited Nathan.[60] On 11 November, the very day that the British government issued additional Orders in Council,[61] Cohen discovered that the *Laura* had still not sailed. Miffed, he wrote Nathan: "I consider you Responsible for these friends in this Transaction."[62]

When Nathan began planning yet another smuggling venture to the Continent via the island of Heligoland,[63] both Hertz and Cohen were startled. "*Mr. R seems not to be aware of the existing difficulties which exist now in Holld* [*sic*] and every where for the introduction of produce," Hertz wrote Fox.[64] "In the present Critical Moment," Cohen wrote Nathan, "a Decision must be taken,"[65] and he abruptly and unilaterally took control of the *Laura* operation. He, therefore, arranged through Baruch Goldschmidt of London (who Nathan had recently insulted) for G. L. Goldschmidt & Co. of Hamburg to take charge of selling the *Laura* cargo on the Continent for a 1 percent commission and, as a condition, G. L. Goldschmidt insisted that Rothschilds have nothing to do with the transaction.[66] A troubled Hertz wrote Fox: "*I know Mr. Rothschild, will be very angry.*"[67]

Winter brought new challenges to Nathan, Cohen, and Fox. Letters were delayed and inevitably crossed each other. Hertz wrote Fox: "you were many times the Topic of Conversation, when the Wind blew hard, which was the Case very often, I said & oftener I thought, where is Mr. Fox now [?]"[68] Fox arrived in Gothenburg in January 1808, leaving the *Laura* blocked in ice three miles from port. He waited impatiently for the thaw, for the winds to subside, and for the Custom House to permit the *Laura* to unload its cargo.[69] When it did, Fox refused to relinquish his authority over the *Laura's* cargo to Goldschmidt, who wanted it shipped to Königsberg on another ship.[70] Instead, Goldschmidt sold the cargo of coffee and sugar in Gothenburg in early March but prevented Fox from participating in the sale. Goldschmidt claimed that, according to his agreement with Solomon Cohen, he had sole authority over the disposal of the cargo and that he should receive the promised 1 percent commission. Moreover, Goldschmidt would only remit the proceeds from the sale to Solomon Cohen, not to Nathan.[71]

Fox reported to Nathan that the sale of the *Laura's* cargo grossed approximately £17,000 with an estimated a profit of more than £4,700.[72] However, Nathan chose not to settle his accounts expeditiously with his Liverpool investors which led to unpleasant encounters. Barber related that William Fawcett "seemed quite out of temper respecting the adventure viz the *Laura*, as so long a time has elapsed since its commencement without any *Account of Sales*, or *return* being made and *Mails* frequently arriving without any letters from Mr. Fox, and Mr. Fox having transferred the property to Mr. Goldschmidt was unaccountable . . . and said it was extremely disagreeable to both *Mr. Holland & himself* to be kept in suspense so long."[73]

The *Laura* smuggling affair did not end well for Fox. In March, he suffered a severe attack of rheumatism in his hands and arms that put him to bed and required a friend to write his letters for him.[74] Hertz tried to comfort him: "I cannot help you even if I was a Doctor, the only Request which I have to make you, is, that in Case you should, by the Receipt of this Letter, be Death [*sic*], not to trouble you to write me an answer, but if you are a life [*sic*] as I heartily wish & hope, then don't lose a moment to assure me of it."[75] But Hertz's charming humor could not help Fox. When Barber learned that Fox had died in Gothenburg, he melancholically acknowledged the sad news: "Poor Fox! To die in a strange land, without a friend to soothe thee in thy affliction or to close thy eyes in death and follow thee to the grave, was indeed very hard—O how short and uncertain is the life of Man! And how uncertain are his hopes!"[76]

The death of Fox in a foreign land cost Nathan Rothschild an agent. Another death at home a short time before would present him with an opportunity.

Notes

1. MAR Fft. to NMR n.p. 10 January 1806, RAL xi/86/oA.
2. Jurgen Jeske, "Introduction" to Carl-Ludwig Holtfrerich, *Frankfurt as a Financial Centre. From Medieval Trade Fair to European Banking Centre* (Munich: Verlag C. H. Beck, 1999), pp. 11–12; and see also pp. 120–121, 126 & 145–147.
3. For the original document, see Melanie Aspey, "Salomon's Archive," *The Rothschild Archive. Review of the Year April 2001–March 2002* (London: The Rothschild Archive, 2002), pp. 27–29.
4. For summaries of the early years, see Corti, chapter I.

Amschel Mayer (1773–1855): Amschel in 1795 married Eva Hannau (1779–1848).

Salomon Mayer (1774–1855): Salomon in 1800 married Caroline Stern (1782–1854).

Nathan Mayer (1777–1836): Nathan in 1806 married Hannah Cohen (1783–1850).

Carl Mayer (1788–1855): Carl in 1818 married Adelheid Herz (1800–1853).

Jacob [James] Mayer (1792–1868): James in 1824 married Betty von Rothschild (1805–1886), Salomon Mayer's daughter.

Jeanette (1777–1859): Jeanette in 1795 married Benedikt Moses Worms (1772–1824).

Isabella/Betty (1781–1861): Betty in 1802 married Bernard Judah Sichel (1780–1862).

Breunle/Babette (1784–1869): Babette in 1808 married Sigmund Beyfus (1786–1845).

Gotten/Julie (1789/1790–1815): Julie in 1811 married Meyer Beyfus (1790–1860).

Jettchen/Henrietta (1791–1866): Jettchen in 1815 married Abraham Montefiore (1788–1824).

5. See Fritz Backhaus, "The Jewish Ghetto in Frankfurt," in Gray & Aspey, pp. 22–33.
6. There is an oft-repeated story about Nathan's arrival in London, which may have been invented by the journalist Lucien Wolf, and which the historian Stanley D. Chapman followed: "M. A. Rothschild sent his third and most able son, N. M., to London immediately after his coming-of-age in September 1798. He was to gain commercial experience with L. B. Cohen and then with Levi Salomons . . . before moving to Manchester to establish an agency on his own account, about May 1799." Neither Wolf nor Chapman cited extant contemporary sources for this contention. Quoted in S.D. Chapman, "The Foundation of the English Rothschilds: N. M. Rothschild as a Textile Merchant 1799–1811," *Textile History*, 8 (1977), 102. See Lucien Wolf, "(A) Early Business Letters of the Rothschilds," in *Essays in Jewish*

History (London: The Jewish Historical Society of England, 1934), p. 262. See also Bill Williams, "Nathan Rothschild in Manchester," in Gray & Aspey, pp. 34–41, passim.

7. Bill Williams, "Nathan Rothschild in Manchester," in Gray & Aspey, p. 34. See also Bill Williams, *The Making of Manchester Jewry 1740–1875* (Manchester: Manchester University Press, 1976). For the series of Nathan Rothschild's business accounts during his Manchester years, see RAL 1/218.

8. Harman & Co. was established from the time of the earthquake in Lisbon, Portugal (1755) and was first known as Gurnell and Hoare; then Gurnell, Hoare, and Harman (the father of Jeremiah); then Harman, Hoare, and Co; and lastly Harman & Co. Jeremiah Harman (1763–1844), the principal partner of the firm, held many prominent positions in the City and was a director of the Bank of England from 1794 to 1827. During the Napoleonic Wars, Harman & Co. was banker to the Russian Court. See *The Times*, 14 February 1844, p. 8. col. d. For this, I am grateful to Jane Waller for consulting with me regarding this matter.

9. Har Lon. to NMR Man. 14; & 23 March 1807, RAL xi/112/4; Har Lon. to NMR Man. 14 March, 3 December 1807, 12 & 21 March & 13 April 1808, RAL xi/112/38.

10. *On chests/cases*: MAR Fft. to NMR Man. 9 July & 20 December 1805, 17 January 1806, RAL xi/86/0A, respectively; MAR Fft. or Ham. to NMR n.p., n.d., RAL xi/86/0A; CMR Ham. to NMR Man. 8 July & 7 August 1807, RAL xi/86/0A, respectively; Joseph Israels, for Israel Levy, Lon. to NMR Man. 18 March 1805 & Hanau Junr. Ams. to NMR Man.15 April 1805, RAL xi/112/39A, respectively.

11. *On invoices*: MAR Fft. to NMR Man. 27 December 1804 (in 5 January 1805), 16 July, 26 November & 20 December 1805, 10 & 17 January, 7 & 28 February, 26 August, 7 October & 18 November 1806, RAL xi/86/0A, respectively; CMR for MAR Altona & Ham. to NMR Man. 22 May & 7 August 1807, RAL xi/86/0A, respectively; H. Ries Lon. to NMR Man. 15 May 1805, RAL xi/112/39B.

12. *On goods not ordered*: SMR Fft. to NMR Man. 21 March 1806 & MAR Fft. to NMR Man. 15 July 1806, RAL xi/86/0A, respectively.

13. *On poor quality of goods*: H. Beyer, for Bramerel & Co. Lon. to NMR Man. 5 March 1805, Joseph Israels, for Israel Levy, Lon. to NMR Man.18 March 1805, N. B. Rindskopf Lon. to NMR Man. 25 March 1805, Hanau Jr. Ams. to NMR Man. 15 April & 17 May, 1805; M. Josephs Lon. to NMR Man. 15 & 20 May 1805; J. E. Jacobs Lon. to NMR Man. 5 August 1805, RAL xi/112/39A, respectively.

14. *On ships and captains*: MAR Fft. to NMR Man. 20 December 1805 & 17 January 1806, RAL xi/86/0A, respectively.

15. MAR Fft. or Ham. to NMR n. p., n. d., RAL xi/86/0A.

16. MAR Fft. to NMR Man. 15 March 1806, RAL xi/86/0A. See also, MAR Fft. or Ham. to NMR Man. 16 July 1805, 10 January, 28 February, 8 April, 5 August, 5 & 7 September 1806, 19 June & 3 July 1807, RAL xi/86/0A, respectively.

17. Lyon de Symons Lon. to NMR Man. 15 December 1806, RAL xi/112/5. Italics mine.

18. Lyon de Symons Lon. to NMR Man. 18 January 1805, RAL xi/112/39B; & see JF Lon. to NMR Man. 30 March 1807, RAL xi/112/4.

19. B. L. Behrens Lon. to NMR Man. 10 May 1805, RAL xi/112/39A. See also, Brothers Behrens Leipzig to NMR Man. 22 December 1804; B. L. Behrens Lon. to NMR Man. 6 May 1805, RAL xi/112/39A.

20. B. L. Behrens Ham. to NMR Man. 10 January 1806, RAL xi/112/5.

21. MAR Fft. to NMR Man. 16 June 1807, RAL xi/86/0A.

22. SMR Fft. to NMR Man. 21 March 1806, RAL xi/86/0A; see CMR for MAR Ham. to NMR Man. 7 August 1807, RAL xi/86/0A.

23. N. L. Hanau Lon. to NMR Man. 26 February 1805, RAL xi/112/39A.

24. Hanau Jr. Ams. to NMR Lon. 1 February 1805, RAL xi/112/39A.

25. See Lyon de Symons Lon. to NMR Man. 29 October 1805, RAL xi/112/39B.

26. An older cousin, Benjamin Cohen (1726–1800) of Amersfort and Amsterdam, gained prominence in the tobacco, grain, silver, and the Brazilian diamond trades. A scholar and an advocate of Jewish emancipation in The Netherlands, he had close ties with the Stadtholder William V. Jozeph Michman asserts that Benjamin Cohen "was undoubtedly the predominant Jewish personality during the second half of the 18th century." Jozeph Michman, *The History of Dutch Jewry during the Emancipation Period 1787–1815* (Amsterdam: Amsterdam University Press, 1995), pp. 15–16 et seq.

27. In Dutch, *Diamantslijper* means diamond cutter/polisher and it is more than likely that this was also Joseph's craft. Levy Barent Cohen's marriage into the Diamantschleifer family may indicate that he traded in diamonds early in his general merchant career.

28. Joseph (1774–1838): Joseph's mother was Fanny. In 1796, he married Marion/Marianne Joachim (1768–1840), daughter of Elias Joachim, London bill broker, and niece of the London financier Abraham Goldsmid.

Solomon/Selig (1776–1864): Solomon's mother was Fanny. He married Hannah (1776–1871), daughter of Moses Samuel, London merchant. From as early as 1807, he signed for L. B. Cohen & Co. and de facto managed his father's firm.

Barent/Berman (1780–c.1807): Barent's mother was Lydia. There is no evidence of marriage and presumably he may have died sometime after he wrote from Lisbon on 7 August 1807, where he was on business for his father. See Barent Cohen Maderia to L. B. Cohen Lon. 7 August 1807, RAL xi/112/4.

Benjamin (1789–1867): Benjamin's mother was Lydia. In 1819, he married Justina Montefiore (1800–1873), sister of Abraham and Moses Montefiore, London merchants.

Isaac (1791–1846): Isaac's mother was Lydia. In 1818, he married Rebecca (1793–1819), daughter of Dr. Joseph Hart Myers and, in 1827, he married Sarah (1810–1879), daughter of Phineas Samuel.

Hannah/Hanna (1783–1850): Hannah's mother was Lydia. In 1806, she married Nathan Mayer Rothschild.

Judith/Jetta (1784–1862): Judith's mother was Lydia. In 1812, she married Moses Montefiore (1784–1885), London merchant.

Fanny/Fania (n. d.): Fanny's mother was Fanny. In 1797, she married Solomon Cohen Wessels of Amsterdam, son of Hyman Cohen Wessels and nephew of Levy Barent Cohen (brother of Hyman Cohen Wessels).

Esther/Ester (1782–1859): Esther's mother was Lydia. In 1803, she married Samuel Moses Samuel (1773–1873), son of Moses Samuel (1740–1839) and Rachel Phillips, and one of the founders of Samuel & Phillips & Co. of London and Rio de Janeiro, which traded in commodities, specie, bullion and diamonds.

Jessy/Jesi (1795–1869): Jessy's mother was Lydia. In 1816, she married Mayer Davidson (d. 1846), principal clerk to Nathan Mayer Rothschild.

Adelaide/Adeline (1799–1877): Adelaide's mother was Lydia. In 1817, she married John Helbert (1785–1861).

29. One rare public notice about him appeared in 1778, when he was cited with another enterprising Jewish merchant for having organized a "combination of merchants," a mechanism to undermine competitive bidding for the purchase of damaged cloth publicly sold by the East India Company. This maneuver antagonized other merchants who sought remedy in court. For this, see Gedalia Yogev, *Diamonds and Coral. Anglo-Dutch Jews and Eighteenth-Century Trade* (Leicester: Leicester University Press, 1978), pp. 74–75, 286.

30. Lydia received the household furniture, plate and £14,604 in cash and, with her children, shares in an unspecified number of British securities. Joseph received £6,000. Solomon received £4,500 "over and above the share he is entitled to in my Business according to the respective entries in my Books" [which have not survived]. Barent, Benjamin, and Isaac each received £3,500. Each spinster daughter, Judith, Jessy, and Adelaide, received £3,200; and each married daughter, Esther, Hannah, and Fanny, received £1,200. Cohen had reservations about Fanny's husband Solomon Cohen Wessels, who was also his nephew, because he stipulated that his bequest to her "shall be her own and for her absolute use of herself and the heirs of her Body." The five daughters of his deceased brother Solomon Cohen would receive a total of £500. His clerks and servants would receive £200. See *Will. LBC.*

31. See Lord Justice Cohen, "Levi Barent Cohen and Some of His Descendants," *TJHSE.* XVI (1952), 11–12; Lucien Wolf, *Essays in Jewish History* (London: The Jewish Historical Society of England, 1934), pp 234–235.

32. See GAA 735/1009–1022, passim.

33. For this affair, see Northbrook Papers A13 & A19; The Baring Archive, ING Group NV & Hope & Co., especially 16 March 1802, GAA 735/411.

34. Barent Cohen Madeira to L. B. Cohen Lon. 7 August 1807, RAL xi/112/4.

35. See his particularly revealing and touching note to her. AH Lon. to NMR Man. 26 October 1807, RAL xi/112/4.

36. See *Will. LBC* & Lord Justice Cohen, "Levi Barent Cohen and Some of His Descendants," *TJHSE.* XVI (1952), 11.

37. See Melanie Aspey, "Mrs. Rothschild," in Gray & Aspey, p. 60.

38. MAR Fft. to NMR Man. 20 December 1805, RAL xi/86/0A.

39. MAR Fft. to NMR Man. 10 January 1806, RAL xi/86/oA.

40. [M.?] Alexander Lon. to NMR Man. 21 February 1806, RAL xi/112/5. My thanks to Mordichae Zucker for this translation. *Kallah* = bride; & *chevra* = friends, see Leo Rosten, *The Joys of Yiddish* (New York: McGraw-Hill Book Company, 1968), pp.165 & 85, respectively.

41. See postscripts to letters from MAR Fft. to NMR Man. 30 Aug 1806, RAL xi/86/oA, Tape 240/Letters 15 & 17.

42. The 3 percent Consol, "the perpetual and redeemable annuity," a "nearly ideal security," was created by the Consolidating Act of 1751 and "essentially gave the holder an equity position in the financial fortunes of the state. But its attractiveness to the investing public depended on the relative ease by which it could be acquired and disposed of, the clear terms of the interest payments, and the readily available information about its current price and the military and political events likely to affect its price." Larry Neal, *The Rise of Financial Capitalism. International Capital Markets in the Age of Reason* (Cambridge: Cambridge University Press, 1990), p.14.

43. "Settlement made previous to the marriage of Mr. Rothschild with Miss Cohen," RAL 000/103, RFam FP/11. Italics mine.

44. "Settlement made previous to the marriage of Mr. Rothschild with Miss Cohen," RAL 000/103, RFam FP/11.

45. Ferguson, p. 59.

46. AH Lon. to NMR Man. 4 December 1806, RAL xi/112/5.

47. AH Lon. to NMR Man. 26 January 1807, RAL xi/112/4.

48. See Paul W. Schroeder, "IV. Peace at Lunéville and Amiens, 1801–1802," in *The Transformation of European Politics 1763–1848* (Oxford: Clarendon Press, 1994), pp. 210–230; Jonker, p. 32.

49. See Jonker, p. 32.

50. ER Liv. to NMR Man. 30 September, 3 & 19 October 1807, RAL xi/112/4. For the *Laura* operation, see also LJ RAL xi/218/30, passim.

51. SC Lon. to NMR Man. 19 October 1807, RAL xi/112/4. Italics mine.

52. SC Lon. to NMR Man. 22 October 1807, RAL xi/112/4.

53. SC Lon. to NMR Man. 21 & 22 October 1807, RAL xi/112/4.

54. ER Liv. to NMR Man. 21 & 26 October 1807; and JF Liv. to NMR Man. 23 & 24 October 1807, RAL xi/112/4, respectively.

55. SC Lon. to NMR Man. 20, 23 & 26 October 1807; &AH Lon. to NMR Man. 24 October 1807, RAL xi/112/4, respectively.

56. SC Lon. to JF Liv. 30 October, JF Liv. to NMR Man. 2 November & Har Lon. to NMR Man. 22 October 1807, RAL xi/112/4, respectively.

57. SC Lon. to JF Liv. 30 October 1807, RAL xi/112/4.

58. JF Liv. to NMR Man. 5 November 1807, RAL xi/112/4.

59. JF Liv. to NMR Man. 2–3 & 5 November 1807, RAL xi/112/4.

60. JF Liv. & SC Lon. to NMR Man. 5–7 & 9 Nov 1807, RAL xi/112/4, respectively.

61. See Eli F. Heckscher, *The Continental System. An Economic Interpretation* (Oxford: Clarendon Press, 1922), pp.114–116 et seq.; François Crouzet, "Wars,

Blockade, and Economic Change in Europe, 1792–1815," *The Journal of Economic History*, XXIV:4 (December 1964), 567–88, passim.

62. SC Lon. to NMR Man. 11 November 1807, RAL xi/112/4.

63. SC Lon. to NMR Man. 16 November 1807, RAL xi/112/4.

64. AH Lon. to JF Got. 24 November 1807, RAL xi/112/38. Italics mine.

65. SC Lon. to NMR Man. 26 November 1807, RAL xi/112/4.

66. See SC Lon. to NMR Man. 21 July, to JF Got. 24 & 27 November & to NMR 24 & 26 November 1807, RAL xi/112/4.

67. AH Lon. to JF Got. 27 November 1807, RAL xi/112/38. Italics mine.

68. AH Lon. to JF Got. 26 January 1808 RAL xi/112/38.

69. JF Got. to NMR Man. 22 January 1808, RAL xi/112/76. See also ER Liv. to NMR Man. 9 & 20 February & 7 March, William Fawcett, Liv. to NMR Man. 19 March, & Fermin de Tastet & Co. to NMR Man. 20, 22, 26 & 29 February & 22 April 1808, RAL xi/112/76, respectively; AH Lon. to JF Got. 26 Jan, 2, 9, 16 & 23 February & 8 Mar 1808, RAL xi/112/38 & RAL xi/112/76, respectively; Jacobs Lon. to NMR Man. 10 May 1808, RAL xi/112/38.; SC Lon. to NMR Man.16 & 19 February 1808, RAL xi/112/76.

70. JF Got. to NMR Man. 22 January 1808, RAL xi/112/76.

71. JF Got. to NMR Man. 26 February & 7 March 1808, RAL xi/112/76. Cohen received the first installment of remittances in March. SC Lon. to NMR Man. 21 March 1808, RAL xi/T (A) 8 [trans. RAL xi/82/10/6] & RAL xi/112/76.

72. JF Got. to NMR c/o L. B. Cohen, Lon. 2 May 1808, RAL xi/112/76. See also, JB Man. to NMR post office Lon. 15 June 1808, RAL xi/38/41A.

73. JB Man. to NMR post office, Lon. 21 May 1808, RAL xi/38/41A. See also William Fawcett's letters, passim, RAL xi/112/76.

74. James Reid Got. to NMR Man. 7 March 1808, RAL xi/112/38.

75. AH Lon. to JF Got. 15 March 1808, RAL xi/112/38.

76. JB Man. to NMR c/o L. B. Cohen, Lon. 11 June 1808, RAL xi/38/41A.

Levy Barent Cohen by Richard Dighton, 1817. Reproduced with the permission of The Guildhall Library, Corporation of London.

From Manchester to London

> Mr. & Mrs. Rothschild are here, and I think they will
> make a longer stay this time than ordinary at Manchester
> there is not much to do and Mr. R finds allways [sic] to
> do here.
>
> —ABRAHAM HERTZ *to* JOHN FOX. *19 April 1808.*[1]

Early Friday morning, on 11th of March 1808, Abraham Hertz—dutiful clerk, trading associate, "honorary member" of the Cohen family and witness to Levy Barent Cohen's *Will*—conducted his routine business affairs saddened by the thought that his old friend would die that day. He wrote to Nathan Rothschild, who was in Manchester, and thanked him for sending the Cohens turkeys for the Jewish Purim holiday "which I am sorry to say don't come in a proper time, M[r.] LBC. being very Ill."[2] Later that morning, he wrote to his friend and colleague John Fox in Gothenburg: "I have nothing new to communicate at least nothing what is good, only an unhappy Event I have to inform you of, that Mr. L. B. Cohen died this Morning and will be buried next Sunday he suffered a great Deal of late and in this point of view it may be call'd a happy release but for his family it is a Melancholy Case this is the End of us all, and must be Content with it, because we cannot alter it."[3]

The funeral was on Sunday because, according to Jewish tradition, Levy Barent Cohen had to be buried within a day of his death but not on the Sabbath. Nevertheless, on Saturday, Hertz wrote to Nathan Rothschild about the "melancholy situation we are in here, and that Mr. S[olomon] Cohen cannot answer your letters which he has received this Day with Remittances."[4]

L. B. Cohen & Co. had come to a standstill but the London community of merchants was confident that the firm would continue to honor its obligations.[5] On Wednesday, 16 March, Solomon wrote to Nathan that he could not answer fully his recent letters owing to the "unhappy conditions we are in and because we have to sit shiva."[6] About the future of L. B. Cohen & Co., Solomon revealed:

> I have not made any arrangements yet concerning our future business. Probably I shall inform you after the shiva. I and my mother together shall make arrangements shortly.
>
> In the meantime I do not want to undertake any new business, until we have this one arranged. But you can certainly rely on the old firm, until I shall inform, how else to do it. . . .
>
> I have to go back to the parlour for Minyan[7] and things like that. After the Shiva I shall write to you in greater detail.[8]

Although there is abundant evidence that Solomon had for some time managed the day to day affairs of the firm, his remarks to Nathan were the first indication that he and his mother would together decide the future of L. B. Cohen & Co. His father's *Will* made no explicit provision that Joseph, the eldest son, who already had his own firm, Joseph Cohen & Co., or any other son or daughter should share in the ownership or management of L. B. Cohen & Co.[9]

Solomon made a personal request to his brother-in-law: "You say Hannah is angry that we did not tell her about the state of our father's health. We did not want to upset her. . . . Console Hannah as much as you can." Solomon also enclosed a separate letter to Hannah:

> Dear Sister.
>
> I hope Rothschild has communicated to you with the utmost caution, the unpleasant intelligence of the Death of Our dear Father, which happened Friday last, in the Morning at 9, and the Funeral was on Purim at eleven which was attended by a numerous and Respectable [attendance] You can imagine a Man of his worth & Merit deserved; he died regretted by all the World, as well as his Family—he was receding all the last 4 weeks, but Still we buoyed ourselves with the hope of his Recovering, and unfortunately were disappointed—we did not wish to alarm You, & therefore thought best not to mention it. We must all however console each other. . . . You can have no Idea what attention Mamma & Judy paid our late Father in his illness.

Mamma of course was inconsolable, but at present is a little reconciled to her Situation, Indeed who can avert the all powerful hand of God? I wish You, Your dear Rothschild & little Girl Long Life, and happiness and hope the Lord will protect us all.[10]

Solomon's action raises an important and puzzling question: why did he choose to deny Hannah knowledge of their father's illness during the final four weeks? Hannah was the daughter of Lydia, their father's second wife, and presumably would have wanted to be with her mother at her dying father's bedside and would have wanted to attend his funeral. There is no evidence that Hannah could not have made a brief trip to London during those four weeks because several days after the funeral she traveled to London. The delicacy of Hannah's absence did not go unnoticed. John Fox, who knew the Cohens and Rothschilds intimately, wrote Nathan Rothschild from Gothenburg: "I am much grieved to hear of the death of Mr. L. B. Cohen, which must occasion Mrs. Rothschild & yourself as well as his whole family, much sorrow.—It must have been a melancholy event for Mrs. Rothschild, who would feel it more severely by reason of being absent from him at the time it took place."[11]

To exclude Hannah meant to exclude Nathan, who would surely have accompanied her to London, as he did shortly after the funeral, and therein lies the probable motivation for Solomon's action. He must have known his father's intention concerning the future ownership of L. B. Cohen & Co. and it was implausible for him to think that Nathan could, by any turn of events, succeed to it. But Solomon had suffered his brother-in-law's arrogance and also his ambition and presumably he wished to keep him at a distance. There seems to be no other compelling reason why he would deny Hannah the opportunity to attend her father at his deathbed and at his funeral.

On Monday, 21 March, Solomon wrote Nathan more details about the future of L. B. Cohen & Co.

> I expect to see you and Hannah here this Wednesday. Even though not all is in order with my family, I hope that your company will make this disagreeable situation better.
>
> I took [a leading role] under the old firm. But now a new arrangement is needed. I think I shall work together with my mother and sign Widow L. B. Cohen and Son. But I shall inform you of this in greater detail. Perhaps I shall write by post, how we decided about it. . . .
>
> My best wishes to Hannah. I received her letter. I wish your little daughter a better health.[12]

In early April, L. B. Cohen & Co. was reorganized into L B Cohen & Son, headed by Solomon Cohen.[13]

Several months later, Nathan and Hannah Rothschild moved from Manchester to London. It is not known precisely when they gave up their residence in Manchester and when they established their new one in London. In the interim, they visited London several times and they most likely stayed with the Cohens, while Nathan collected his mail at the post office and at L B Cohen & Son, Angel Court. The first time that Joseph Barber, Nathan's principal clerk, wrote and shipped their household effects, plates, linens, and carpets to them at 12 Great St. Helens, Bishopsgate Street, their new residence and place of business, was on 17 August 1808. Lionel, the Rothschild's second child, was born there on 22 November. As early as March 1809, Nathan contemplated moving again[14] and, in May–June, took possession of No. 2, New Court, St. Swithin's Lane, which has remained a Rothschild establishment to this day.[15]

Because no extant contemporary source reveals Nathan's reason for moving to London at that time, historians have speculated about his motivations. S. D. Chapman believed that Hannah Cohen Rothschild's inheritance made it financially feasible for him to move to London: "In October 1806 he had married Hannah Cohen and two years later acquired his first permanent office in London, at 12 Great St Helen's Street. The death of his father-in-law the same year suggests a connexion between the two events; quite possibly his wife's inheritance provided the means and occasion for the change of address."[16]

Cohen's *Will* does not support this view. The money he left to his daughters was not intended for their husbands' use. His bequest to Fanny, who had married his nephew, contained language similar to the language of the marriage trust bestowed on Hannah: "shall be her own and for her absolute use of herself and the heirs of her Body." By itself, the £1,200 in cash he left to Hannah, while not a trifling sum, is not likely to have triggered Nathan's move to London, even if she had turned it over to him.[17]

What probably precipitated Nathan Rothschild's move to London was the simple fact of Levy Barent Cohen's death. The demise of the patriarch of the prosperous Cohen mercantile establishment may have inspired hope within Nathan that he might take control of the firm. At a minimum, he had interests to protect. The firm had been his most lucrative client and he had relied on its financial resources to back his own business ventures.

Numerous *Journal* entries and correspondence demonstrate how financially dependent Nathan was on his in-laws.[18] He was in considerable arrears to Solomon Cohen, who did not trust Nathan's arithmetic. About two weeks before Levy Barent Cohen died, Solomon upbraided him:

> am sorry to observe that the Acct Court. can be of no use to me, you begin in 1806, at which I was amazingly surprized, you Know, yourself, that you have received since that time several Account Courts. which have been, examined, reexamined, rectified, alterd [*sic*], discussed, and every thing done & adjusted according to your Wishes & Suggestions, which you will find by the many Letters which have been written on both sides on the Subject and according to my Books, have been alter'd, and now after all, you overthrow every thing & begin anew, you will excuse Sir my refusal to submit to it, if your Books are Kept in such a manner, as to make it easy to alter, correct & alter again after so many alterations have taken place, I Confess that Mine are not, I shall therefore be under the Necessity to send back your Act. Court. and send you one from the 1st of August last at that period you received one which was corrected.[19]

Further, for a four-week period soon after Levy Barent Cohen died (13 April–11 May 1808), the value of the bills drawn on Solomon's new firm, L B Cohen & Son, amounted to £10,613.[20] And, at the end of August 1808, Nathan, by his own arithmetic, owed Solomon at least £27,000.[21]

The financial value of Nathan's trading transactions with the Cohens was second only to that with his father.[22] There are two London *Ledgers* covering the periods May–December 1809 and January–December 1810 (including one entry dated 1811), which are problematic financial sources because Nathan did not follow the guidelines of double-entry bookkeeping.[23] These *Ledgers* testify to his slipshod bookkeeping practices. The data in the *Ledgers* cannot be verified but they yield unique information about the *relative* value of his trading transactions. During the period May–December 1809, his *Ledgers* show two accounts with Solomon Cohen, separate accounts for L B Cohen & Son, Joseph Cohen & Co., and the other Cohen sons. The value of his transactions with the Cohens was almost £200,000.[24] In 1810, the value of these transactions more than doubled to about £444,000.[25]

Of utmost importance to Nathan were the bills of exchange of L. B. Cohen & Co. which were readily accepted throughout the international trading community, as Nathan's own bills were not. The bill of exchange—in the absence of specie, bullion, or an accepted paper currency—was the essential financial instrument in mercantile transactions to balance accounts between buyers and sellers. John Orbell, historian and archivist of The Baring Archive, ING Group NV, London, has lucidly explained what a bill of exchange was and how it functioned:

> The bill of exchange was a well established widely used instrument for making payments between international centres, but it was an agreement to receive payment after delivery, and possibly sale, of goods. The seller's confidence in the standing of the buyer was essential but the bill's usefulness broke down when such confidence did not exist or where the standing of the two parties was unknown to one another. In such cases a third party, in whose creditworthiness the seller had confidence, and who had confidence in the ability of the buyer to meet his obligations, would accept the bill, i.e. he would guarantee to meet payment of the bill when it fell due, the buyer placing him in funds immediately prior to this.[26]

Once established in London, Nathan remained close to the Cohens, who continued to provide him with financial backing and participated with him in trading ventures, but there is no evidence that they invited him to join their mercantile establishment.[27] For his part, Nathan did not announce what he intended to do with his firm in Manchester. For more than a year, Barber, who corresponded with Nathan almost daily, continued to refer to it as the *Manchester Concern* or the *Manchester House*, separately from the *London Concern*.[28] But on 1 May 1809, with no forewarning, Nathan wrote him "of a new arrangement in our business, and an alteration in the Firm."[29] In the past, when he had received letters from Nathan that had not made sense, Barber had scolded him: "it is quite impossible to ascertain *your meaning . . .* as it abounds with *contradictions*."[30] Now, Barber was confronted with a serious challenge to the present and the future existence of the firm he had given years of service and he chose a different approach to seek out Nathan's intentions:

> . . . but as your letter is not quite so explicit on the subject as it should have been, I will now state to you what I suppose to be your meaning respecting the *new arrangement*, which if not exactly correct, I hope you will inform me per return—
> 1st That the firm be still "N M Rothschild" in *London*.
> 2nd That the firm in *Manchester*, be altered immediately to "Rothschild, Brothers."—
> 3rd That for all goods purchased by the Concern in Manchester, Bills be drawn by "Rothschild, Brothers" on "N M Rothschild, St. Swithins Lane, London"—

4th That Barber sign the Bills for "Rothschild, Brothers," by procuration—
If this new arrangement is an *actual* partnership between yourself and *one*
or *more* of your brothers, have you not engaged in the same rather too pre-
cipitately? As you ought most certainly to have ascertained the *exact state* of
your *own* Concern, by balancing all the Accounts, taking Stock etc. previous
to the commencement of a Partnership Concern—I have no doubt you will
inform me in your next if the alteration is to be a *real partnership*, and if so,
with *which of your brothers*; as I am fully persuaded you know me sufficiently,
that you can make any communication to me in the fullest confidence of *secrecy* and *safety*.[31]

There is no evidence that Nathan ever replied to these questions or ever
identified the brother or brothers, who supposedly made up "Rothschild,
Brothers." Perhaps it was simply a business ruse to distinguish it superficially
from "N M Rothschild." All we do know is that when his youngest brother
Jacob [James] visited London in October 1809, Nathan made him his partner in the specie and bullion trade.

No annual accounts survive that reveal the profitability, or lack thereof,
of the Manchester firm about the time Nathan moved to London. Shortly
after the reorganization of the firms, Barber requested that he compile balances for the *Manchester Concern* and the *London Concern* but they are not
extant, if they were ever done.[32] Subsequently, he asked that the firm "N M
Rothschild" balance its account with "Rothschild, Brothers" but there is no
evidence that this was done before it closed its doors in 1811.[33]

There is, however, impeccable evidence about the estimated material
worth of the London firm "N M Rothschild" and, as well, about Nathan
and Hannah Rothschild's personal property. Just one month after Nathan
wrote to Barber about the reorganization of the two mercantile houses, the
Imperial Insurance Company of London issued, on 2 June 1809, a "Policy
for Insurance from Loss or Damage by Fire" to N. M. Rothschild of No 2 St
Swithins Lane on:

> *Household goods, linen, printed books, wearing apparel, plate and wine, in his
> house situate as aforesaid;*
> **Five hundred pounds.**
> *And on stock in Trade and utensils in his warehouse adjourning,*
> **Four thousand five hundred pounds.**[34]

Whether in London or Manchester, Nathan was always in want of bills
of exchange to pay his creditors. To meet his needs, he created credit where

none actually existed. He teamed up with Peter Fawcett (of Moulsen & Fawcett, Manchester), a brother of William, with whom he collaborated in smuggling operations. Nathan's relationship with Peter Fawcett was unusual and the latter pretended it was even intimate. Nathan relied very much on Fawcett's ingenuity and gave him, surprisingly, considerable authority to handle accounts at his Manchester firm.[35]

Fawcett covered Nathan's outstanding balances by the employment of "accommodation bills" (known also as "kites," "windmills," or "wind bills") whereby:

> **A** may accept a bill for the accommodation of **B** the drawer, who is in need of money. **A** receives no consideration and does not expect to be called upon to pay the bill when due. **B** raises the necessary funds by discounting the bill, expecting that, at maturity, he will be in a position to meet the bill himself.[36]

Fawcett passed these bills of exchange through his firm's merchant accounts before sending bills to Nathan's creditors. He also lent several thousand pounds of his firm's bills with flexible repayment dates to Nathan: "You may have 6000£ as usual, whenever you have a mind."[37]

Fawcett never missed an opportunity to ingratiate himself with the Rothschilds. "I am very thankful that Charlotte [Nathan's daughter] is so much better. Make my best respects to Mrs. R.—the candles are arrived, and I am much obliged to her for the trouble she has had about them—but I am determined to pay for them."[38] Before it was generally known that Nathan would move to London, Fawcett wrote him (in April 1808), as if he had already given up his Manchester home: "I hope to see you here, a bed is purposely made up for you."[39] The birth of Lionel Rothschild on 22 November allowed for his eloquence and prophecy: "It affords me infinite satisfaction to understand your dear lady is likely to do well after her accouchement, and I congratulate you most heartily on the birth of a son and heir, to inherit a handsome fortune which will some time hereafter fall to his lot."[40] He often intermingled delicate personal matters, feelings, and attitudes with business affairs and those letters reveal how complex and troubled he must have been:

> All the bills you sent me . . . will never see the light until payment is demanded for them— . . . you must send me 10,000£ worth of bills to negotiate for you, . . . Send me these bills immediately—I do not care who they are upon; . . . five or six thousand may now be upon Mr. Cohen—I wish you would come down and cheer us with your presence and that of your dear Mrs. R—and her little infant—I am quite lost for want of you all!—and am

like a fish out of water—I have been very ill of a bowl [*sic*] complaint but am now got well again—Write me a long letter, send me a deal of bills to negotiate for you—and all in a few days—let me know how Charlotte goes on, and remember me most respectfully to Mrs. R—Miss Judith Cohen and all the family—You Know how busy I always am, and will excuse the inaccuracies of long a letter scribbled late in the evening—You Know I am a night crow!!!⁴¹

In the fall of 1808, Nathan generated more bills by employing "Pig Upon Bacon"or "Pig on Pork," whereby the Manchester house would draw bills on the London house, as if they were two entirely separately owned firms. Thus, he became the drawer of the bill and also the acceptor of the bill.⁴² Barber hesitated to go along with what appeared to him to be a manipulation of bills of exchange and he registered his disapproval in an uncommonly elliptical letter:

> I am unable at present, to decide on the measure you propose "of the person we buy Goods from, drawing upon you in London", it is certainly a measure of great importance and delicacy and will require much deliberation and discussion, before it can be adopted with propriety; and from the attention I have been able to devote to this subject, am inclined to hazard the following opinion that it would not be either wise or prudent to propose or adopt that measure unless it was generally understood that we have a separate and permanent establish[ment]—in London; in that case there is not the smallest doubt, but paper to any extent might be drawn and issued by the Manchester House on the house in London, without prejudice and would be equally acceptable to those Bills we have been in the habit of drawing—I have reasons for the above opinion, which I do not feel at liberty to state to you by letter—perhaps I am wrong in the opinion, but I feel persuaded I am right—You well know, how averse I am to the System of accomodation [*sic*] beyond a reasonable extent, and should be very glad to exert myself to the utmost, either to devise or execute a wise plan, to do without it, as much as possible—⁴³

Barber's caution did not deter Nathan from generating bills of exchange wherever he could, especially in the face of mounting obligations in October and November 1808. This burdened Barber greatly: "I have never before been besieged by so large a host of applicants for Bills, as I have been last night and today and notwithstanding all my maneuvers, have been obliged to draw rather largely" on L B Cohen & Son.⁴⁴ One such maneuver that failed was when he signed his own name on behalf of Barber & Co. He was fully aware that such a "scheme of finance" would not work "as my signature is now become too notorious, to be used for a purpose of that nature," and, instead, he drew "Bills for Mr. Fawcett on Messrs. Joseph Cohen & Co."[45] The Cohens had become indispensable to Nathan Rothschild.[46]

By late December 1808, Rothschild's and Fawcett's bill manipulation schemes faced greater challenges. Although Fawcett had just sent £22,781 in bills to Nathan's creditors, he soon found there was yet another £10,117 due in January 1809. He once again intervened: "I am rather low in suitable bills. . . . However, I think I may be able to do you a few thousands, perhaps from six to ten, for the two months."[47] On Christmas Eve, a worried Fawcett cautioned Nathan about their dealings: "My drafts on Devaynes & Co. . . . you will please always to discount with De Tastet in order to keep them out of the bank. . . . I have drawn on D & Co. rather too freely of late, and I should not have discounted a bill of this size, at this time, for any other person in the world—but my friend N: M: R: nor for you, if I did not know you would send my draft on them to De Tastet."[48] A few days later, he frantically wrote that the bills on Devaynes & Co. with Fermin de Tastet had to be kept "out of the money market;" and "never put your name on the back of our drafts on D & Co. as it does not look well to see you and us dealing together in bills— . . . You may have another £6000 as usual whenever you like!"[49] Just before the year was out, Fawcett confessed he could no longer send Nathan's bills to Devaynes & Co. because "they would be holders of more of your acceptances than it is usual for me to send them upon any one house—especially one so recently established as that of yours is."[50]

The pressure on Fawcett mounted and he reluctantly drew back from his earlier declaration that Nathan was a *banker*. At that time, Fawcett had not only created a fiction, but also a myth which has endured to this day, when he addressed an envelope to Nathan:

N: M: Rothschild Esq.
Banker
London[51]

"Although I consider you as *a banker*," he wrote Nathan, "and am as well satisfied with your acceptance as I should be with that of any banker in London, they may reply that upon reference to the printed list of *London bankers*, they could not find your name amongst them."[52]

The unsavory relationship between these two men continued until August 1810, when Nathan precipitously gave up bills of exchange that had been accepted by Devaynes & Co. This prompted Devaynes & Co. to do the same with bills Moulsen & Fawcett had accepted. This time, Fawcett could not make good on these bills and his firm's creditors caused an investigation into his dealings. Fawcett accused Nathan of bad faith.[53] At least £14,000 in bills were at stake.[54] In addition, Fawcett owed thousands of pounds to Solomon Cohen who subsequently sought legal redress to get back his money.[55] At the end of October 1810, Fawcett again wrote to Nathan: "I am a close prisoner to my room, and very much reduced in body, as well as mind," and, finally, "Under these circumstances it was not possible for me to settle my affairs in any other way, than what I have done namely—a friendly commission of bankruptcy," and "to quit this country for ever."[56]

Nathan must have repeated (or even boasted) to his father what Peter Fawcett had said about him being a *banker*. But his father was not impressed. Nathan's relationship with his father had not improved appreciably. It might have been expected that, after more than a decade, the father-son business association would have become less strained but the temperament of one seemingly could not accommodate the temperament of the other. Although meager, their extant correspondence reveals details of their unusual and quarrelsome relationship. "I shall see myself oblige[d] to break off all banking business with you," the senior Rothschild wrote his son in August 1809, "unless you mention at the time of your Remittance, the Exchange of every Bill and for how many £ you debited my Acct. as it is the Custom with others [*sic*] Bankers."[57]

Mayer Amschel Rothschild's criticism of his son is especially worthy of note because it was leveled just prior to the time when he supposedly entrusted to Nathan the purchase of securities for Wilhelm, the Elector of Hesse-Kassel.

The Rothschild-elector connection is the central conundrum of the historiography of the Rothschilds. Writers have used it to offer speculative answers to important questions, such as how Nathan made and disposed of his money during 1809–1810, how he was able to fund his specie and bullion trade, and how he was able, at the same time, to make substantial purchases of 3 percent Consol securities.

In 1983, Richard Davis, in his book *The English Rothschilds*, stated: "but there is no doubt that beginning in 1809 very large sums of the Elector's money were put into this British stock, with Nathan acting on the Elector's behalf. . . . for long periods Nathan had a great deal of money and valuable assets in his own hands." In this regard, Davis wrote, "see Count Corti, *The Rise of the House of Rothschild.* . . . Corti had access to Continental archives since destroyed."[58]

Count Egon Caesar Corti had researched the correspondence of Carl Friedrich Buderus (Buderus von Carlshausen), the elector's financial adviser, and found substantial information about Mayer Amschel Rothschild's involvement in the investment of the elector's money. According to Corti, in February 1809, the close relationship between Buderus and Mayer Amschel Rothschild was: "actually embodied in a written agreement between them which virtually made the electoral official a secret partner in the firm of Rothschild." Buderus invested 20,000 gulden and "promised to advise that firm in all business matters to the best of his ability and to advance its interests as far as he may find practicable." In return, Rothschild would provide Buderus "a true account of the profits made" on the 20,000 gulden. Corti states that "Buderus now had a personal interest in securing for Meyer Amschel Rothschild a monopoly in the conduct of the elector's business."[59] This cozy relationship between Buderus and the house of Rothschild continued for years.[60]

According to Corti, Buderus was successful in having the elector authorize Mayer Amschel Rothschild to invest his money in British securities. "A sum of £150,000 had been invested as recently as December 18, 1809, in three per cent British Consols from *interest* received on behalf of the 'poor' elector."[61] Corti does not state whether this was the first or the second investment of £150,000 but, from another letter in November 1810, to the elector, Buderus referred to a third investment, which would presumably bring the total to £450,000. "'After long arguments, and as the result of great efforts . . . I have persuaded the crown agent, Rothschild, in effecting *the third investment of £150,000 sterling*, to charge one-quarter percent less commission, so that he will deliver the stock *for 73¾*, involving a saving of £4,521. . . . The younger son of Crown Agent Rothschild will bring over the document relating to the first purchase of stock, as soon as means can be found for sending it safely.'"[62]

In December 1810, the elector wrote Buderus that he was satisfied with Mayer Amschel Rothschild's service:

> I have decided to increase this investment by a further £100,000 . . . but on the understanding that I shall pay this amount in instalments [*sic*], and that I am not to be worried about it in any way. At the same time you are to see that *the document regarding the first investment* reaches me as soon as possible,

and *that I receive the others shortly afterwards.* I note with pleasure that the House of Rothschild has shown its traditional devotion to me. . . . You will kindly convey to them my satisfaction and gratitude.[63]

This letter raises a puzzling question as to why the elector had not received "the document regarding the first investment" at least one year after £150,000 was supposedly invested on his behalf. Nathan, in his "My dear Father" letter of 8 September 1809, mentioned that he had visited the elector's London banking firm of Messrs. Peter & Charles van Notten & Co. but said nothing about any investment on behalf of the elector.[64] From October through December 1809, Jacob [James] Rothschild visited his brother in London and could have conveyed the Consol document to his father but, in the extant correspondence about his visit, there is no mention that such an investment was made.[65] Later, Joseph Barber related that Jacob had visited London, Manchester, and Liverpool in June and July 1810, and, while it would not be likely that any discussion of the elector's 3 percent Consols would be found in Barber's letters, Jacob certainly had another opportunity to collect and deliver the important Consol document to his father.[66] By April 1811, the elector had still not received title to the Consols. "'Young Rothschild,'" Buderus wrote to reassure the elector, "'is actually on his way to London to fetch the certificates of title regarding your investment of capital.'"[67] But several months later the situation had not changed, and the elector again wrote to Buderus: "*I am exceedingly worried about this matter.*'"

> . . . In the meantime you are *to cease making any further payments with respect to these stocks, neither are you to invest in them any further English interest payments. I am still waiting in vain for the documents regarding the capital which I have invested*; and in spite of all the confidence which I have in Rothschild, I cannot tolerate this delay any longer. Neither has the registration of the older stocks been effected yet. . . . You must see that [*chargé d'affaires,* Lorentz] is kept fully informed of all my financial affairs in England, and especially of *the investments effected through Rothschild, in order that he may keep an eye on them.*[68]

Buderus chose to execute the elector's orders selectively and it was probably indicative of the way he handled the elector's business with the Rothschilds. Buderus never informed Lorentz, the elector's *chargé d'affaires* in London, as the elector had instructed.[69] This undoubtedly is why Lorentz does not mention it in his 1811 and 1812 reported conversations with Nathan from whom he wanted to borrow money for his personal affairs.[70]

Missing from Corti's quotations from Buderus's correspondence is any reference to how the investment transactions were executed; whether via Mayer Amschel Rothschild and Nathan Rothschild, or via Mayer Amschel Rothschild and the elector's London banker, van Notten & Co., with or without Nathan Rothschild's participation. Also missing is Nathan Rothschild's name or even an oblique reference to him. In the context of the correspondence, Buderus's reference to "'Young Rothschild'" could mean any of Mayer Amschel Rothschild's sons but it most likely referred to Carl or Jacob Rothschild, who frequently traveled on business for the Frankfurt house, and certainly not Nathan Rothschild, who already resided in London. Finally, Corti relates that during the spring of 1812, the Rothschilds succeeded "in smuggling over to the Continent a certificate for £189,500 sterling, and this was immediately forwarded to the elector. William now again consented to the interest on his capital being used for effecting investments."[71] Corti does not state what this £189,500 represented and it may be that his search through the paper trail of interest money derived from the elector's investments ended with this communication.

In the received version of the historiography of these events, there is the implication that Nathan made use of the elector's funds for his own operations. If he did, that could explain why the certificate for £189,500 was not delivered to the elector prior to the spring of 1812. Corti's interpretation of this matter fueled this assumption, although it was vague and betrayed his ignorance as to how Nathan purchased 3 percent Consols, which in reality was a simple transaction. He wrote that Nathan would not have had any difficulty in "getting possession of the documents certifying the purchases of stock, this being not so difficult for Nathan to arrange, in view of his numerous Jewish and non-Jewish connections." He further suggested that Nathan might have made use of the elector's money for his own purposes "as considerable periods of time could be made to intervene between the purchase and the payment of the securities, he sometimes had temporary control of very substantial sums of money." However, Corti did not document that this actually occurred.[72]

The most recent survey of these events and historiography is found in Niall Ferguson's 1998 *The House of Rothschild. Money's Prophets 1798–1848*. Chapter two is entitled: "The Elector's Treasure." In it, he related how the elector made a lot of money from selling the services of his Hessian army to England and concluded: "This money was paid not in the form of cash, but in (non-interest-bearing) bills of exchange which were initially paid to William's account at the London bank of Van Notten & Son. . . . his object in realising such bills was more usually to invest his earnings so that they yielded the highest possible interest." Ferguson calculated the elector's estimated wealth in 1806 to be more than £4 million, of which about 10 percent "was invested in English annuities."[73]

Ferguson appropriately added that: "the myth of the elector's treasure has been related so often and with so much embroidery that it has never seriously been questioned. Yet a close scrutiny of the surviving records suggests that the elector's significance has been exaggerated—or at least misunderstood."[74]

However, Ferguson made his own contributions to this misunderstanding. One was the epigraph he chose to introduce chapter two—"The Old Man . . . made our fortune"—which expresses the traditional notion about how Nathan Rothschild achieved his early prosperity.[75] Ferguson quoted this from a letter written by Carl Rothschild to Amschel Rothschild on 9 September 1814—that is, several years after the transactions supposedly took place. There are two translations of Carl's letter at The Rothschild Archive. The first was made several decades ago and the translator actually warned readers: "this letter seems to define a frequently misinterpreted fact."[76] In the most recent translation of that letter, which contains a good deal of routine business reportage, the mention of "the old man" is found midway in the letter and the words "made our fortune" are found at the bottom of it. It was by combining those two that Ferguson developed his epigraph. Moreover, the author of the latter part of the statement was not Carl but Nathan, whose letter to Carl is not extant. Carl merely restated to Amschel what Nathan had written to him: "He has written about the Elector again saying that the Elector has made our fortune. If he hadn't had £300,000 in his hands he would have been nothing and he writes as though, I don't know, there might be something to think about. I would rather eat dry bread myself, may God be with me."[77]

There is a problem with another statement made by Ferguson. In the opening paragraph to this chapter, Ferguson elaborated on the relationship of the Rothschilds to the elector: "Indeed, even Mayer Amschel's own sons themselves tended to regard his relationship with William IX, Hereditary Prince, Landgrave and after 1803 Elector (Kurfürst) of Hesse-Kassel, as the real foundation of their fortune."[78] To support his assertion, Ferguson cited a letter from Amschel in April 1814. But Amschel's letter does not contain such a statement. What Amschel wrote was that: "Buderus has been here. He said to me, 'You have made your fortune out of *the old man*. Don't leave him in the lurch.'"[79]

There is yet another oft-quoted and widely circulated story about how and when Nathan first came to handle the elector's money. It also is difficult to verify in order to determine if it is true. On 14 February 1834, Sir Thomas Fowell Buxton wrote a letter to his daughter: "'We yesterday dined at Ham House to meet the Rothschilds; and very amusing it was. He (Rothschild) told us his life and adventures.'"[80] At the end of the letter, Buxton wrote: "'The Prince of Hesse-Cassel,' said Rothschild, 'gave my father his money; there was no time to be lost; he sent it to me. I had £600,000 arrive unexpectedly by the post; and I put it to such good use, that the prince made me a present of all his wine and his linen.'"[81]

This story is contrary to Corti's scholarship in several respects. First, the sum of money is greater than £450,000–£550,000; second, the conveyance of the money is different; and, third, there is no mention of the installment investments during 1809–1812. Corti's research implies that the money—interest on the elector's British investments—was on deposit in London, presumably at the elector's banker, Messrs. Peter & Charles van Notten & Co., and that Buderus simply authorized its use by the Rothschilds, with Nathan Rothschild in London acting on behalf of his father in Frankfurt.

Ferguson provided a different set of details. "At the start of his time in exile [circa 1807], William already had a very substantial English portfolio, primarily annuities with a nominal value of £635,400 paying interest of £20,426 a year."[82] But it is obvious that to accumulate £450,000 to £550,000 of interest at that rate would take decades, and it should also be noted that as of July 1818 the elector's investment portfolio in London was £782,150 and produced a half-year dividend of £11,732.[83]

Ferguson, therefore, suggested additional sums of the elector's money from which the investments could have been made. The Prince of Wales and his brothers, the dukes of York and Clarence, owed the elector "a considerable sum" and in 1812 the debts including back interest amounted to £225,361.[84] But, while this figure is correct, according to a report dated 21 December 1815 by Robert Gray, secretary to the Prince of Wales's commissioners, no interest was paid to the elector during 1809–1816 and so none could have been invested for him.[85]

Ferguson also identified another possible source of funds for the elector. "As an ally of the crown, he also received subsidies totalling £100,150 between 1807 and 1810."[86] But Ferguson did not provide any data on the interest that this subsidy would accrue nor did he establish whether it was paid to the elector, let alone invested by the Rothschilds on behalf of the elector.

"The critical question," Ferguson wrote, was "what should be done with the interest payments and subsidies as they were paid to William's current account with Van Notten." Without explaining why van Notten could not itself have made the purchases of securities for the elector, Ferguson instead speculated—without accompanying source citations—how Mayer Amschel Rothschild might have benefited from differing exchange rates by sending his own bills of exchange to Nathan, who would purchase 3 percent Consols for the elector's account instead of using the money already on deposit at Peter & Charles van Notten & Co.[87]

There is no existing contemporary evidence for the period 1809–1812 to support the view that Nathan Rothschild used the elector's money for his own purposes. In fact, the extant contemporary sources reveal quite a different story about Nathan's purchases of 3 percent Consols. What undermines the veracity of the received version of the Rothschild-elector historiography and what has not been explored until now is the important role that Harman & Co. played in facilitating the commercial and financial transactions of the Rothschilds. The extant accounts and correspondence of Harman & Co. contribute not only to the reconstruction of Nathan's early business enterprises but also to the resolution of crucial elements in the received historiography.

Harman & Co. purchased, sold, and shipped for Nathan specie and commodities—among the latter, barilla, cotton, currants, flax, hemp, indigo, bar iron, logwood, madder, olive oil, silk, soap, tallow, and tobacco—and purchased and sold securities for him and his father.[88] Nathan had from time to time purchased 3 percent Consols either for himself or for his father and, at times, those securities were held in Nathan Rothschild's name or in the name of Jeremiah Harman, who would later transfer them into Nathan's or his father's account. According to Nathan's 1809–1810 problematic *Ledgers*, his transactions with Harman & Co amounted to £96,297 (£46,530 in 1809, and £49,767, in 1810) of which his stock account amounted to £57,225.[89] Moreover, the *Ledgers* separately list under his father's name: "Stock Account" (1809 = £105,310) and "Stock Purchases"(1809 = £56,714; 1810 = £211,604; and 1811 = £122,463).[90]

In March 1809, a critical month in the growth of his mercantile career—when he contemplated moving from 12 Great St. Helens to No. 2, New Court, St. Swithin's Lane—Nathan purchased 3 percent Consols through Harman & Co. for £20,000: "Said Sum is placed for the present, as agreed between us, in the name of our Jer[emiah] Harman."[91] In early April, Nathan purchased an additional £25,000 3 percent Consols, [92] and in May yet another £35,000 through Harman & Co.[93] Nathan remitted cash and bills of exchange to Harman & Co. to be credited to his stock account.[94] Thus, for the period 4 March–26 May 1809, there are bona fide sources that Nathan purchased £80,000 in 3 percent Consols through Harman & Co. On 5 July, 1809, Harman & Co. credited his account with the half-year dividend "on your £80,000 Consolidated 3 pCt standing in the name of our Jeremiah Harman." The placement of this stock sum was not altered until 1811.[95]

Where did Nathan Rothschild obtain the money for these purchases? The extant contemporary evidence demonstrates conclusively that he obtained the funds from his recent entry into the specie and bullion trade and from his father, who substantially underwrote it as his partner. While the following chapter examines this trade in detail, it is important at this time to note several important and well-documented facts. In March–April, 1809, his father sent him about £49,999 in bills of exchange through the auspices of Braunsberg & Co. of Amsterdam, which forwarded them to Harman & Co.;[96] and, for the entire year 1809, about £101,000.[97] During October–December 1809, Braunsberg & Co. sent him advances of about £59,000 against future sales of specie and bullion.[98] Nathan used these funds to pay for the specie and bullion he would ship to Amsterdam and Frankfurt and, until his invoices became due, he parked some of this money temporarily in safe 3 percent Consols, as will be shown in the next chapter.

There is no extant contemporary evidence for the purchase of £150,000 "as recently as December 18, 1809, in three percent British Consols from interest received on behalf of the 'poor' elector," as Corti-Buderus related. In March 1810, Nathan instructed Harman & Co. to sell £30,000 of 3 percent Consols belonging to his father that were being held in Jeremiah Harman's name. Additional sales also were anticipated.[99] Although the extant record attests that most of Nathan's Consol transactions were handled by Harman & Co., at least three were handled by John Mann at the Royal Exchange: on 10 May 1810, he sold £10,000 and purchased £10,000; and, on 20 September, he sold £20,000.[100] Again, it is not known whether these transactions were for

Nathan or for his father. During the remainder of the year, Nathan continued to fill his stock account at Harman & Co.: he deposited £17,125 on 16 August; £10,000 on 16 October; £6,800 on 19 October; and £11,780 on 17 December.[101] On 23 October, Harman & Co. wrote him that it had "transferred into your Name the Sum of Forty thousand Pounds 3 pCt Cons. Ann. which completes the amount purchased by our House for your account."[102] In December 1810, Harman & Co. again credited Nathan's account with the half-year dividend on his £80,000 3 percent Consols standing in the name of Jeremiah Harman.[103] However, ten months later, in October 1811, Harman & Co. informed Nathan that his stock account had a balance of merely £196. The above-mentioned £80,000 in 3 percent Consols had been transferred into his father's account.[104]

It may be, as Corti suggested, that the Rothschilds were employed by the elector to purchase and manage British securities on his behalf from the interest on his investments in England. But there is no evidence in the extant contemporary record to support the view that Nathan and/or his father either received the estimated £450,000 to £550,000 that the elector had supposedly authorized during the period 1809–1811, or that either or both purchased that amount of Consols for the elector. Further, evidence is lacking that such a huge sum could have been generated in interest from the elector's known investments and/or from outstanding debts owed to him by personages or by the British government. And, hearsay to the contrary, there is no sustainable evidence that Nathan and/or his father made even "temporary" use of such money for their own business ventures.

It is not possible to say, on the basis of currently available contemporary documents, what Nathan or others may have meant by the comment that the elector or "the old man" made the Rothschilds' fortune. Any conclusions or inferences in that regard can only be speculation and nothing more.

Notes

1. AH Lon. to JF Got. 19 April 1808, RAL xi/112/38.
2. AH Lon. to NMR Man. 11 March 1808, RAL xi/112/76.
3. AH Lon. to JF Got. 11 March 1808, RAL xi/112/76.
4. AH Lon. to NMR Man. 12 March 1808, RAL xi/112/38.
5. For example, A. L. Annesby, a London merchant, condoled with Nathan Rothschild and requested bills on L. B. Cohen & Co. because he knew he could still negotiate them. Annesby Lon. to NMR Man. 12 March 1808, RAL xi/112/76.

6. *Shivah*: "The seven solemn days of mourning for the dead, beginning imme-diately after the funeral, when Jews 'sit *shivah*' in the home of the deceased." Leo Rosten, *The Joys of Yiddish* (New York: McGraw-Hill Book Company, 1968), p. 342.

7. *Minyan*: "The ten male Jews who are required for religious services." Ibid p. 243.

8. Selig [Solomon] Cohen Lon. to NMR Man. 16 March 1808, RAL xi/82/10/3.

9. See *Will. LBC*.

10. SC Lon. to Dear Sister [Hannah Cohen Rothschild] Man. 16 March 1808, RAL xi/82/10/3.

11. JF Got. to NMR c/o L B Cohen. Lon. 8 April 1808, RAL xi/112/76.

12. Selig [Solomon] Cohen Lon. to NMR Man. 21 March 1808, RAL xi/82/10/6.

13. See JB Man. to NMR n.p. 13 April 1808, RAL xi/38/41A.

14. JB Man. to NMR Lon. 2 March 1809, RAL xi/38/41B.

15. AH Lon. to JF Got. 15 March 1808, PF Man. to NMR Lon. 13 April 1808 & Horstman letters from Amsterdam, RAL xi/112/38, respectively; JB Man. to NMR Lon. 31 March–31 August & 21 September 1808 & NMR Man. to JR Lon.13–14 & 16 July 1808, RAL xi/38/41A, respectively; & Imperial Insurance Company Policy No. 35457, RAL 000/573.

16. S. D. Chapman, "The Foundation of the English Rothschilds: N. M. Roth-schild as a Textile Merchant 1799–1811," *Textile History*, 8 (1977), 111.

17. See *Will. LBC*.

18. See *Bills of Exchange Ledgers*, RAL 1/218/3; LJ RAL 1/218/30 & 41; JB Man. to NMR Lon. 13, 19 & 29 April; 15 & 21–22 June, 11, 27 & 30 July, 3, 10, 17 & 25 August 1808, RAL xi/38/41A; & PF Man. to NMR Lon. 13 August & 19 November 1808, RAL xi/112/76.

19. SC Lon. to NMR Man. 22 February 1808, RAL xi/112/76.

20. JB Man. to NMR post office, Lon. 6 April, 11–12, 16, 18, 21 & 25 May; & 4 June 1808, RAL xi/38/41A.

21. SC Lon. to NMR Man. 29 December 1808, RAL xi/112/76.

22. His transactions with other merchants were relatively insignificant. In 1809, with Moulsen & Fawcett (Man.), about £54,000, and J. Aldebert & Co.(Man.), about £55,000; in 1810, with S. M. Samuels (Lon.), about £32,000, and Moulsen & Fawcett, about £79,000. See RL RAL VI/10/0 (1809–1810), ff. 1–2, 10 & 43; & RAL VI/10/1 (1810), pp. 3, 7 & 36.

23. RL RAL VI/10/0; & RAL VI/10/1.

24. RL RAL VI/10/0 (1809–1810), ff. 20–23, 83, 121–122, 164–166.

25. RL RAL VI/10/1 (1810), pp. 40, 50–51, 119, 144, 173 & VI/10/0 (1810), ff. 83, 123–124. Nathan had several different accounts with his father and together they repre-sented a substantial trading and financial position, even though the detailed nature of the transactions that made up each account cannot be determined. For the period May–December 1809, Nathan's transactions with his father amounted to an estimated £300,000, and for 1810 they almost tripled to £867,000. RL RAL VI/10/0 (1809–1810), ff. 30, 130–133, 142–147, 153, 236–239, 244 & RAL VI/10/1 (1810), pp. 35, 77–78.

26. Orbell, p. 5. See also Joshua Montefiore, *A Commercial Dictionary: Contain-ing the Present State of Mercantile Law, Practice, and Custom. Intended for the Use of*

the Cabinet, the Counting House, and the Library (London: Printed by the Author, 1804).

27. See L B Cohen & Son Lon. to NMR Lon. 16 March 1809, RAL xi/112/38; & L B Cohen & Son Lon. to NMR Lon. 30 May, 1, 6 & 10 August & 7 September 1810, RAL xi/112/3, respectively.

28. JB Man. to NMR Lon. 19 September 1808 & 13 May 1809, RAL xi/38/41A & B, respectively. See also, LJ, RAL 1/218/30, p.145 & passim.

29. JB Man. to NMR Lon. 3 May 1809, RAL xi/38/41B.

30. JB Man. to NMR Lon. 25 April 1809, RAL xi/38/41B.

31. JB Man. to NMR Lon. 3 May 1809, RAL xi/38/41B.

32. JB Man. to NMR Lon. 13 May 1809, RAL xi/38/41B.

33. As of 31 August 1810, the firm N M Rothschild owed "Rothschild, Brothers" "nearly *£10,000.*" See JB Man. to NMR Lon. 15, 17, 22 & 29 September 1810, RAL xi/38/41C, respectively. On 25 June 1811, the *Manchester Exchange Herald* carried the following notice: "'the business heretofore carried on by the undersigned Nathan Meyer Rothschild, at Manchester, under the firm of 'Rothschild, Brothers' will cease to be carried on by him from this day, and any person having dealings with that firm, are required to send their demands or pay their accounts to N. M. Rothschild, at his Counting-house, in No. 2 New Court, St Swithin's-lane, London.'" Reproduced and quoted in Gray & Aspey, p. 93.

34. *Imperial Insurance Company Policy*, No. 35457, RAL 000/573.

35. PF Man. to NMR Lon. 4 & 23 June 1808, RAL xi/112/76; & JB Man. to NMR post office, Lon. 28–29 June 1808, RAL xi/38/41A.

36. William Thomson, *Dictionary of Banking*, 6th ed. (London: Pitman, 1926), p. 9. Bold font is mine. I am grateful to Dr. John Orbell and Dr. Joost Jonker for consulting with me regarding this matter.

37. PF Man. to NMR Lon. 23 June 1808, RAL xi/112/76 & PF Man. to NMR Lon. 26 July 1809, RAL xi/112/34.

38. PF Man. to NMR Lon. 23 June 1808, RAL xi/112/76. See also PF Man. to NMR Lon. 28 May & 4 June, RAL xi/112/76.

39. PF Man. to NMR Angel Court, Lon. 13 April 1808, RAL xi/112/38. Italics are mine.

40. PF Man. to NMR Lon. 24 November 1808, RAL xi/112/76.

41. PF Man. to NMR Lon. 13 June 1808, RAL xi/112/76.

42. William Thomson, *Dictionary of Banking*, 6th ed. (London: Pitman, 1926), p. 519. I am grateful to Dr. John Orbell and Dr. Joost Jonker for consulting with me regarding this matter.

43. JB Man. to NMR post office, Lon. 19 September 1808, RAL xi/38/41A.

44. JB Man. to NMR Lon. 26 October 1808, RAL xi/38/41A.

45. JB Man. to NMR Lon. 27 October 1808, RAL xi/38/41A.

46. JB Man. to NMR Lon. 2–3, 9, 12, 15, 23–24 & 30 November, 7 & 10 December 1808, RAL xi/38/41A.

47. PF Man. to NMR Lon. 19 December 1808, RAL xi/112/76.

48. PF Man. to NMR Lon. 24 December 1808, RAL xi/112/76.

49. PF Man. to NMR Lon. 28 December 1808, RAL xi/112/76.

50. PF Man. to NMR Lon. 30 December 1808, RAL xi/112/76.

51. For example, see PF Man. to NMR Lon. 17 August 1808, RAL xi/112/76.

52. PF Man. to NMR Lon. 30 December 1808, RAL xi/112/76.

53. PF Man. to NMR Lon. 28 August 1810, RAL xi/112/34. See also JB Man. to NMR Lon. 1, 4, 8, 11, 14 & 20–21 August 1810, RAL xi/38/41C.

54. PF Man. to NMR Lon. 20 & 25 October 1810, RAL xi/112/34. See also JB Man. to NMR Lon. 13 & 15 October 1810, RAL xi/38/41C.

55. See JB Man. to NMR Lon. 29 October, 3 November, 3–4 & 31 December 1810, RAL xi/38/41C.

56. PF & JB Man. to NMR Lon. 29 October 1810, RAL xi/112/34 & RAL xi/38/41C, respectively. On the bankruptcy proceedings, see JB Man. to NMR Lon 31 October, 3, 7, 15, 20, 22 & 27 November, 4, 22, 26 & 31 December 1810, RAL xi/38/41C.

57. MAR Fft. to NMR Lon. 2 August 1809, RAL xi/86/0A. For similar criticisms, see MAR n.p. to NMR, n.p. 28 June 1809, German original, RAL xi/86/0A (trans. RAL xi/T5/6) & MAR Fft. to NMR n.p. 20 August 1809, RAL xi/86/0A. See also, NMR Lon. to MAR Fft. 8 September 1809, RAL xi/86/0A.

58. Richard Davis, *The English Rothschilds* (Chapel Hill: University of North Carolina Press, 1983), pp. 29, 248, n. 34, respectively.

59. See Corti, pp. 69 *et seq.* & 411, n. 41.Carl Friedrich Buderus, Buderus von Carlshausen (1759–1819) was variously the principal revenue officer of Hesse and administrator of Wilhelm's estates.

60. A letter exists that indicates that the Rothschilds managed the elector's security investment in England in 1818 and paid Buderus £1500. MAR & Sons Fft. to NMR Lon. 21 October 1818, RAL xi/86/0A.

61. Corti, p. 79. Italics mine.

62. Quoted in Corti, p. 89 & see p. 411, n. 53. Italics mine.

63. Quoted in Corti, p. 91 & see p. 411, n. 56. Italics mine.

64. NMR Lon. to MAR Fft. 8 September 1809, RAL xi/86/0A.

65. MAR Fft. to NMR Lon. 24 September, 10 & 13 December 1809 & CMR Fft. to JMR Lon. 29 October & 15 November 1809, RAL xi/86/0A, respectively.

66. JB Man. to NMR Lon. 14 May, 16 & 25 June, 2 & 25 July 1810, RAL xi/38/41C.

67. Quoted in Corti, p. 93 & see p. 411, n. 58 (7 April 1811).

68. Quoted in Corti, p. 96 & see p. 412, n. 62 (28 August 1811). Italics mine.

69. Quoted in Corti, p. 97.

70. Lorentz, Lon. to NMR Lon. 14 January, 27 June, 8 August, 28 October, 8 November 1811, 13 April, 23 June, 11 July & 24 November 1812, RAL xi/112/33.

71. Corti, p. 99; & see pp. 96–99 & p. 412, notes 63–67.

72. Ibid, pp. 112–113. For "the relative ease" by which the 3 percent Consol "could be acquired and disposed of," see supra chapter 1, note 42.

73. Ferguson, p. 61.

74. Ibid, p. 60.

75. Ibid, p. 60 & p. 494, n. 1.

76. CMR Fft. to AMR n.p. 9 September 1814, RAL xi/T27/105.

77. CMR Fft. to AMR n.p. 9 September 1814, RAL xi/82/1, Tape 123.

78. Ferguson, p. 60.

79. Ferguson, p. 494, n. 2; & AMR Fft. to SMR & JMR Paris, circa April 1814, RAL xi/82/9/1, Tape 247/Letter 18.

80. Quoted in Charles Buxton (ed.), *Memoirs of Sir Thomas Fowell Buxton, Baronet* (Philadelphia: Henry Longstreth, 1849), p. 292. See Victor Gray, "An off-hand man: The character of Nathan Rothschild," in Gray & Aspey, pp. 14–21.

81. Quoted in Charles Buxton (ed.), *Memoirs of Sir Thomas Fowell Buxton, Baronet* (Philadelphia, Henry Longstreth, 1849), p. 294.

82. Ferguson, p. 66.

83. For these sums, see MAR & Sons Fft. to NMR Lon. 21 October 1818, RAL xi/86/0A.

84. Ferguson, pp. 66 & 495, n. 41.

85. See Robert Gray, "Debt to the Elector of Hesse," 21 December 1815, *HP* BLAddMss. 57416, ff. 91–92 & GH Lon. to NMR Lon. 25 March 1816, RAL xi/38/59C.

86. Ferguson, p. 66.

87. Ibid, pp. 66–67.

88. See Harman & Co. correspondence with Nathan Rothschild, 1808–1810, RAL xi/112/38 & RAL xi/112/3, passim; in particular, Har Lon. to NMR n.p. 20 May, 11, 22–23 June, 25 August, 15 & 20 September, 6 & 21 October, 18 November & 6 December 1808, RAL xi/112/38; "Mr. N. M. Rothschild his account current with Harman & Co." 31 December 1808–31 December 1809, RAL xi/112/3; & Har Lon. to NMR Lon. 1 March, 21 May, 27 June & 25 October 1810, RAL xi/112/3. See also LJ RAL 1/218/30 & 41, passim.

89. RL RAL VI/10/0 (1809), ff. 125–126; & VI/10/1 (1810), pp. 11–12, 154.

90. RL RAL VI/10/0 (1809–1810), ff. 130–133, 153, respectively.

91. £10,000 @ 67¼ & £10,000 @ 67 ⅜, Har Lon. to NMR (Private) Great St. Helens, Lon. 4 March 1809, RAL xi/112/3; & see LJ RAL 1/218/30.

92. £10,000 @ 67⅝ & £15,000 @ 67⅞, LJ 5 & 12 April 1809, RAL 1/218/41 & Har Lon. to NMR Great St. Helens, Lon. 6 April 1809, RAL xi/112/3.

93. £10,000 @ 68½, £10,000 @ 68⅜, £10,000 @ 68⅝ & £10,000 @ 68⅛, LJ RAL 1/218/41 & Har Lon. to NMR Lon. 25 May 1809, RAL xi/112/3.

94. Har Lon. to NMR Lon. 25 May 1809 & "Mr. N. M. Rothschild his account current with Harman & Co." RAL xi/112/3.

95. LJ 5 July 1809, RAL 1/218/41, pp. 32 & 141, Har Lon. to NMR New Court, Lon. 17 December 1810, RAL xi/112/3 & Har Lon. to NMR Lon. 5 October 1811, RAL xi/112/33 (RAL xi/112/34).

96. BB Ams. to NMR Lon. 25 March & 5 April 1809, RAL xi/38/55A.

97. BB Ams. to NMR Lon. 25 March, 5 April, 15 & 22 July, 15 September, 10, 16, 19, 23, 27 & 30 December 1809, RAL xi/38/55A.

98. BB Ams. to NMR Lon. 30 September, 10, 14, 21 & 24 October, 11, 21, 25 & 29 November, 5, 13, 18–19, 23 & 29 December 1809, RAL xi/38/55A.

99. £10,000 @ 67¾; £10,000 @ 68; & £10,000 @ 68⅛. Har Lon. to NMR New Court, Lon. 13 March 1810, RAL xi/112/3.

100. At 70½, 64, and 66¼, respectively, John Mann, Stock Exchange, Lon. to NMR Lon. 10 May & 26 September 1810, RAL xi/112/34, respectively.

101. Har Lon. to NMR New Court, Lon. 16 August, 16 & 19 October & 17 December 1810, RAL xi/112/3, respectively.

102. Har Lon. to NMR New Court, Lon. 23 October 1810, RAL xi/112/3.

103. See Har Lon. to NMR New Court, Lon. 17 December 1810, RAL xi/112/3, Har Lon. to NMR Lon. 5 October 1811, RAL xi/112/33 (RAL xi/112/34) & LJ 10 January 1810, RAL 1/218/41, p.147.

104. See Har Lon. to NMR Lon. 5 October 1811, RAL xi/112/33 (RAL xi/112/34) & LJ RAL 1/218/41, p.147.

PART TWO

Gold and Silver

Portrait of Nathan Rothschild by Moritz Daniel Oppenheim, n.d. Reproduced with the permission of The Rothschild Archive.

THREE

Nathan Mayer Rothschild's Trading Network

1808–1812

> Have you not lately had brought to you a great quantity
> of Gold which cannot be exported?
>
> —It is very scarce now; but there is a great deal that
> we melt down, which cannot be exported, because it
> cannot be sworn off as foreign Gold.
>
> Has there not come to you a great quantity within
> the last twelvemonth?
>
> —No, it has been very scarce, we can hardly supply
> the trade . . . owing to the shortness of supply; and, I
> apprehend, a great deal is smuggled out of the country.
>
> —FRANCIS HORNER, *in the Chair.*
> WILLIAM MERLE, *banker & gold refiner, house of*
> *Cox and Merle, Examined.*
> *24 February 1810.*[1]

> Whereas great Quantities of the Gold Coin of this
> Realm, have been clandestinely and illegally exported
> from various parts of England: And whereas it is highly
> expedient to prevent such unlawful Practice, and to
> discover and punish the Offenders.
>
> —*Gold Coin. Custom House. London.*
> *12 September 1811.*[2]

By the time Nathan Rothschild moved to London in the summer of 1808, it had become clear to him, as it had to many other commodity and textile merchants who depended very much on having access to overseas markets for their livelihood, that the traditional way of doing business was no longer profitable. Access to overseas markets had become severely restricted by the double constraints of Napoleon's Continental Blockade (1806) and Great Britain's Orders in Council (1807). So, not unlike other British merchants, Nathan engaged in smuggling not only commodities and textiles, as the *Laura* operation had shown, but also specie and bullion to the Continent.

Nathan was repeatedly warned about the risks involved in smuggling. For example, Fermin de Tastet & Co., a London firm with which Nathan worked closely, wrote to him one week before Levy Barent Cohen died in March 1808, about the large balance he owed the company and about its expectation that he would remit bills to pay off his account "when convenient" for him to do so. "We say, when convenient, because we are sensible of the disappointment you must experience with the present irregularity in the intercourse with the Continent, or to speak more accurately we experience it ourselves with [the] rest of merchants; victims of the turn the war has taken, which consequently must affect the manufactures, agriculture, and so forth [of] all the nation, unless Heaven finds soon a remedy for us all. Amen."[3] Several months later, Fermin de Tastet & Co. again wrote him about the higher cost and danger of continuing his smuggling operations: "You know, we presume, that some people are shipping for Amsterdam, insuring at 40 perCt captures in port included. These shipments, although certainly susceptible of great profits, are, in our opinion, very hazardous, owing to the illegality of the practices."[4]

Nathan disregarded this advice. Instead he seized the opportunity presented by the rapidly rising market price of gold and silver in England and on the Continent to create for himself a niche in the international specie and bullion trade. It would prove to be a fateful decision for it was his role as a specie trader that would lead the British government to turn to him in 1814 to find and deliver French specie to pay Wellington's troops. And it was that relationship, based though it was on illegality and smuggling, that established Nathan as a dependable international banker, which became the basis for the creation of the Rothschild financial dynasty.

The escalation in the market price of gold and silver was caused, in general, by the war against France, which had been going on for more than decade prior to Nathan's move to London and, in particular, by events taking place in Great Britain. At the end of 1796, rumors were rife that the French intended to invade Britain and, by the third week of February 1797, fearful depositors across the country had withdrawn enough gold from banks to cause some of them to stop payment in that coin. The gold reserve at the Bank of England had fallen from less than £2,000,000, at the beginning of 1797, to a little more than £1,000,000, on 21 February. Merchants, bankers, and government officials hurriedly called meetings to deliberate what could be done to resolve the financial crisis that pervaded the country. The most crucial meetings were attended by the king, prime minister, cabinet members, the Privy Council, and officials of the Bank of England. In the evening of 26 February—"Black Sunday"—an Order in Council was issued prohibiting the Bank of England from paying out gold until the sense of Parliament could be taken. The Government instructed the Royal Mint to stamp large quantities of Spanish dollars stored at the Bank of England and also authorized the Bank to issue new one-pound and two-pound notes. By mid-March, the suspension had taken effect, the panic to a large extent had subsided, and Parliament made the suspension of cash payments the law. English gold coins ceased to circulate as currency and could not legally be exported. British merchants who were engaged in overseas trade were especially burdened because they could make payments abroad only with bills of exchange and scarce foreign specie and bullion.[5]

The cost of the war against Napoleon placed enormous demands on Great Britain's diminishing supply of specie and bullion. In particular, in 1808, Great Britain dispatched an expeditionary force to the Iberian Peninsula to support Spanish and Portuguese patriots against the increasing French military presence there. To pay for this, in addition to the specie purchased locally and regionally, Great Britain sent more than one million pounds in specie from home.[6]

During the summer of 1808, the market price in London for gold in bars rose above His Majesty's Mint price of £3.17.10½. per oz. (standard fineness) and sold for £4 per oz. In 1809, the market price fluctuated between £4.9. and £4.12. per oz. and, during the first three months of 1810, it moved between £4.10. and £4.12. per oz. Gold in bars of standard fineness selling at £4.10. per oz. was about 15½ percent above the Mint price.[7]

On the Continent, the demands by the French army placed a premium on foreign coins because they were portable and more marketable in foreign countries than gold in bars. This was particularly true for the gold Spanish-American doubloon and the gold coins of Portugal–Brazil.[8] This was noted in England: "From what I have heard," a bullion dealer testified before a parliamentary committee in February 1810, the higher price of gold "has greatly arisen from the practice of the French armies, who in their progress through the Continent carry Gold in order to pay the demands upon them; and as a proof of the probability of this circumstance, since the war in Spain, doubloons have borne a greater premium on the Continent in proportion to other Gold."[9]

The market price of silver also rose. The English East India Company, a major purchaser of silver, shipped large amounts to India and to China to balance its trade accounts and, occasionally, it resorted to "panic purchases," depleting the market of large amounts of silver in the course of one week. Silver also flowed to France. The continual drain of Great Britain's silver supplies led the Bank of England to "re-tariff the Spanish dollar," that is, to revalue it upward in 1797, 1804, and 1811.[10]

In 1808, the price of standard silver at the Royal Mint in London was 5s. 2d. (5 shilling 2 pence) per oz. and the value of the new Spanish dollar was 4s. 4d. or 4s.11½ per oz. In 1809, the London market price of new Spanish dollars advanced considerably and fluctuated between 5s. 5d. and 5s. 7d. per oz. In October 1810, new Spanish dollars were quoted even higher at 5s. 8½d. per oz.[11]

The market price of foreign gold and silver in England continued to climb and declined only when the war against Napoleon was nearing its end, as Table 3.1 illustrates.

Compounding this fluid situation in gold and silver was sterling's unfavorable exchange rate which, from the end of 1808, significantly undermined Great Britain's trade with the Continent. During the last six months of 1809 and first three months of 1810, the exchange rate for sterling at Hamburg and Amsterdam fell between 16 and 20 percent below par and at Paris it dipped even lower.[12] The convergence of these two circumstances—the rise in the market price of gold and silver and the fall in the exchange rate—meant that an English merchant who traded in specie and bullion to the Continent, while taking extraordinary risks, could reap extraordinary profits.

The most informative contemporary source revealing the complexities of the specie and bullion trade is the Parliamentary Select Committee on the High Price of Gold Bullion, which opened its inquiry on 22 February 1810 and published its findings on 8 June 1810.[13] Aaron Asher Goldsmid, the 25-year-old partner in Mocatta & Goldsmid, bullion broker to the Bank of England from the time of its establishment in 1694,[14] was the first to testify about the considerable profit that could be made in purchasing specie and bullion in England and selling it on the Continent. Francis Horner, in the

TABLE 3.1

Fluctuation in Market Price of Foreign Gold and Silver in England: 1811–1815

Year	Price of Standard Gold in Bars (per oz.)			Price of Portugal Gold in Coin (per oz.)			Price of Standard Silver in Bars (per oz.)			Price of New Spanish Dollars (per oz.)		
	£.	s.	d.	£.	s.	d.	£.	s.	d.	£.	s.	d.
1811[a]												
Low:	4	11	0	4	15	0	0	5	11½	0	5	10
High:	4	19	6	4	19	6	0	6	4	0	6	2
1812[b]												
Low:	4	15	0	4	14	0	0	6	3½	0	6	1
High:	5	7	0	5	11	0	0	6	7	0	6	8½
1813[c]												
Low:	4	17	0	5	1	0	0	6	7½	0	6	6
High:	5	10	0	5	11	6	0	6	11	0	7	0½
1814[d]												
Low:	4	4	0	4	4	0	0	5	6½	0	5	3½
High:	5	10	0	5	10	0	0	6	11½	0	6	11½
1815 January[e]												
Low:	4	6	6	4	6	6	0	5	9	0	5	7
High:	4	6	6	4	8	0	0	5	9	0	5	7

[a] *MPG & S: 1810–1811* & *MPG & S: 1811–1813.*
[b] *MPG & S: 1811–1813.*
[c] *MPG & S: 1811–1813* & *MPG & S: 1813–1814.*
[d] *MPG & S: 1813–1814* & *MPG & S: 1814–1815.*
[e] *MPG & S: 1814–1815.*

chair for the committee, asked him: "If a person in possession of 100 guineas of full weight [£105] were to melt them into bars and sell them in the market, what sum in Bank of England paper would he be able to obtain for them?" Goldsmid replied: £121. 11s. 6d.[15]

John Louis Greffulhe, a member of a respected general merchant banking family in London and Paris, also testified with detailed first-hand information.

Q: HORNER: Supposing you had a pound weight troy [*12 oz.*] of Gold of the English standard at Paris, and that you wished by means of that to procure a Bill of Exchange upon London, what would be the amount of the Bill of Exchange which you would procure in the present circumstances?

A: GREFFULHE: I find that a pound of Gold of the British standard at the present market price of 105 francs, and the exchange at 20 livres, would purchase a Bill of Exchange of £59. 8s.

Q: HORNER: At the present market price of Gold in London, how much standard Gold can you purchase for £59. 8s.?

A: GREFFULHE: At the price of £4.12s. I find it will purchase 13 ounces of
Gold, within a very small fraction.

Q: HORNER: Then what is the difference per cent. in the quantity of
Standard Gold which is equivalent to £59. 8s. of our currency as at Paris and in London?

A: GREFFULHE: About 8½ per cent.

Horner asked Greffulhe the same questions but substituted Hamburg and
Amsterdam for Paris and Greffulhe answered accordingly:

> At the Hamburgh price of 101, and the Exchange at 29, the amount of the
> Bill purchased on London would be £58. 4s. [which would purchase 12 oz. 13
> dwts., making a difference of about 5½ per cent.] At the Amsterdam price of
> 14½, Exchange 31.6 and Bank agio[16] 1 per cent. the amount of the Bill on
> London would be £58.18s. [which would purchase 12 oz. 16 dwts., making a
> difference of about 7 per cent.][17]

The testimony of Goldsmid and Greffulhe demonstrated how the business of arbitrage works; that is, the simultaneous purchase and sale of mon-
eys in different markets to profit from unequal prices. Merchants, bankers
and even British government officials engaged in arbitrage during the difficult wartime years. John Charles Herries, sometime banker, career bureau-
crat, and from 1811, commissary-in-chief, adroitly manipulated monetary
transactions to become extraordinarily influential during the last several years
of the Napoleonic Wars. The British government's desperate need for money
led him in February 1815 to propose raising from £400,000 to £500,000 on
the Continent by selling guineas borrowed from the Bank of England—
despite the prohibition on their export—and he calculated a net profit of
almost 13 percent above the price of gold at the Royal Mint in London.[18]

The circumstances were much different and more difficult for the ordi-
nary merchant or banker who wanted to engage in such arbitrage. The buying and selling of specie and bullion was a challenging trade. The price of
specie and bullion and the rate on bills of exchange fluctuated every trading
day.[19] This meant that a merchant or banker could only increase his profit
margin by shaving a fraction from the price he had to pay for specie and
bullion and the rate he had to pay for a bill of exchange. Nathan Rothschild
understood this market mechanism quite well and exploited it to the fullest.
He never simply accepted the quotes from dealers, brokers, and bankers but
bargained and bullied his way through every transaction.

Before gold or silver could be exported legally, the government required an oath to be sworn before the Court of Aldermen that the specie or bullion for export was foreign in origin or, as one refiner declared: "You swear that no part of the Gold you produce has been the current coin, or clippings or meltings [*sic*] of the current coin of this country."[20] Mocatta & Goldsmid actually required two witnesses during the melting process and all its transactions were entered into the books of the Bullion Office of the Bank of England. Mocatta & Goldsmid fixed the price of gold it bought and sold and received a brokerage fee of ⅛ percent from each party. Most of the gold it purchased came from "West Indies merchants," primarily Jamaican merchants, who found it more advantageous to remit gold because of its high market price in England, than bills of exchange. A fair amount of gold was also purchased from English bullion dealers.[21]

English gold refiners and dealers had to account precisely for every grain of gold and not solely because it was precious. The law defined what a "heavy" and "light" guinea weighed. According to a noted gold refiner and banker, a guinea, when coined, weighed "Five pennyweights [5 dwts.] nine grains and a fraction: the Bank allows a grain for circulation and rubbing and so on," but "a guinea must not now be under 5 dwts. 8 grains." If there were a mass of guineas in circulation "they would weigh about five pennyweights seven grains and a half: if it is only a fraction of a sixteenth under five pennyweight eight grains, they are considered as light." A light guinea was then valued at the average price of £1. 0s. 9d. not £1. 1s. 0d.[22]

William Merle, banker and gold and silver refiner, traded on a large scale and supplied gold and silver to goldsmiths for their own manufacture and for exportation. His firm, Cox and Merle, purchased foreign gold specie and bullion from a variety of people and sources—from the Bank of England, goldsmiths, private persons, and merchants who received remittances in foreign gold. "I swore off near 4,000 ounces of Gold dust that I had from Africa: I believe I have got near 3,000 ounces coming now," Merle told the committee. His firm also sold about 20,000 ounces of Spanish dollars a month to the trade and to merchants. Cox and Merle paid Mocatta & Goldsmid a commission to sell his exportable gold and silver, much of which went to Holland.[23]

Merle also testified that in the past his firm had melted down millions of light guineas into bars and sold them to the Bank of England but his profit margin was thin. The Bank of England never paid more than £3. 17s. 6d. per oz., that is, several pence less than the Mint price. However, he had to pay £3.

17s. 2d. or £3. 17s. 2½d. per oz. and, with melting costing him two pence, he was left a profit of only 1½ pence per oz. Moreover, Merle's goal of turning over a large volume of light guineas was no longer achievable: "we see no Gold now; my Clerks, who are out collecting every day, do not perhaps bring me perhaps a seven-shilling piece." During the past six months, the high price of gold bullion had kept the guinea out of circulation: "I have no doubt they are collected up to be sent abroad . . . the exchange making it so much more favourable to transmit it than bills." He said he could no longer supply his clients as he had just a year before: "my consumption for the trade is as nearly as can be about two thousand ounces of Gold a month. . . . fine Gold, quite pure" but now "we can hardly supply the trade . . . owing to the shortness of supply; and, I apprehend, a great deal is smuggled out of the country."[24]

English Customs was aware that "great Quantities of the Gold Coin of this Realm, have been clandestinely and illegally exported from various parts of England," and it gave "*Notice*" that offenders would be punished and in-formants would be rewarded: "*that in case any Person or Persons will give In-formation of any such illicit Practices, so that any Seizures shall be made of any such Gold Coin in consequence thereof, the Person or Persons given such Infor-mation*, shall, immediately after such Coin shall have been condemned, re-ceive One Third Part of the Value of such Seizures, without any Deduction whatever."[25]

It could be expected, therefore, that exporters would take the greatest care when testifying before the committee. Aaron Asher Goldsmid's firm did business with about twenty merchants but he knew of none devoted solely to exporting specie and bullion. Most of the gold bars and coins his firm sold went to French and Dutch merchants, who were aware that "all com-modities coming from England are liable to confiscation," and that the costs of transportation and insurance premiums were not insignificant, varying between 5½ and 7 percent.[26] Moreover, Goldsmid was reluctant to say spe-cifically how much his firm traded in a month: "Perhaps thirty or forty thousand, or perhaps fifty thousand pounds sterling or more in a month; perhaps eighty thousand or more in a month." Yet, he estimated that well over £500,000 of gold had been exported during the past twelve months and that more of it went to Holland than to any other place.[27]

Abraham Goldsmid, partner in Aron Goldsmid Son & D. Eliason, re-sponded quite differently from his cousin to the questions put to him by the committee: "There has been no bar silver exported from this Country to

Amsterdam" during the past five or six months. He was unaware that any specie had been sent to France. His firm had "not sent any Gold direct to Hamburgh these five years; none has gone, except either by Amsterdam or through Heligoland, and some by Gottenburg;" and that owing to "the recent political changes" for the past month to six weeks "it is really impossible to send Gold to Holland."[28]

Nathan Rothschild did not testify before the committee and his name is nowhere to be found among the more than two hundred pages of committee documents.[29] It would be fair to conclude that, in early 1810, he was but one of the many anonymous incidental bullion and specie traders or, as Aaron Asher Goldsmid had characterized them, one of those "new hands," into which the specie and bullion trade had recently fallen.[30] The record of Nathan's early specie and bullion trades is spotty but at least one significant trade dates from the time of his move from Manchester to London. In June 1808, he purchased 38,959 Spanish dollars from Jamaica. Harman & Co. handled the transaction for which Nathan deposited bills of lading, an insurance policy for £9,000, and bills of exchange totaling £8,047 to cover the basic cost of the consignment.[31] During the following months, Nathan transacted many modest trades with a variety of merchants and bullion and specie dealers.[32] In early 1809, he sold through Harman & Co. two parcels each of 2,000 new Spanish dollars, and both sales were above the silver Mint price of 5s. 2d. per oz. and within the fluctuating market price of 5s. 5d.– 5s.7d. per oz.[33]

But in March 1809, a dramatic change took place in Nathan's business circumstances when his father began investing heavily in his specie and bullion operations. Mayer Amschel Rothschild sent Nathan £31,434 in bills of exchange, the first of many sums sent through the auspices of the prominent Amsterdam merchant banking house of Braunsberg & Co., which in turn sent them to Harman & Co. The bills of exchange were sent without explanation, except that Nathan was to credit them to his father's account.[34] Employing Braunsberg & Co. as a conduit was a safe and clever maneuver because that firm had been a player in specie and bullion operations between Mexico, the United States of America, and Europe vis à vis Hope & Co. and Baring Brothers & Co.[35] The role that Braunsberg & Co. was to play was made clear in a letter that Mayer Amschel Rothschild wrote to Nathan in November 1809: "You would I believe do well to continue with Remitt. of gold and Silver to Ms. Braunsberg & Co. and as I have recommended you very heartily to them."[36]

This infusion of money could not have come at a more fortuitous time for Nathan because, as was shown in the previous chapter, he faced a rather precarious financial situation during the closing months of 1808 and the first two months of 1809. These investments evolved into a specie and bullion partnership between Nathan and his father and, when Jacob [James] visited Nathan at the end of the year, he also became Nathan's partner. Although there is no extant source that documents its provisions, a partnership certainly existed not only because their subsequent bullion and specie transactions confirm it but also because Nathan's father and Amschel Rothschild, his brother, said so: "We are partners and he [Nathan] has so much of ours in his hands, which he uses to his advantage [and] we have a share of his profit;"[37] and "we ask you as a partner, to write everything to us accurately and to state everything openly to us."[38]

This partnership in the specie and bullion trade between Nathan and his father may resolve a puzzling aspect of the received version of the Rothschild historiography as to why Nathan was not listed as a partner in *Mayer Amschel Rothschild und Söhne*, which was subsequently and formally established on 27 September 1810 in Frankfurt-am-Main. The Frankfurt house was referred to as Mayer Amschel Rothschild & Sons, or simply as M. A. R. The document of the firm opened by stating "that a trading company has been brought into being between those Jewish bankers of this place, Mr. Meyer Amschel Rothschild and his two longest married sons, namely Mr. Amschel Rothschild and Mr. Salomon Rothschild." The partners named were Mayer Amschel Rothschild with 370,000 gulden, Amschel Rothschild with 185,000 gulden, and Salomon Rothschild with 185,000 gulden of special trading capital. Carl Rothschild was mentioned as having 30,000 gulden special trading capital and Jacob [James] Mayer Rothschild with 30,000 gulden to be kept for him until he came of age, at which time he would be taken into the business as a partner. The document made clear that Mayer Amschel Rothschild was the controlling force in the firm, and upon the marriage of Carl and/or Jacob [James], he would have the power to redistribute shares in the firm upon them. The document also provided for an elaborate arrangement to be followed on the death of any of the partners or with regard to disputes that might arise among them. Nathan Rothschild was nowhere mentioned or alluded to.[39]

By its nature, overseas trading in specie and bullion required a great deal more vigilance than in other commodities, especially those that did not lend themselves to pilferage. To be successful, Nathan not only needed to exert more personal diligence in London but also needed to have a trustworthy person looking after his interests on the other side of the Channel. For some time, he had wanted one his brothers to join him in London but his father had been reluctant to allow any son to leave Frankfurt, except when traveling on business. Yet, Mayer Amschel Rothschild could not deny that assisting Nathan would ultimately benefit the Frankfurt house and, finally, he agreed to allow Jacob [James] to go to London.[40]

James arrived in London in October 1809 with £10,167 that Braunsberg & Co. had given him for his father's account with Nathan.[41] In the absence of extant contemporary sources, it can only be speculated as to what the two brothers agreed on but the known facts immediately following demonstrate that Nathan had made James his partner with the responsibility of supervising the operation in Amsterdam, Paris, and along the French Channel coast. To get him started, Nathan authorized Braunsberg & Co. to give James more than £6,000 on his return to Amsterdam in January 1810.[42]

Nathan Rothschild bought specie and bullion from anyone, anywhere. For example, almost weekly, during 1809–1810, Isaac Spiers [Heksher Izak Speyer], a small specie and bullion trader from Gosport, dispatched insured parcels to Nathan and apprised him of the availability of this or that coin, asking him to bid on such and such a parcel at a particular price by a certain time. In turn, Nathan placed orders with Spiers for certain coins at specified prices. Located between the seafaring towns of Portsmouth and Southampton, Spiers had access to the local specie market supplied by military personnel and also to auctions of prize goods. He crossed over to France where he bought coins from private and military persons. He had accounts with refiners, such as Cox and Merle, and he charged ¼ percent commission on transactions. Nathan paid his outstanding balances into Spiers's account at Barclays bank in London.[43]

In 1810–1811, Nathan joined Fermin de Tastet & Co. of London in shipping 200,000 Spanish dollars from Lima to Cadiz.[44] In 1811–1812, Nathan's clients in Curaçao and St. Thomas sent him doubloons, dollars, and gold bullion valued in thousands of English pounds sterling to pay for consignments of merchandise he sent to them.[45] From late 1812 onward, Samuel & Phillips & Co. of Rio de Janeiro and London supplied him with gold specie and bullion from Brazil.[46] There is also evidence suggesting that, in 1813, he purchased bullion and specie for export from Cox and Merle.[47]

Nathan employed no fewer than a dozen couriers to cross the Channel and deliver his specie and bullion to an extensive network of clients—dealers, brokers, and bankers—in The Netherlands and France. They cooperated and at times competed with each other to sell his specie and bullion and to remit bills of exchange to him at the best rates. Among others, they included: Braunsberg & Co.; D. Crommelin & Sn., Amsterdam; J. Charles Davillier & Co., Paris; Frederick Faber & Co., Dunkerque and Paris; Hottinguer & Co., Paris; Mallet Frères & Co., Paris; Veuve Dominique Morel & Co., Dunkerque and Paris; John Osy & Co., Rotterdam; and Perregaux Laffitte, Paris.[48] This integrated network, it seems to me, was one reason for the British government's decision in January 1814 to engage Nathan Rothschild to supply Wellington with specie to fund his campaign against Napoleon.

During 1809, Nathan and Braunsberg & Co. had a secure and flexible business arrangement. Nathan sent his consignments of specie and bullion to Braunsberg & Co. who sold them on the Amsterdam market or forwarded them to his father in Frankfurt. Braunsberg & Co. remitted bills of exchange to Nathan or to the Frankfurt house frequently in advance of sales, since Mayer Amschel Rothschild guaranteed all transactions. Braunsberg & Co. also acted as a clearing house for Rothschild correspondence and it communicated regularly about market conditions: about prices of certain coins, silver and gold bullion, about rates of bills of exchange on London and their availability at Amsterdam, Hamburg, and Paris, and even about how best to ship his cargoes. The available evidence suggests that sometime in September Nathan consigned about £11,000 in specie and bullion to Braunsberg & Co.,[49] which the latter acknowledged with the comment: "You may depend on us Keeping Secret any thing relating to this or any Similar transaction which may take place between us and though we feel not inclined to take a share in the same, you may depend on our managing your interests as our own."[50]

The year 1809 was a good year for Nathan Rothschild. His father passed through Braunsberg & Co. bills of exchange amounting to at least £101,000.[51] From October through December 1809, Braunsberg & Co. remitted Nathan a minimum of £59,000 against sales.[52] Altogether, Nathan received at least £160,000 to buy specie and bullion and 3 percent Consols.[53]

In 1810, the Amsterdam market proved more difficult for Nathan and, despite his increased consignments of Spanish dollars, doubloons, and gold bars to Braunsberg & Co., other traders filled the market with specie and bullion. Demand slackened, producing lower prices, delayed sales, and narrower profit margins. It took more and more Dutch guilders to buy bills of exchange on London.[54]

The changing political situation in Holland also had the effect of dampening commercial and financial activities. Napoleon's decision to incorporate Holland into the Grande Empire, the abdication of Louis Napoleon as King of Holland, and the increasing presence of French troops "produced serious unrest, and this in turn led to general stagnation on the Stock Exchange."[55]

By year's end, the well-known Amsterdam houses of R. & Th. Smeth and L. H. Keyzer "stopped payment."[56] According to Braunsberg & Co., communications between Amsterdam and London had become by midyear "rather dangerous" and it stopped sending remittances directly to Nathan in London.[57] Thus, the bookkeeping of Nathan's specie and bullion operations became more and more complex and less complete as the year progressed. In February, March, and May—three months for which there is a detailed record—Mayer Amschel Rothschild funneled at least £60,000 in bills of exchange to Nathan through Braunsberg & Co. but there is no available evidence of similar transfers for the second half of the year.[58] From January through May, Braunsberg & Co. remitted advances of about £112,000 to him in London[59] but afterward it sent about £37,000 to his father in Frankfurt[60] and also handed about £33,000 to James in Amsterdam.[61] For the year 1810, Braunsberg & Co. remitted at least £182,000 to the Rothschilds. Notwithstanding these challenges, it appears that Nathan may have had about £242,000 to work with in 1810, about 50 percent more than he had had in 1809.

Braunsberg & Co.'s cautious business practices dissatisfied Nathan, who not only wanted more remittances but also complained about the way he was being treated. This led to angry exchanges. "We do not find we deserve your upbraiding on account of Remittances and must observe that it grows more and more difficult at present to purchase Bills,"[62] Braunsberg & Co. wrote to Nathan. It stated that it would have sent more remittances had the exchange not declined, had market prices not fallen, and had first rate bills on London not been scarce. It dismissed Nathan's charge that it had offered other merchants in London more favorable quotes on gold by citing the firm's *Copy Book of Letters* as proof, and claimed that in all important matters it had merely executed James's orders.[63] It cautioned Nathan that "owing to the present critical State of matters there is So much risk attending Business" with London that "we must wait till a more propitious opening Shows itself to continue making advances on your Consignments."[64] Finally, Braunsberg & Co. wanted an "Extraordinary Commission" because of "the present most extraordinary Circumstances."[65]

Consequently, toward the end of the year 1810, Nathan began redirecting his landing operations to the French Channel coast. The French government had, by a decree of 15 June 1810, permitted gold and silver imports by ship into France at the small port of Gravelines.[66] Situated between Calais and Dunkerque, Gravelines was in easy reach of Folkestone on the English coast, a legendary haven for guinea smuggling activities and home to the Cullen family which served Nathan's transporting interests.[67]

By early 1811, Nathan had significantly modified his operations and had determined where, how, and with whom he would continue trading in specie and bullion on the Continent. Braunsberg & Co. lost its lead position but would continue to serve his interests when called on.[68] In France, Veuve Dque Morel Frères & Co. (Dunkerque) and Faber & Co. of (Dunkerque and Paris) became Nathan's principal clients, who would receive and transport his specie and bullion to Paris, Lille, and Amsterdam for sale.[69]

Richard Faber & Co. of Dunkerque dealt in diamonds, snuff boxes, and dozens of coins from almost as many countries and passed his accounts through his father's office, Frederick Faber & Co. in Paris.[70] Although the early correspondence is fragmentary and difficult to interpret, numerous transactions took place comprising Spanish, Portuguese, and French coins and the sale of 45,000 diamonds. From May through December 1811, the Fabers remitted an estimated minimum of £260,000 in bills of exchange, about what Braunsberg & Co. had remitted in 1810. In addition, Frederick Faber & Co. of Paris opened substantial credit accounts for M. A. Rothschild & Sons and for James Rothschild.[71]

Nathan did much more business with the Morels than he did with the Fabers and, at the end of 1811, the Morels opened two additional houses: Morel Frères & Co. in Paris and Gravelines.[72] Extant remittance records from December 1810 through 1811, indicate that transactions amounted to a staggering £486,000. Moreover, the Morels opened credit accounts for the Rothschilds with merchant-banking houses in Paris and Amsterdam for about £375,000.[73]

In 1811, the London market price of gold rose as high as 28 percent above the English Mint price,[74] and Nathan sold much more gold bullion and specie on the Continent than he had during the previous two years. One shipment alone, in May, contained 8,007 bars of gold bullion.[75] He traded tens of thousands of Spanish dollars and doubloons and Portuguese gold coins ("Heavy and Light Ports").[76] He also traded hundreds of thousands of coins, referred to in the correspondence as "Pictures."

The word "Pictures" is not included in traditional numismatic nomenclature.[77] But it is clear from the available contemporary evidence that "Pictures" was the code word that Nathan and his clients in France used for English guineas to keep their smuggling operation secret from English officials who might intercept their correspondence. While it might be a coincidence, in 1811 in France, the average market price of a Picture was £1.8s. 8¼d., which was the approximate market price of an English guinea. This is confirmed by a contemporary invoice stipulating that Nathan and James sold tens of thousands of English guineas smuggled out of England to a Paris banker.[78]

Two additional sources also confirm Pictures to be English guineas. In their correspondence with each other, the Rothschilds used the code words "Rabbi Moses" to mean English guineas.[79] In one such letter, on 17 August 1811, James wrote that he suspected that authorities were onto Nathan: "Why don't you want to buy any more Rab[bi] Moses? Is it attracting attention? Do you think the people know you are doing the business?"[80] Additionally, Bertrand Gille cites the minister of the Treasury's letters to Napoleon in March 1811, in which the former declares that James was importing hundreds of thousands of English guineas via the Channel coast and was selling them to bankers in Paris.[81]

Pictures were valuable and marketable but had to be handled with care, as Morel attests: "we will be your debtors of 20 à 30,000 Pounds St upon which more than 30,000 Pictures still are in our hands from which stock we every day send a few thousand to the best near market place, but only a few thousand at once as we would find too much risk to trust more than two or three thousand at once to the same Wagoner your Pictures being so valuable."[82]

One indication of the relative value of Pictures to the whole of Nathan's specie and bullion trade is indicated in eleven detailed "Account of Sales" for "Mr. Langbein" [code words for Nathan Rothschild] for 2–16 November 1811. The total amount of these sales was about £95,000, of which ports and doubloons represented 14.2 percent, gold bullion in bars 21 percent, Pictures 31.2 percent, and snuff boxes 33.5 percent.[83]

Morel alone received more than 400,000 of Nathan's Pictures during the period February–November 1811. At their 10-month average French market price of £1. 8s. 8¼d., their sale could be estimated at more than £570,000, which Morel would credit to the Rothschilds. But because Morel's sales accounts and correspondence often lumped the proceeds from Pictures together with snuff boxes, bars of gold, Spanish doubloons, and Portuguese Ports, it is impossible to determine which proceeds were credited solely to Nathan from the sale of only Pictures. Nevertheless, the extant record for 1811 supports an estimated minimum of more than £250,000.[84]

It could have been expected that, because Nathan moved so much merchandise so frequently across the Channel by a dozen different couriers, some slippage might have occurred in the packing, transporting, and counting except for the fact that merchandise of such extraordinary value per unit weight/volume should have received more care than bulky commodities. It was easier to pocket gold and silver coins, diamonds, and even snuff boxes than it was coffee, sugar, indigo, logwood, and textiles. But Nathan again demonstrated that he was by temperament not a hands-on manager, and apparently he did not employ someone who was. If he was at all sensitive to his shortcomings, the warning his father made years before must now have haunted him: "if then you are so disorderly . . . you will be the victim of thieves all round."[85] And so he was.

There were too many incidents of mismanagement to recount all of them, but several are illustrative. In November 1809, John Osy & Son of Rotterdam reported that the captain of the ship carrying Nathan's cargo of gold bars and specie found the seal of one sack "spoiled" and Braunsberg & Co. found "near 3 Ounces of the Species are wanting."[86] In January 1810, James Cullen, who with other members of his family became Nathan's most trusted couriers, delivered not 1,000 doubloons as had been quoted but 800.[87] In March, it could not be determined if a parcel containing three large bars of gold, one small bag of doubloons, and two bags of French gold coins belonged to Nathan or to L B Cohen & Son.[88] In July, Morel wrote Nathan that James, with whom Morel had formed a close business friendship, "thinks just as we do that you must have been deceived many times by those from whom you bought the goods or those who packed them," the proof of which was their finding an iron box in the parcel marked gold snuff boxes.[89] Morel repeatedly cautioned that, unlike other traders, Nathan's bales arrived not tied or sealed properly and the specie count wrong.[90] "All this we Confess is very disagreeable," and while Morel could not expend the time and workmen to unpack, sort, count and re-pack the contents of each bag of coins, his clients to whom he sold the specie and bullion did and they complained of discrepancies. "Those errors we conceive accrue from the hurry you sometimes are in and of the great number of your business . . . and we entreat you to cause your Packers to be more exact in future on that head."[91] He reminded Nathan that, unlike others in the trade, he was losing not only money but the confidence of his clients, a situation that James witnessed.[92]

Although 1811 was a very profitable year, Nathan was not satisfied. Nathan's profit margin was determined by the difference between what he paid for specie and bullion in England and the rate he paid on bills of exchange on London, which he received in payment for the sale of his specie and bullion on the Continent. As late as June 1811, bills of exchange on London sold in Paris at a rate of $fr.16.80 = £$; but, in the second half of the year, it drifted upward to ƒr.18.80. Nathan sought to maximize his profit by insisting, during the first half of the year, that his French clients not pay on his behalf a rate higher than ƒr.17.00 = £ and, during the second half of the year, no higher than ƒr.18.00–18.09 = £.[93]

When the Paris market could not accommodate these limits, couriers were sent to scour the Amsterdam market for an equivalent rate.[94] Despite their efforts, Nathan reproached Faber and Morel for paying higher rates for bills than he had stipulated and also for not sending him remittances soon enough. Morel called these charges unjust,[95] and Faber wrote Nathan that he did not know how the market worked.[96]

By insisting that his French clients buy bills of exchange on London only at his predetermined rates rather than just relying on their professional judgment, Nathan had charted an unrealistic course. James oversaw—and implicitly sanctioned—Morel's and Faber's operation in France and knew what was going on all the time and even assisted in drafting the Morel–N M Rothschild Account Currents and Account Sales.[97]

Nathan even accused his brother of holding back remittances. This, of course, "did not merely irritate me," James retorted, "you write in each of your letters that I am taking your remittances. I swear to you it is quite the opposite, so help me God. . . . it pains me to read in every letter 'you should be sending money.' . . . You have just written to me as though I were a stranger and a rogue."[98] James must have regretted capitulating months earlier to Nathan's jealous protests over his joining with Morel to set up a separate account to trade in French goods.[99] Now, he was "extremely angry," enough to quit his business partnership with his brother:

> I would prefer to leave this place and not get involved in any of your business. . . . I am sending you the money I owe you. I shall not draw a farthing even for a cup of coffee and I shall stop everything so that at least I will be sure not to get any disagreeable letters. . . . I am going to leave all your bickering behind me now because I don't like being smeared by your quarrelsome letters. . . . I am working like a packhorse and all I get is quarreling. . . . You can see that I am keeping the books properly, praise God, and that your account is exact to the nearest farthing. . . . I get up at 5 o'clock every morning . . . but I continue to get quarrelsome letters.[100]

The specie and bullion business had expanded considerably by the end of 1811 and it required more orderly administration and accounting procedures. For this purpose, M. A. Rothschild & Sons furloughed Rabbi Asher Leib, its bookkeeper, to Paris to work with James.[101]

This decision was smart and timely. Gold had become extremely scarce everywhere Nathan traded and he must have worked wonders to procure the volume of specie and bullion he exported to France and The Netherlands. For example, Isaac Spiers wrote from Gosport that he was "sorry to say that never was gold scarcer at this place than it is now. . . . any Doubloons they are generally sold to officers going abroad" and that "so many troops embarking daily for Spain & Portugal which makes the scarcity of the gold you desire to purchase."[102] And from Curaçao, Levinson & Coster informed him: "Dollars & Dubloons are getting very Scarce here. . . . we therefore anticipate that if we Cannot Muster Specie enough we shall remit you part Bills."[103] As a consequence of such scarcity, the 1812 London market price of foreign gold coins of English standard fineness rose by 42.5 percent and standard gold in bars rose by 37.4 percent above the English Mint price.[104]

That year was a banner year for the Rothschilds. The estimated minimum value in bills of exchange remitted from France and The Netherlands to Nathan alone was about £2,500,000, the overwhelming amount of which resulted from the sale of specie and bullion and, to a much lesser extent, diamonds, snuff boxes, carnelian stones, commodities (such as indigo, coffee, and sugar), and bill of exchange transactions. The sale of Pictures alone amounted to a minimum of about £500,000.[105]

James was very much responsible for this success story. He not only organized and centralized much of the Rothschild client network on the Continent, but also made it work effectively. During the two previous years, each client had remitted bills of exchange directly to the Rothschilds in London and Frankfurt and this frequently caused confusion and created irritating moments for Nathan. However, in 1812, James personally collected most of the bills from the client houses in Paris—Davillier, Faber, Hottinguer, Mallet, Morel, and Perregaux Laffitte—and sent them directly to Nathan or to Frankfurt.[106] He oversaw the delivery and sale of Nathan's valuable merchandise and regularly informed his brother when it would be propitious to slow or accelerate shipments.[107] He purchased bills at the Paris exchange where he said he became a familiar figure and even an influence: "now the exchange gets a little up as some speculators are taking trusting that I will take at any rate but they will find them self [sic] mistaken as I am determined not to take any till it will be lower."[108] Occasionally, he had misunderstandings with clients[109] but, on the whole, they cooperated with him and accepted his advice and instructions. Finally, he maintained readable, orderly, and regular business accounts. To accomplish this, James was on the road a great deal of the time from Paris to Boulogne, to Dunkerque, to Gravelines, to Amsterdam, and back to Paris.[110] These journeys frequently sapped his energy, as he wrote in his imprecise English to Hannah Cohen Rothschild: "I was very sick but thank God, quiet well now. It is 3 weeks that I did not left my room and I am intend to go out for half a hour to day [*sic*]."[111] To alleviate his recurrent fatigue, James later asked Nathan to send him boxes of *James's Analeptic Pills.*[112]

Nathan probably did not appreciate James's aggrandizing authority and he must have sensed that his operation in France was slipping from his personal control. In this regard, two examples are telling. During the early months of 1812, the rate on bills of exchange on London had risen above fr.19 = £.[113] Therefore, with James's acquiescence, Frederick Faber refused any longer to accept Nathan's rate restrictions: "Thus you may depend on Speedier returns, as I shall not suffer myself to be controlled by Limits."[114] Morel respected and frequently welcomed James at his home and, when Nathan reproached Morel for not writing directly to him, Morel revealingly replied: "we cannot send you our letters from here without having previously sent them to Paris which must be Known to you. . . . Now all our accounts being carried on with Mr. J M R—according to his orders it deprives us of the pleasure of having occasion as formerly, to write to you."[115]

James's commanding presence on the Continent augured well for the growth prospects of Rothschild's specie and bullion business. His experience also prepared him for the greater challenge of supplying specie to Wellington, who would soon engage Napoleon in France.

Notes

1. *P. P. Gold Bullion, 1810,* "Minutes of Evidence," p. 49 (24 February 1810).
2. PROT 1/1470/No. 987.
3. Fermin de Tastet & Co. Lon. to NMR Man. 5 March 1808, RAL xi/112/76.
4. Fermin de Tastet & Co. Lon. to NMR Man. 23 July 1808, RAL xi/112/76. In Amsterdam, bills on London were suspended in September 1807; the number of ships entering the harbor in 1808 fell to 357 (down from a peak of 3,539 in 1802); and imports of raw sugar dropped from 50,000 metric tons in 1807 to 9,100 tons in 1808 and to 1,800 in 1809. See Jonker, p. 32.
5. I am grateful to G. P. Dyer, librarian and curator, of the Royal Mint, for sharing with me his excellent unpublished paper "Suspension and Restriction," 14 pages (Great Britain, 2001). See also John M. Kleeberg, "The International Circulation of Spanish American Coinage and the Financing of the Napoleonic Wars," *XII. Internationaler Numismatischer Kongress Berlin 1997. Akten—Proceedings—Actes II.* (Berlin:

Herausgegeben von Bernd Kluge under Bernhard Weisser, 2000), p. 1168; & Kelly, pp. 13–15 *et seq.*

6. See Charles J. Esdaile, *The Duke of Wellington and the Command of the Spanish Army 1812–14* (New York: St. Martin's Press, 1990), pp. 1–26; Muir, pp. 32–59, 62–63, 118; Sherwig, pp. 222–224; Severn, in Gash, pp. 34–36; & S. G. P. Ward, *Wellington's Headquarters. A Study of the Administrative Problems in the Peninsula 1813–1814* (Oxford: Oxford University Press, 1957), ch. III. "The Maintenance of the Army in the Peninsula," pp. 66–101,passim.

7. *P. P. Gold Bullion, 1810*, "Report," p. 1.

8. Portuguese gold coins had about the same fineness as the English standard but Spanish gold coins had less. The fineness of Spanish gold was "from 4½ to 4¼ grains worse than standard, making about a 4s. difference in value." *P. P. Gold Bullion, 1810*, "Minutes of Evidence," p. 35 (22 February 1810). Dealers in Portuguese coins used short-hand descriptions to distinguish them: "Heavy Ports" (full-weight ports) and "Light Ports" (owing to their wear from circulation), and the market price reflected the difference in their weights. In England, in 1809–1810, Spanish doubloons and Light Ports sold between 84 and 89 shillings (£4.4s. to £4.9s.) per oz., and Heavy or full-weight ports sold for 91 and 92 shillings (£4.11s. to £4.12s.) per oz. See correspondence between Isaac Spiers [Heksher Izak Speyer] and Nathan Rothschild, in particular, 7 & 12 May, 6 & 26 June, 22 September, 12 November & 27 December 1809, RAL xi/112/3, 2 & 29 January, 15 February, 22 March, 3 April, 1810, RAL xi/112/34; *MPG & S: 1810–1811*; & discourse on Portuguese gold and silver coins, PRO Mint 13/179. See also Oscar G. Schilke and Raphael E. Solomon, *America's Foreign Coins* (New York: The Coin and Currency Institute, Inc. Book Publishers, 1964), p. 50; & Raphael E. Solomon, "Foreign Specie Coins in the American Colonies," ch. 4 in Eric P. Newman and Richard G. Doty, eds., *Studies on Money in Early America* (New York: The American Numismatic Society, 1976), p. 34.

9. *P. P. Gold Bullion, 1810*, "Minutes of Evidence," p. 56 (26 February 1810), and "Report," pp. 2–4 and 6; & see John M. Kleeberg, "The International Circulation," p. 1174.

10. John M. Kleeberg, "The International Circulation," pp. 1168–1169. See G. P. Dyer, "Suspension and Restriction," unpublished, 14 pages (Great Britain, 2001), passim, & Kelly, chs. III–IV & VI–VII, passim. See also the data for Great Britain's imports and exports of silver and gold coin and bullion from the late eighteenth century to 1810 in *P. P. Gold Bullion, 1810, Appendix of Accounts*, passim; & No. 13. "Average Price Paid by the Company for New Dollars, from 1791," p.168; Oscar G. Schilke and Raphael E. Solomon, *America's Foreign Coins* (New York: The Coin and Currency Institute, Inc. Book Publishers, 1964), p. 170; Raphael E. Solomon, "Foreign Specie Coins in the American Colonies," ch. 4 in *Studies on Money in Early America*, Eric P. Newman and Richard G. Doty eds. (New York: The American Numismatic Society, 1976), pp. 30–31; John M. Kleeberg, "The Silver Dollar as an Element of International Trade: A Study in Failure," *Coinage of the Americas Conference at the American Numismatic Society, New York, October 30, 1993*, (NY: The American Numismatic Society, 1995), p. 88; & Albert R. Frey, *Dictionary of Numis-*

matic Names (New York: Barnes & Noble, Inc., 1947), pp. 69, 198 & passim for varieties and early coinage of the Dollar.

11. *P. P. Gold Bullion, 1810*, "Report," p. 2 & *MPG & S: 1810–1811*.

12. *P. P. Gold Bullion, 1810*, "Report," p. 2.

13. *P. P. Gold Bullion, 1810*.

14. For this extraordinary extended family, see S. R. Cope, "The Goldsmids and the Development of the London Money Market during the Napoleonic Wars," *Economica*, IX:33–36 (May 1942), 180–206; Paul H. Emden, "The Brothers Goldsmid and the Financing of the Napoleonic Wars, "*TJHSE*. XIV (1940), 225–246; L. Alexander, *Memoirs of the Life and Commercial Connections, Public and Private, of the Late Benj. Goldsmid, Esq. of Reohampton* (London: Printed by and for the author. Entered at Stationers Hall, 1808); "*The Circular Letter of Our Daniel Eliason,*" 31 December 1811; "*Circular Goldsmid Son & Salomons,*" 1 January 1812; "*Circular Goldsmid & Salomons,*" 30 June 1812; & "*Circular Goldsmid & Salomons,*" 10 July 1812, RAL xi/112/34 & xi/112/33, respectively.

15. *P. P. Gold Bullion, 1810*, "Minutes of Evidence," p. 57 (26 February 1810).

16. The Oxford English Dictionary defines "agio" as the percentage of a charge for exchanging paper money into cash. Similarly, converting a less valuable metallic currency into one of greater value. Thus, *agio* is the "excess value of one currency over another."

17. *P. P. Gold Bullion, 1810*, "Report," p. 14 & "Minutes of Evidence," p. 100.

18. "Memorandum for the payment of any Sums to the extent of 4 or 500,000 £ immediately wanted on the Continent." in H Lon. to V. Lon. 8 February 1815, *HP* BLAddMss. 57394, ff. 73–74.

19. John Louis Greffulhe testified on 14 March about the exchange rates he knew about at that time. But between 2 March and 3 April the exchange rates had fluctuated: at Paris, between 19.16 and 21.11; at Hamburg, between 29.4 and 31; and at Amsterdam, between 31.8 and 33.5. *P. P. Gold Bullion, 1810*, "Report," p. 2.

20. *P. P. Gold Bullion, 1810*, "Minutes of Evidence" of William Merle, p. 50 (24 February 1810).

21. *P. P. Gold Bullion, 1810*, "Minutes of Evidence" of Aaron Asher Goldsmid, pp. 36–43, passim (22–23 February 1810). For the Bullion Office, see "Minutes of Evidence" of John Humble, pp. 146–147 (18 April 1810).

22. *P. P. Gold Bullion, 1810*, "Minutes of Evidence," of William Merle, pp. 48–49, passim (24 February 1810).

23. *P. P. Gold Bullion, 1810*, "Minutes of Evidence," pp. 50–54, passim (24 February 1810).

24. *P. P. Gold Bullion, 1810*, "Minutes of Evidence," pp. 46–53, passim (24 February 1810).

25. "Gold Coin" Custom House Lon. PROT 1/1470/No. 987 (12 September 1811).

26. *P. P. Gold Bullion, 1810*, "Minutes of Evidence," of Mr.—, a Continental Merchant (5 March 1810) & Abraham Goldsmid (12 March 1810), pp. 76 & 91, respectively.

27. *P. P. Gold Bullion, 1810*, "Minutes of Evidence," pp. 36–43 (22 February 1810).

28. *P. P. Gold Bullion, 1810*, "Minutes of Evidence," pp. 91–92 (12 March 1810).

Abraham Goldsmid (1770–1812), son of George Goldsmid, partner in Aron Goldsmid Son & D. Eliason, at times, was referred to as Abraham Junior.

29. Denis Gray's contention in *Spencer Perceval. The Evangelical Prime Minister 1762–1812* (Manchester: Manchester University Press, 1963), pp. 370–371, that "N. M. Rothschild, appearing modestly before the bullion committee as Mr.—, a continental merchant" is wrong. A careful reading of the style and content of this anonymous testimony, appearing on pp.73, 75, 82–85 in *P. P. Gold Bullion, 1810*, "Minutes of Evidence," precludes any attribution to Nathan Mayer Rothschild.

30. *P. P. Gold Bullion, 1810*, "Minutes of Evidence," p. 40 (23 February 1810).

31. Har Lon. to NMR n.p. 9 June 1808, RAL xi/112/38; & LJ 9 June 1808, RAL 1/218/30, p. 19.

32. See LJ 1808–1809, RAL 1/218/30 & 41, passim.

33. Har Lon. to NMR Lon. 31 January & 8 February 1809, "Mr. N. M. Rothschild, his account current with Harman & Co.," 31 December 1809, RAL xi/112/3; & LJ RAL 1/218/30 & 41, passim.

34. BB Ams. to NMR Lon. 25 March, 30–31 May & 9 November 1809, RAL xi/38/55A.

35. F. L. Braunsberg, a German immigrant (d. 1815), founded Braunsberg & Co. (1770?–1782); Braunsberg & Streckeisen (1782–1794); Braunsberg, Kluppel, Faesch & Co. (1794–1800); & Braunsberg & Co. (1800–1844). See Jonker, pp.193, 228–229, 320; & Buist, p. 318.

36. MAR Fft. to NMR Lon.15 November 1809, RAL xi/86/0A.

37. MAR Fft. to JMR Paris, 9 June [1811 ?], RAL xi/86/0A, Tape 240/Letter 6. For this, my thanks to Mordichae Zucker and Dr. Rainer Liedtke.

38. AMR Fft. to JMR Paris, 23 June [1810 ?], RAL xi/82/9/1/6 & RAL xi/82/1/1, Tape 247/Letter 14 or Tape 257/Letter 10. For this, my thanks to Mordichae Zucker and Dr. Rainer Liedtke.

39. See "Meyer Amschel Rothschild und Soehne," RAL 000/231.

40. See MAR Fft. to NMR Lon.16 July & 24 September 1809, RAL xi/86/0A.

41. BB Ams. to NMR Lon.15 September & 18 October 1809, RAL xi/38/55A.

42. BB Ams. to NMR Lon.16 December 1809 & 10 January 1810, et seq., RAL xi/38/55A.

43. See correspondence between Isaac Spiers and NMR for 1809–1810, RAL xi/112/3 & RAL xi/112/ 34; & LJ RAL 1/218/30 & 41, passim.

44. Fermin de Tastet & Co. Lon. to NMR Lon. 13 June 1810 & 20 September 1811, RAL xi/112/34.

45. See correspondence between Levinson & Coster, Curaçao & E. Sarguy, St. Thomas, (1811–1812) and NMR, RAL xi/112/33 & 32B.

46. The founders of the firm Samuel & Phillips & Co., Rio de Janeiro and London, descend from the marriage of Moses Samuel (1740–1839) and Rachel Phillips; one of the founders was their son, Samuel Moses Samuel (1773–1873), who in 1803 married Esther Cohen (1782–1859), daughter of Levy Barent Cohen, and, thereby, became in 1806 a brother-in-law to Nathan Mayer Rothschild and in 1812 also to Moses Montefiore (1784–1885), who married Judith Cohen (1784–1862). Samuel &

Philips & Co. traded in commodities, specie and bullion, and diamonds. See RAL xi/38/215A & B & RAL xi/112/2.

47. See Montefiore Brothers, Lon. to NMR Lon. 15 November 1813, RAL xi/112/2.

48. Nathan Rothschild's couriers were most often identified by their initials or abbreviated names. Some of Nathan's clients belonged to branches or houses headed by members of their extended family in different cities and occasionally the names of the firms varied.

49. BB Ams. to NMR Lon. 30 September, 10, 14, 21 & 24 October, 9, 11, 15, 18, 21, 25 & 29 November, 5, 8–9, 13, 16, 18–19, 23 & 29 December 1809 RAL xi/38/55A; LJ RAL 2/128/41; & *Bullion Listed Cash Book, 1809–1812*, RAL VII/16A/1, ff. 1–11, passim.

50. BB Ams. to NMR Lon. 10 October 1809, RAL xi/ 38/55A.

51. BB Ams. to NMR Lon. 25 March, 5 April, 15 & 22 July, 15 September, 10, 16, 19, 23, 27 & 30 December 1809, RAL xi/38/55A.

52. BB Ams. to NMR Lon. 30 September, 10, 14, 21 & 24 October, 11, 21, 25 & 29 November, 5, 13, 18–19, 23 & 29 December 1809, RAL xi/38/55A.

53. Har Lon. to NMR Lon. 6 April & 25 May 1809, RAL xi/112/3. Nathan Rothschild's problematic *Ledger* recorded transactions with the Bank of England of slightly more than £99,000 for May–December 1809. RL. RAL VI/10/0 (1809–1810), ff. 125–126, 199–203 & 252–256.

54. See Braunsberg Co.'s 1810 correspondence with Nathan Rothschild, passim, RAL xi/38/55A.

55. Buist, p. 231. See also, BB Ams. to NMR Lon. 4 July 1810, RAL xi/38/55A.

56. BB Ams. to NMR Lon. 5 & 7 December 1810, RAL xi/38/55A.

57. BB Ams. to NMR Lon. 12 June 1810, RAL xi/38/55A.

58. BB Ams. to NMR Lon. 3 & 9 February, 17, 21, 24, 28 & 31 March, 9 & 12 May 1810, RAL xi/38/55A.

59. BB Ams. to NMR Lon. 3, 8, 10–11, 15, 17 & 31 January, 28 March, 14, 18, 21, 25 & 28 April, 9 & 29 May 1810, RAL xi/38/55A.

60. BB Ams. to NMR Lon. 12, 15, 19, 22 & 26 June, 10 & 28 July, 2 August & 24 December 1810, RAL xi/38/55A.

61. BB Ams. to NMR Lon. 4, 10, 18 & 21 August, 18 & 26 September 1810, RAL xi/38/55A. An additional £6,000 appears to have been sent to Nathan in December, see BB Ams. to NMR Lon. 1 &12 December 1810, RAL xi/38/55A.

62. BB Ams. to NMR Lon. 29 October 1810, RAL xi/38/55A.

63. In particular, see BB Ams. to NMR Lon. 24 & 29 May, 30 October, 7 & 23 November, 7 & 12 December 1810, RAL xi/38/55A.

64. BB Ams. to NMR Lon. 7 November 1810, RAL xi/38/55A.

65. BB Ams. to NMR Lon. 12 December 1810, RAL xi/38/55A; & BB Ams. to NMR Lon. 30 January 1811, RAL xi/38/55A.

66. Bertrand Gille, *Histoire de la Maison Rothschild* (Genève: Libraire Droz, 1965), I, 45.

67. See Michael B. Cullen, *The Cullen's Family Association with the de Rothschilds*. Copyrighted typescript, 1989, deposited in RAL T66.

68. See BB Ams. to NMR Lon. 30 January & 16 February 1811, RAL xi/38/55A.

69. There is evidence in the *Bullion Listed Cash Book, 1809–1812*, RAL VII/16A/1, ff. 3–20, passim, that in late 1809 and in early 1810, Nathan Rothschild had initiated transactions with Faber & Co. and Veuve Dque Morel Frères & Co. (also known as Morel Brothers & Co.and Morel & Son). Curiously, the Fabers addressed their early 1811 letters to Nathan by his nick- or code-name: "Mr. N. Langbein for Mr. N. M. R. Lon.," which only James Rothschild could have given them. See Frederick Faber and his son, Henry, to "Mr. N. Langbein for Mr. N. M. R. Lon." 5 & 8 February 1811, RAL xi/112/34.

70. Faber Dun. to NMR Lon. 2 February 1811, RAL xi/112/33 RAL xi/112/34.

71. See Faber correspondence, 1811, RAL xi/112/34, passim.

72. See Morel Dun. to NMR Lon. 13 November & 17 December 1811, RAL xi/112/33.

73. See entries in *Bullion Listed Cash Book, 1809–1812*, RAL VII/16A/1, ff.18, 20, et seq., & Morel correspondence for 1810–1811, RAL xi/38/180 & RAL xi/112/33, passim.

74. See supra Table 3.1. Fluctuation in Market Price of Foreign Gold and Silver in England: 1811–1815.

75. Morel Dun. to NMR Lon. 30 May 1811, RAL xi/38/180.

76. See Morel correspondence for 1810–1811, RAL xi/38/180 & RAL xi/112/33, passim.

77. My thanks to David T. Alexander, Stack's; Barry Cook, curator of medieval coins and medals, The British Museum; Richard G. Doty, curator of numismatics, Smithsonian Institute; Robert W. Hoge, curator, American Numismatic Association; and John M. Kleeberg, sometime curator of modern coins and currency, The American Numismatic Society.

78. Castinel Boulogne to JMR n.p. 18 December 1811, RAL xi/85/0. See also Castinel's 1812 correspondence with Nathan Rothschild, RAL xi/112/10, passim.

79. See JMR [Paris] to MD Lon. 21 February 1811, JMR Paris to NMR Lon. 17 August 1811 & JMR[Got.?] to NMR Lon. 18 November 1811, RAL xi/85/0; & AMR Fft. to JMR Paris 17 June 1811, RAL xi/82/9/1/5; & RAL xi/82/1, Tape 247/Letter 14 [1811?].

80. JMR Got.? to NMR Lon. 17 August 1811, RAL xi/85/0.

81. Bertrand Gille, *Histoire de la Maison Rothschild* (Genève: Libraire Droz, 1965), I, 45–50 et seq.

82. Morel Dun. to NMR Lon. 1 May 1811, RAL xi/38/180.

83. Morel Dun. to Mr. Langbein Lon. 2–16 November 1811, RAL xi/112/33.

84. See Morel Dun. to NMR Lon. 18 June 1811, RAL xi/38/180 & RAL xi/112/33, passim.

85. MAR Fft. or Ham. to NMR n.p. n.d., RAL xi/86/0A.

86. John [Jean/Johann] Osy & Son, Rot. to NMR Lon. 29 November 1809, RAL xi/112/3.

87. BB Ams. to NMR Lon. 31 January 1810, RAL xi/38/55A.

88. BB Ams. to NMR Lon. 7 & 10 March 1810, RAL xi/38/55A. For L B Cohen & Son's specie and bullion activities, see SC Lon. to NMR Lon. 24 August 1811, RAL xi/112/34.

89. Morel Dun. to NMR Lon. 6 July 1811, RAL xi/38/180.

90. Morel Dun. to NMR Lon. 12 August 1811, RAL xi/38/180.

91. Morel Dun. to NMR Lon. 1 May 1811, RAL xi/38/180.

92. Morel Dun. to NMR Lon. 29 September 1811, RAL xi/112/33.

93. In almost every letter, the exchange was noted or commented on; see Faber's and Morel's 1811 correspondence, passim, RAL xi/112/34, RAL xi/112/33 & RAL xi/38/180, respectively.

94. Morel Dun. to NMR Lon. 27 & 29 September, 7, 17, 21 & 26 December 1811, RAL xi/112/33.

95. Morel Dun. to NMR Lon. 13 & 18 June & 3 July 1811, RAL xi/38/180.

96. Faber Dun. to NMR Lon. 23 June, 6 & 9 August, 2 September, 14 & 19 November 1811, RAL xi/112/34.

97. See Morel Dun. to NMR Lon. 10 April & 1 May 1811, RAL xi/38/180.

98. JMR [Paris] to NMR Lon. 17 August 1811, RAL xi/85/0.

99. Morel Dun. to NMR Lon. 21 & 30 May & 23 June 1811, RAL xi/38/180.

100. JMR [Paris] to NMR Lon.17 August 1811, RAL xi/85/0.

101. SMR Fft. to JMR Paris, Lon. 6 & 13 December 1811, RAL xi/87/0A, Tape 171/Letter 4 & RAL xi/86/0A, Tape 240/Letter 26, respectively; & AMR Fft. to JMR Paris, 5 March 1812, RAL xi/82/9/1/Tape 247/Letter 17.

102. Spiers Gos. to NMR Lon. 21 & 23 April 1812, RAL xi/112/32B.

103. Levinson & Coster, Curaçao to NMR Lon. 26 March 1812, RAL xi/112/32B.

104. See supra Table 3.1. Fluctuation in Market Price of Foreign Gold and Silver in England: 1811–1815.

105. See 1812 correspondence of James Rothschild, RAL xi/85/0, passim.

106. For correspondence of Davillier & Co., Faber & Co., and Hottinguer & Co., RAL xi/112/33; for Mallet Frères & Co., and Perregaux Laffitte & Co., RAL xi/112/32B; & Veuve Dque Morel Frères & Co., and Morel Frères & Co., RAL xi/112/32B & RAL xi/38/180.

107. See JMR Paris to NMR Lon.15 May (No. 6) & 24 July 1812, RAL xi/85/0.

108. JMR Paris to NMR Lon. (No. 2), 6 April 1812, RAL xi/85/0.

109. See JMR Paris to NMR Lon. 28 March 1812, RAL xi/85/0.

110. See Faber Paris to NMR Lon. 15 January 1812, RAL xi/112/33, and Morel to NMR Lon. 8 February 1812, RAL xi/112/32B.

111. Quoted from postscript to Hannah Cohen Rothschild in JMR Paris to NMR Lon. 18 November 1811, RAL xi/85/0, Tape 79.

112. See NMR Lon. to JMR Ams. 23 September 1814, RAL xi/82/7/4/37 & MD Ams. to NMR Lon. 23 September 1814, RAL xi/112/72. My thanks to Carol Reynolds, MD, consultant, Mayo Clinic, Division of Anatomic Pathology, for recommending William H. Helfand, "James Morison and His Pills: A Study of the Nineteenth Century Pharmaceutical Market," in *Transactions of the British Society for the History of Pharmacy*, I:3 (1974), 101–135.

113. See James Rothschild's 1812 correspondence, RAL xi/85/0, passim.

114. Faber Paris to NMR Lon. 24 January 1812, RAL xi/112/33.

115. Morel Gravelines to NMR Lon. 20 May 1812, RAL xi/112/32B.

The Duke of Wellington with Colonel Gurwood at Apsley House by Andrew Morton, n.d.
Reproduced by kind permission of the trustees of The Wallace Collection, London.

FOUR

Nathan Mayer Rothschild and Wellington

1812–1814

> I think that Government have been wrong in employing
> the Bank to make their purchase of bullion to supply this
> army . . . instead of employing their agents to purchase
> it as the dealers in coin do. . . . I am quite convinced
> that if Government were to employ an agent to purchase
> £100,000 every month, the circulation in England would
> not feel the drain, and we should be very much relieved,
> and the exchanges would be much improved.
>
> —WELLINGTON *to* EARL BATHURST.
> *18 August 1812.*[1]

> We have an operation going on in Germany & the
> neighbouring countries to collect Specie for Lord
> Wellington's Army. It is of the most private nature . . .
> & has all the appearance of an individual speculation,
> but ships of war will from time to time be sent to
> Helvoet, or off the Dutch Coast to take the money on
> board. . . . The principal Agent is a great Jew Broker
> named Rothschild.
>
> —NICHOLAS VANSITTART *to*
> LORD CLANCARTY. *27 January 1814.*[2]

"Sometimes the most determined of invaders, equipped with strong armies
and copious intelligence about its enemy, can make myopic blunders that
later seem close to madness. . . . And such, at the dawn of the nineteenth
[century], was Napoleon's in Spain," opines Robert Hughes in his masterly

study of Goya. "The Peninsular campaign turned out to be as grievous a disaster for Napoleon's Grande Armée as its failure to conquer the immense winter wastes of Russia."[3]

Hughes knows what he is writing about. "Compared with his Grande Armée, the Spanish armed forces were nothing in Napoleon's eyes, a joke: riddled with nepotism and corruption, top-heavy with incompetent officers, antiquated in organization, badly equipped, ill-trained, and small. . . . But the Spanish army's worst and apparently insoluble problem was not the lack of men . . . but the shortage of money."[4]

Indeed, the catalyst that united Arthur Wellesley (1769–1852), the 1st Duke of Wellington, the "military genius," and Nathan Mayer Rothschild, the "financial genius," in the war against Napoleon and made both of them unforgettable figures was money. Wellington wanted it and Rothschild supplied it.[5]

All generals want more troops and Wellington was no exception. But his plaint took the form of a cry for more money, not only to pay his British troops but to train and put soldiers from Spain and Portugal into the field. Wellington never believed he had enough specie to feed and pay his men. In victory or defeat, he never missed an opportunity to ask for additional money to meet his military expenses and the British government did its best to meet his requests; but it was never enough, given its diminishing supply of gold and silver. Because he doubted the efficacy of his government to secure and send him the specie he needed, a prescient Wellington recommended in August 1812 that the government hire an agent to collect and deliver it to him. By the end of 1813, after repeated victories in Portugal and Spain—the Peninsular War—Wellington was prepared to challenge Napoleon's hegemony in France itself. But, before he would send his troops into battle, he requested the funds necessary to pay and feed them. On 21 November 1813, from his headquarters just south of Biarritz and Bayonne, at St. Jean de Luz, France, he wrote two letters and, while they might be viewed as the *casus nexus* for the British government's decision several weeks later to employ the services of Nathan Mayer Rothschild, they really cannot be interpreted as extraordinary or even surprising because they were just the latest round of similar letters he had sent his government the preceding two years. Wellington continued to send more such letters until he was absolutely convinced he would receive the funding he required. Yet, it was not until the British government recognized how desperate was its quest to secure more of the scarce coins that it decided to employ Rothschild to collect and supply the money to Wellington.

In March of 1808, the month in which Levy Barent Cohen died, Carlos IV of Spain abdicated his throne. In May, his son, Ferdinand VII, resigned his claim to the throne and Napoleon chose Joseph, his elder brother, to rule. Great Britain feared that the increasing presence of French troops in the Iberian Peninsula might deny it access to Latin American markets, so when the Spaniards rose up against the French, Britain sent expeditionary forces into the Peninsula to assist them. In August, Wellington defeated the French in Portugal,[6] and the British continued to support Spanish and Portuguese patriots with matériel, troops, and money. The commissary-in-chief in London and his agents in the field administered the military chest, which provided pay and sustenance to the soldiers and subsidies to the Portuguese government. In 1808, Britain filled the military chest with specie purchased locally and regionally with bills of exchange on London and with £1.6 million in specie from home, which undoubtedly influenced the increasing market price of specie in Great Britain.[7]

In 1809, the British government gave Wellington command of British forces to defend Portugal and he defeated the French at Oporto (Portugal) and Talavera (Spain). The £230,000 in Spanish dollars, doubloons, and Portuguese gold coins the British government had sent him, however, did not reach him before the battle began and, because he feared his desperate troops would plunder the countryside, he broke off his campaign. He criticized the Treasury and requested £100,000 immediately and £200,000 in specie for each of the following several months.[8] He even threatened to withdraw British and Portuguese armies from the field, if he and the Portuguese government did not receive more money. William Huskisson, the secretary of the Treasury, asked him: "'How can you expect us to buy specie here with the exchange thirty percent against us, and guineas selling at twenty-four shillings?'"[9]

The British government sent more than £2.6 million (£466,000 in specie) to the Peninsula in 1809 and, in 1810, its allocation increased to more than £6 million (£679,000 in specie).[10] Wellington was assured that, in 1811, £2,000,000 would be set aside to aid Portugal and more than £3,000,000 to aid Spain.[11]

But Wellington wanted more than just money. He also wanted power over the subsidy money that went to the Portuguese and Spanish governments so that he could enforce his will over their undisciplined and ineffective troops.

It may have been his victories at Ciudad Rodrigo and Badajoz in early 1812 or simply his aggrandizing ambition that emboldened him to write his brother, Henry: "If I had the command of that sum of money really, I should have the efficient control over all their operations."[12] He wrote more explicitly to the Earl of Liverpool, the secretary-at-war: "If I was enabled to pay them, I would force them to learn and to perform their duty. . . . it is my opinion that all the supplies sent to this country for the Spanish Government should be at the disposal of the Commissary in Chief of the King's troops." Nonetheless, he asserted: "I was not desirous of creating an impression that I wished to accumulate power into my own hands."[13]

To some extent, Wellington got his way. In 1812, about half the British subsidy to Portugal and a small portion of the recently increased British subsidy of £1,000,000 to Spain passed through his commissary general.[14] Yet, it was not enough: "we are really in terrible distress; I am afraid, in greater distress than any British army has ever felt." In July, Wellington wrote to Earl Bathurst, the newly appointed secretary-at-war: "Our principal and great want is money, with which I am afraid you cannot supply us sufficiently."[15]

After his victory at Salamanca later that month, Wellington wrote Bathurst: "I hope that you will be pleased with our battle."[16] Bathurst replied that he was and sent him another £100,000.[17] The following month, Wellington complained that his troops had gone without pay for months. "We are in the greatest distress," he wrote Bathurst, "The want of money in the army is become a most serious evil; and we may trace to this want many of the acts of plunder and indiscipline by which we are disgraced every day. We must be regularly supplied, or we cannot go on." He recommended to Bathurst that he no longer depend on the Bank for its specie but employ a private agent to collect and deliver it to him.[18]

Wellington's advice was timely and may have encouraged Bathurst to take extraordinary and courageous measures. In letters dating from the end of August, Bathurst related to Wellington how he came to circumvent, in the name of national security, the spirit and letter of the law regarding the export of gold and silver. Because the Bank of England would only give him slightly more than £76,000 in foreign gold and refused to surrender its English gold in bars to the government,[19] Bathurst submitted a proposal to the Bank: "The *legality* of what was proposed to them yesterday is a little questionable; but we have told them that the responsibility shall not rest upon them." This prompted the Bank to give Bathurst another £100,000 in foreign gold specie and bars.[20] But he wanted more and he continued to press the Bank until he reached an "Arrangement" with it in September 1812. The gravity of the situation was expressed by the Earl of Harrowby, Lord President of the Council. "I hope you will not lose your head for your dealings with the bank," he wrote Bathurst. "You and all of us should deserve to lose it, if we refrained from using a vigour beyond the law to enable Lord W[ellington] to pursue his successes, and it is fortunate that you have a decent legal cloak for so good a deed."[21]

On 22 September, Bathurst wrote at length to Wellington about the "Arrangement."

> The Bank truly believes, indeed I may say am sure, have no more foreign Gold & thus they have also parted now with the little Bar Gold, which they had. There is nothing left for us to get from them but Guineas: and you know it is illegal either to export them, or to part with them for more than their nominal value: and yet if we could not have got the Bank to spare us some Guineas, we could not in the present state of things have hold out to you hopes of being able to furnish you with Money. What has been done therefore is this. By the Act which restricts the Bank not to issue any Guineas &c in exchange for their Notes, there is a Clause by which the Privy Council has a power of issuing an Order of Council requiring the Bank to advance Gold for the payment of the troops. . . . we think we may issue an Order upon the Bank for the payment of the Troops: altho' the Clause was certainly not intended to refer to the pay of troops abroad; nor has it even been so construed. The Bank has certainly a right, & if it went too far, would have a duty to remonstrate. They have however consented to make only a private representation, on our understanding that this Order is not to be renewed. The Order will be for four hundred thousand pounds, to be paid by instalments, one hundred thousand pounds the middle of October, and so on the middle of the succeeding Months by which time the whole will be paid—Up to this we are within the *letter* of the Law. The transgression of the Law will be on my part, in the Instruction I shall think it proper to give you— Namely that you may dispose of it in the manner the most advantageous for the Service of the British Army; if circumstances should require you not to confine it to the *pay* of the troops under your Command. If things turn out well, I shall probably never hear much about it, but if there is a great alarm again on the subject of Specie, and there should not have been any brilliant success *at the time*, this transaction, if it comes out, will I am aware open me to some trouble. Of course I cannot wish you to write differently from what you feel & think: but on receiving the Instruction, it would be desirable for me, to have an Answer, in which the serious difficulties to which the Cause of the Peninsula would be exposed without this Advance should be fully stated.[22]

Two weeks later, the Earl of Liverpool, the prime minister, confirmed the "Arrangement," stipulating that Wellington would receive £100,000 in English guineas for four months beginning mid-October 1812. He also hinted that more specie might be forthcoming because he anticipated imports of bullion and specie from the East Indies. Nevertheless, he worried whether it would be enough "considering the scale of your expenditure."[23]

About this time, Wellington became commander of Spain's armies, estimated at 46,000 troops.[24] Contemporary intelligence had calculated that it would cost £1,000,000 per annum to pay 50,000 Spanish troops and that meant Wellington would need at least another £600,000 just to cover their pay from October 1812 to October 1813.[25] In November 1812, Bathurst sent Wellington £100,000 in foreign gold, which reduced the demand on the English guineas he had obtained from the Bank of England, and wrote Wellington: "We shall not send the second one hundred thousand pounds in Guineas, until next Month [December], wishing to have the Guineas for the times when we cannot send foreign Gold."[26]

In 1813, the British government's demand for gold of all kinds significantly increased. In February, Bathurst raised to £150,000 (£100,000 in foreign gold and £50,000 in English guineas) the money he was sending Wellington.[27] In early March, he promised Wellington £150,000 per month for the next three months, of which £300,000 would "probably" be in English guineas "*in consequence of a new arrangement made with the Bank.*"[28]

Bathurst was optimistic about sending Wellington more specie. One gold shipment had arrived from the East Indies, which the Bank had the Royal Mint coin into guineas; another was expected sometime in the summer; and the Bank had recently purchased a cache of specie from a private account. Together they would produce about £300,000 in guineas. He also had £129,000 in Spanish dollars. In May, he sent Wellington £200,000 in Portuguese and Spanish specie and £72,000 in guineas.[29]

These monies undoubtedly supported Wellington's rout of the French army at Vitoria on 21 June, a victory that brought him honor and promotion to field marshal in the British army.[30] Northern Spain was now open to his advancing armies, which in July laid siege to San Sebastian and Pamplona.[31] Bathurst was able to continue his shipments of specie to Wellington in August and September, largely owing to the arrival of gold from India.[32]

If it had not been for Bathurst's "Arrangements" with the Bank of England, John Charles Herries, the commissary-in-chief, whose job it was "to supply the first Wants of the Armies Employed in France & Spain by the purchase of Coin & Bullion," could not have supplied Wellington with the specie he desperately needed. Between March and November 1813, Herries ordered the Royal Mint to coin £512,537 in English guineas, and he sent 519,900 English guineas to the Peninsula that year.[33]

Herries also envisaged expanding this minting operation to include various foreign specie to supply the British forces on the Continent. He requested information from the Royal Mint about the weight and fineness of the Austrian ducat, French Louis d'Or, and Spanish doubloon relative to English standard gold.[34] Yet, the only action he took at this time was to direct the Royal Mint to strike Hanoverian gold coins, variously known as George d'Or, pistole, and Hanoverian five thaler. The date on the document respecting this decision was 12 August;[35] but he also drafted a memorandum, dated 18 August, presumably intended for Chancellor of Exchequer Vansittart's use, wherein he provided his *rationale* for his extraordinary action and its subsequent legitimation. Because it had become extremely difficult to procure money in the north of Germany to pay troops in the service of Great Britain, he requested that Vansittart obtain the authority of the prince regent to strike the coin of His Majesty's Hanoverian electorate.[36] Thus, during September–November 1813, the Royal Mint struck 321,145 Hanoverian gold five thaler pieces, and Herries shipped them to northern Europe for the maintenance of British troops and the assistance of the allied powers.[37]

Herries had established an important prerogative and precedent. For the year 1813, the specie and bullion he disposed of amounted to £2,625,304. In testimony to the Commissioners for Auditing Public Accounts (1815), Herries admitted that he had exceeded the coinage and shipment of specie "by a considerable Sum the Amount for which I have received the express written authority of their Lordships, altho I have always acted under the sanction either of a particular, or a general authority *verbally* communicated."[38]

Notwithstanding all their efforts, Herries and Bathurst could not meet Wellington's monetary needs. On 21 November, Wellington wrote two discouraging letters to Bathurst from St. Jean de Luz, France. In the first, he expressed his frustration for not having received the 300,000 Spanish dollars from Cadiz, which had been promised him two months earlier, to pay his Spanish troops, and also that he could not cover payments to his British troops beyond 4 December. Finally, almost as if he were laying down an ultimatum, he added: "[U]nless this army should be assisted with a very large sum of money at a very early period . . . however desirable that I should continue in operation, and however favorable the circumstances of the moment and the season, it will be quite impossible for me to do any thing."[39]

In his second letter that day, he opined about the state of Napoleon's affairs, praised the French locals for their support of his invasion, and commended the behavior of his Portuguese and British troops. But he despaired over the Spaniards, who "plundered a good deal, and did a good deal of mischief. . . . Some were executed, and many punished; and I sent all the Spanish troops back into Spain to be cantoned." He would bring them back into France only on the condition that he had the money to feed and pay them:

> If I could now bring forward 20,000 good Spaniards, paid and fed, I should have Bayonne. If I could bring forward 40,000, I do not know where I should stop. Now I have both the 20,000 and the 40,000 at my command, upon this frontier, but I cannot venture to bring forward any for want of means of paying and supporting them. Without pay and food, they must plunder; and if they plunder, they will ruin us all.[40]

Weeks passed but Wellington heard nothing about his requests for additional funding. He wrote Bathurst on 8 December: "It is vain to expect to be able to continue to carry on our operations through the winter, unless we should be supplied with money from England."[41] He repeated his appeal on 21 December:

> I am now in a commanding situation on the most vulnerable frontier of France, probably the only vulnerable frontier. If I could put 20,000 Spaniards into the field, which I could do if I had money and was properly supported by the fleet, I must have the only fortress there is on this frontier, if it can be called a fortress, and that in a very short space of time. If I could put 40,000 Spaniards into the field, I should most probably have my posts on the Garonne. Does any man believe that Napoleon would not feel an army in such a position more than he would feel 30 or 40,000 British troops laying siege to one of his fortresses in Holland?[42]

By January 1814, Wellington was completely frustrated and indicted the process that had plagued his command: "it is still incontestible that this army, and all its departments, and the Portuguese and the Spanish army, are at this moment paralysed for want of money." He claimed that British forces were "in debt in all parts of Spain, and are becoming so in France." The army had not been paid in seven months; muleteers had not been paid in over two years; and the ship with the promised money from Cadiz had still not arrived, which necessitated the redeployment of 16,000 Spanish troops.

While he acknowledged the monthly allotment of £100,000 was helpful, it did "not cover the expense of this army. . . . besides the subsidies which must be paid in ready money, such as for meat for the troops, hospital expenses, Commissariat labourers, &c. &c., for which no provision can be made out of the monthly £100,000 received from England." Finally, although he declared he was ready "to push the enemy to the Garonne during the winter," he would not move his troops because "there is not in the military chest a shilling to pay for any thing that the country could afford, and our credit is already gone in this country. . . . It is obvious that an immediate and large supply of money from England is necessary."[43]

Before this severely critical letter reached London, the British government had taken decisive action to deliver specie more effectively to Wellington. On 4 January 1814, Herries invited Nathan Mayer Rothschild "to favor him with a short conversation."[44] After several such meetings, Herries recommended him to Liverpool and Vansittart as the person to collect and deliver French specie to Wellington in the south of France.[45]

There is only one extant contemporary source in which Herries discussed his nomination of Nathan Rothschild.[46] Although undated and unsigned, the draft "Report" is in Herries's hand and must have been written on or just prior to 11 January, the day he appointed Nathan. In it, he accepted responsibility for "the direction of this important & delicate operation of collecting secretly . . . [F]rench Coin in Holland & Germany for the use of the army under Lord Wellington, in France through the agency of Mr. Rothschild." He "carefully considered the various suggestions of Mr. Rothschild as to the most efficient mode of executing this Service, together with the information received from him and from other quarters respecting the state of the Exchanges & the money market in Holland and Germany." He detailed how the purchase of bills of exchange would be made by "Mr. R." and how remittances would be paid to "Mr. R." He approved of advancing to Rothschild "some Money to execute his Commission with dispatch," for which amount Rothschild would "deposit omnium & Stock,"[47] as security, with the office of commissary-in-chief. He also approved of Rothschild's request for "a Commission of 2 per cent for this service" because "The Magnitude of the object, the dispatch and the services required may justify payment of such a remuneration." He cited that the same commission had been given to another merchant for lesser services in arrangement with the Bank of England. Herries was convinced that "it is the Greatest importance that Lord Wellington should speedily be supplied with a large Sum in specie applicable to his expenditure in France," and that because "the Bank of England is unable to meet the demand for this pressing occasion by its purchases in this Market," another way had to be found.[48]

Was there no other merchant-banker—one, perhaps, more traditionally established and more socially accepted—whom Herries could have charged with a mission so vital to the country's national interest? Alexander Baring might have been an obvious choice, except that Baring Brothers & Co. did not have a hands-on network on the Continent, and Hope & Co. of Amsterdam, with which he had a close relationship, was essentially inactive at this time. And politically, Alexander Baring was unsuitable because he criticized government policies in Parliament.[49] Moreover, his enemies complained to Liverpool about his loan policies to the United States: "consequently British money is now used in the vindictive war carried on against us."[50] Socially, there was no intercourse between Herries and Baring, if one accepts the latter's incidental comment to Herries: "I fear I can hardly claim that of being known to you."[51]

Reid, Irving & Co., which the British government had already employed in northern Europe to service the British military's financial needs and, therefore, had hands-on experience, should also have been a logical choice for the Wellington operation.[52] But Herries and Vansittart had reservations about that firm's present effectiveness and doubted it could take on new responsibilities. In fact, at the time of his discussions with Nathan Rothschild, Herries suspended Reid, Irving & Co.'s exchange operations in Holland "until the arrangements of Mr. R. shall have been completed."[53]

What undoubtedly prompted Herries to focus his attention on Nathan Mayer Rothschild was his overseas bullion and specie operations, which had grown so sizable by the end of 1813 that they could hardly have gone unnoticed by any astute London merchant or banker. Jeremiah Harman, director of the Bank of England, whose own merchant bank had handled Nathan's accounts, could have discreetly informed Herries that Nathan was the kind of person he was looking for.

Except for the comments Herries made in his "Report" to Vansittart, there is no existing record of the several conversations he had with Nathan in early January 1814. Nathan could have told Herries that he had an extraordinary network of clients and correspondents in the major financial and commercial centers of Europe, a network superior to any other British merchant-banker who traded overseas in specie and bullion. He could have also told Herries that his brothers knew their way around the Amsterdam, Frankfurt, Hamburg, and Paris exchanges, that merchant-banking houses always accepted their bills of exchange, and that his brothers could activate an operation in any of the key European financial power centers.

Nathan might have impressed Herries with his knowledge of the fluctuating price of specie and bullion and exchange rates to demonstrate his *Fingerspitzengefühl* of the market. For example, in 1813, the London price for legally exportable foreign gold and silver exceeded that of 1812. In 1813, the price of foreign gold in bars rose by 10.4 percent and foreign silver in bars by 16 percent above 1812 prices. In 1813, the lower prices were higher and the higher prices were higher than they had been for bullion and specie in 1812.[54] During the same period, the Paris rate on bills of exchange on London also increased from fr.19 = £ in 1812 to fr.20 = £ in 1813. It was only during the second half of 1813 that the rate fell back to about fr.18.50 = £. While Nathan would not have told Herries that in 1813 James alone remitted to him an estimated minimum of £1,780,000 in bills of exchange on London (of which £460,000 was derived from the sale of Pictures, that is, English guineas),[55] he would have been comfortable in relating to him that on two days in June 1813, he legally exported from Harwich on board His Majesty's packets £20,000 in gold[56]—not an insignificant sum, when compared to Bathurst's specie shipments to Wellington at that time.

Herries might have wanted to know more about Nathan's expanded trade with Russia, and he would have speculated on how the Rothschild presence in St. Petersburg might one day be useful to the British government. Russia needed foreign bullion and specie to pay off its enormous domestic war debts and Great Britain had already committed itself to subsidize Russian military forces against Napoleon. The Russian market was lucrative, as Bathurst had recognized when he informed Wellington about the scarcity of specie and bullion in England: "Such is the depreciation of Paper in Russia, & so unfavorable is the exchange, that any person purchasing Gold or Silver . . . will make more than thirty per Cent by sending it to Russia."[57]

Nathan Rothschild was just such a person. In 1813, his principal clients in St. Petersburg were Meyer & Bruxner, J. M. Jantzon (about whom little is known),[58] and Stieglitz & Co. (which later would become Russia's leading merchant-bank).[59] The extant sources reveal more about Nathan's dealings with Meyer & Bruxner than they do with the others. Nathan must have known that Henry Hope & Co. had vested a great deal of business and responsibility in J. C. Meyer, who was "prudent, incorruptible and opposed to hazardous draft speculations." Hope & Co. considered Meyer & Bruxner an "excellent house."[60]

In May 1813, in addition to a cargo of cochineal, indigo, logwood, and sugar, Nathan sent gold to Meyer & Bruxner. Because there was so much gold entering the St. Petersburg market, regulations had become cumbersome and the effective sale of the gold was significantly delayed. For example, Meyer & Bruxner had first to deliver the gold to the St. Petersburg Mint, which would melt and assay it. In return, the St. Petersburg Mint gave Meyer & Bruxner a bond in silver rubles, redeemable in July, for the gold's intrinsic value. But, in the meantime, Meyer & Bruxner remitted £4,000 in bills on London to Nathan against the sale of the gold (which eventually fetched £6,386) and also sent him a cargo of Russian bristles and tallow.[61]

Meyer & Bruxner repeatedly advised Nathan that his agents had to declare the specie and bullion cargo on arrival, otherwise custom officials could seize it. It also strongly recommended that Nathan not continue to risk transporting bullion and specie solely by sea to St. Petersburg. The firm's experience had shown that it was safer and speedier to ship from Harwich via Gothenburg-Stockholm-Åbo and overland with armed guards to St. Petersburg. If Nathan would ship by that route, Meyer & Bruxner would take £20,000 in Spanish dollars and Portuguese gold coins.[62] Nathan accepted this advice and in equal account with B. A. Goldschmidt & Co. of St. Helen's Place, shipped specie to St. Petersburg.[63] During the next several months, the average shipment of specie and bullion to Meyer & Bruxner amounted to about £9,500.[64]

Nathan Rothschild's continuing success depended on the continuing scarcity of specie and bullion, his skill as an entrepreneur and his ability to execute a trade. He depended greatly on those he contracted to transport his specie and bullion from England to Continental markets, especially on Richard Cullen (1754–1835) and his several sons, who were experienced mariners from Folkestone in easy reach of Calais, Gravelines, and Dunkerque on the French coast. Richard owned or had interest in several boats, among them, the Rover and the P.O., each of which he leased to Nathan for £100 a month. Because some of Cullen's boats were named Lionel, Anthony, and Hannah, it has been thought that Nathan shared in their ownership. The Cullens became indispensable to the execution of Nathan's operation in supplying Wellington with specie.[65]

The contractual arrangement between the British government and Nathan Rothschild was sealed on 11 January 1814, and it would have a positive effect not only on the outcome of Wellington's campaign against Napoleon's forces in the south of France, but also on the future prosperity of the merchant-bank N M Rothschild in London. Two contemporary sources contain the terms of the agreement: Vansittart's letter to Herries on 11 January and Herries's letter to Nathan that same day, although the two documents are not identical. Nathan and his agents were to procure, within two months and with "much secrecy," in Germany, France, and Holland at the approximate current exchange rates, no less than £600,000 in "Gold and Silver French coin," and they were to deliver the specie on board British ships of war stationed off the Dutch port of Hellevoetsluis,[66] which would convey the specie to Wellington's headquarters in the South of France. Nathan would be responsible for all risks and losses prior to delivery on board, for weighing the specie in the presence of naval officers, and for shortages discovered by commissary officials at the final destination. The office of the commissary-in-chief would reimburse him in London for purchases and expenses on submission of invoices and certificates of delivery.[67]

The language covering Nathan's commission was wanting. In Vansittart's letter to Herries, it is "2% with all charges necessarily incurred on the sums actually delivered" and in Herries's letter to Nathan, it is "a commission of two per cent upon the Sterling cost of the specie which you may deliver, together with the necessary charges of the transport and collection of it." Consequently, Nathan could expect to receive £12,000 in commission on the stipulated £600,000 of specie to be delivered to and accounted for by commissary agents. All expenses for transportation, insurance, and brokerage were reimbursable. However, in many of the invoices subsequently submitted to Herries during the Wellington operation, Nathan stipulated a *commission* of 6 pence per ounce (not a charge for transportation, insurance, or brokerage expenses) over and above the cost of the specie and bullion he purchased, handled, or delivered to Herries. Therefore, in calculating the commission Nathan could have expected to receive from the Wellington operation, it would be fair to estimate the £12,000 as the *minimum* sum. By any contemporary standard of measure, a commission of £12,000 was an extraordinary sum of money for two months' work. For example, in 1814, it was greater than the annual salary (although not the total compensation) of each of the British ambassadors at Paris, St. Petersburg, and Vienna;[68] and in 1815, it was greater than the British subsidy to Hanover or any other German state for the military service of 1,000 soldiers per year.[69]

Nathan wasted no time in organizing the operation. He immediately wrote to the prominent merchant-banking houses of D. Crommelin & Sn. and Braunsberg & Co. in Amsterdam, which began purchasing French specie for him.[70] On 13 January, he sent Mayer Davidson, his principal clerk and close associate, to Amsterdam to supervise the operation but unfavorable winds prevented his packet boat from sailing from Harwich for several days.[71] On 14 January, Nathan deposited £39,464 in bills of exchange and a "Bank Receipt for 125000" omnium with the commissary-in chief against "an advance in Money made to him for the purchase of specie abroad."[72] Herries later reported: "I received from Mr. R. at the outset of this business, and I still retain in my hands property of his to the amount of about 100,000 as a security . . . for his Conduct & for any advances that may be made to him."[73] Nathan received his advance and sent a little more than £25,000 in bills of exchange to Davidson in Amsterdam for deposit in "Account G"— the designation for the British government account from which Nathan would earn a commission on every transaction.[74] Four days later he sent another £24,500 to Davidson with a brief comment: "I hope you will be able to accomplish the object of your voyage."[75]

The British government had every intention of keeping the contractual arrangement a secret and would inform only those who needed to know. Colonel Henry Bunbury, military under-secretary, was entrusted to deliver a letter to Wellington informing him that Rothschild would deliver to him an average of about £300,000 in French specie for each of the next two months;[76] in the meantime, Bathurst was also sending him £400,000 in guineas.[77] Vansittart informed Lord Clancarty, the British ambassador to Holland, because "in case of an unforeseen difficulty the parties may apply for your assistance, though they will avoid it, if possible in order to escape suspicion." But Sir George Burgmann, the commissioner to the "federative paper" commission in Amsterdam, who was responsible for the payment of British subsidies to the allied powers, was not to be told.[78]

However, when Davidson finally arrived in Amsterdam with eight bars of Nathan's own gold for sale, his worry was not about keeping secrets that Braunsberg & Co. had already guessed was his mission. "I did not make a secret of it and told them about the commission, especially because the gentlemen promised me to keep everything we do together secret." There is no evidence to suggest that, once *the secret* was no longer *a secret*, the operation was compromised. Buying coins on the "open" market could not be kept quiet for very long. At best, the British could hope that the activities of the Rothschilds would be interpreted as a private speculation. It remained problematic whether Nathan could actually execute his commission and on schedule. Davidson wrote him that "we were misled in our hope" because French coins are "very rare here. My friends tell me that since the French left, these kinds of coins also disappeared."[79]

Davidson was pessimistic about collecting large quantities of the coins quickly on the Dutch market. He asked the Rothschild brothers in Frankfurt to buy up French specie anywhere they could.[80] Private hoards were elusive as well. One person possessing 10,000 Napoléon d'Or refused to exchange them for other gold coins even at a premium. Another agreed to sell 14,000 Napoléons but only for bills of exchange and that sent Davidson scurrying to Braunsberg & Co. to borrow back the bills he had just deposited. He read in the newspaper that the Dutch Mint in Utrecht would become operational again and he recommended that the British government persuade the Dutch government to permit the striking of Napoléon d'Or: "this would be a nice thing. Then I would buy the entire gold in bars and make Napoleons from the gold. This would also hold up the price of gold and would be good for our private things. . . . I could make 'R Meir Regensburg' [Napoléon d'Or] from 'Reb Moshe' [English gold]." Because these expedients would take time, he wrote Nathan "that it will be necessary for you to extend your engagement for at least 3 month instead of the original stipulated time of 2 month, which I hope will be granted."[81]

James visited London at the end of January to report on "the State of Paris" to Vansittart and Liverpool,[82] and then went to The Hague to request that Lord Clancarty obtain permission from the Prince of Orange "to have such quantities of Gold of other nations as he may be able to collect coined into Napoleons, the dies existing for this purpose in the Mint at Utrecht."[83] He also wanted Clancarty to arrange for a British warship to collect at Hellevoetsluis about £100,000 in French specie that was in Amsterdam awaiting shipment to Wellington's forces but Clancarty was uncertain if a warship could rendezvous in time.[84]

When Davidson arrived at the port to supervise the loading of the specie, the HMS Comus, the designated British warship, was nowhere to be seen. He could not find a safe place to store the specie temporarily and registered his frustration to Nathan: "I can not let 100/m lay in the street, there is no British solders in this place [sic]." He, therefore, ordered the cargo loaded on the HM Gun Brig Earnest that was lying off shore to be taken to England. While the loading was taking place, an additional three wagons containing 29 chests of specie from D. Crommelin & Sn. and a parcel of specie from Braunsberg & Co. arrived, which Davidson also placed on board the Earnest. William Cullen sailed with the cargo—54 chests of French silver coins and seven chests of Napoléon d'Or and Louis d'Or—to arrange for it to be weighed and counted.[85]

Davidson was still not sanguine about succeeding in his mission. He wrote despondently to Nathan:

> you maintain your opinion that 600/m can be obtained, I differ wth [sic] you on that subject. If you could only form an idea of the trouble & anxiety connected wth [sic] the business, I think you would not persevere at least my good Sir I am ready to do any thing for you, but I can not undertake to finish this transaction to Satisfaction; here is no Store house, no seals, no weights, & no lodging to be got for money, I have no place where to wright [sic] a letter, & Cullens are not the people who even assist much in *regular* transactions they are not used to it. Therefore I can not be here for ever, hope you will soon release me, I . . . do not See a prospect to finish the business to Satisfaction.[86]

By the end of February, Davidson's negative attitude had stiffened. He opined that the market just could not supply the huge quantity of French specie that the British government wanted purchased. There was a shortage of French coins, especially in Germany, and those that could be found were too dangerous to transport because "troops snoop around day and night." He regretted that Nathan had undertaken a commission where "one spends one's time here for nothing." With only two weeks remaining to complete the total purchase of £600,000 in French specie, Davidson candidly wrote Nathan—"My opinion it is simply impossible."[87]

Davidson did not exaggerate the difficulties he had encountered in purchasing French specie. As the 11 March contract expiration deadline neared, Rothschild agents exhibited frenetic, if not frantic, activity in scouring the mercantile centers of northwestern Europe for French coins. D. Crommelin & Sn. reported every few days on purchases in Amsterdam and other Dutch towns, in Antwerp, Brussels, and Bremen.[88] However, while Braunsberg & Co. lamented its meager purchases for Account G, the merchant bank separately sold significant amounts of gold specie and bullion for the private accounts of Nathan and M. A. Rothschild & Sons.[89]

Despite the extraordinary efforts of his brothers and associates, Nathan did not execute his contract to deliver £600,000 in French specie to British authorities in the south of France by 11 March 1814. The HMS Comus and the HMS Thais had only arrived in the iced Dutch waters off Hellevoetsluis in early and late March, respectively, and collected about £450,000 in French coins.[90] By the time those ships arrived in Bordeaux, Wellington's forces had reached Toulouse, Emperor Alexander of Russia had entered Paris, and Napoleon had abdicated.[91]

According to the "Statement of Funds provided for the Public Service," which stipulated the number, kind and the market price of the coins denominated in English pounds sterling, the Rothschilds delivered a total of 1,085,800 coins valued at £552,335.[92] But the British government did not complain that Nathan had not fulfilled his contract. Rather, he was to continue to supply Wellington with French specie,[93] and to continue to receive his commission of 2 percent.[94]

Nathan Rothschild received praise for his service to the British government. On the eve of the dissolution of the commissariat in 1816, Herries submitted a "Memorandum" to Liverpool and Vansittart wherein he acknowledged that "operations were undertaken . . . through the agency of Mr. Rothschild . . . which proved highly efficacious: the Chest in the South of France was furnished with French Gold from Holland by shipments at Helvoetsluys so rapidly & completely that the Commissary General was abundantly supplied for all his wants, without having occasion to negotiate a bill; and from that time no military Debt . . . was created on the Continent." Herries went on to state—with Nathan Rothschild in mind—that the success of this operation "led to the adoption of the same Course for providing Specie afterwards, required for the greater & more important objects of our Expedition abroad."[95]

Notes

[Please note that citations to letters, especially those to and from Wellington, do not always stipulate the place of recipient, as they were not included in those letters.]

1. W Madrid to B Lon. 18 August 1812, *WD* IX, 369–370.
2. V Lon. to Clancarty Hague 27 January 1814, *VP* BLAddMss. 31,231, f. 14.
3. Robert Hughes, *Goya* (New York: Alfred A. Knopf, 2003), ch. 8, "War with Napoleon," pp. 261 and 262, respectively.

4. Ibid p. 261.

5. See Neville Thompson, "The Uses of Adversity," in Gash, pp.1–10; & Eli F. Heckscher, *The Continental System. An Economic Interpretation* (Oxford: Clarendon Press, 1922), p. 354. Arthur Wellesley, like Nathan Rothschild, had four brothers who helped to prepare him for greatness. The most instrumental was Richard, the eldest (the 2nd Earl of Mornington and later, Marchquess Wellesley), who provided the political base. Richard was governor-general of India (1797–1805); British envoy to the Spanish government in exile; and foreign secretary (1809–1812). Henry, the youngest brother, developed diplomatic skills and Arthur experienced military successes, while serving in India with Richard. Henry (Lord Cowley) later succeeded Richard as ambassador to Spain. See Edward Ingram, "Wellington and India," and John K. Severn, "The Wellesleys and Iberian diplomacy, 1808–12," in Gash, pp. 11–33 & 34–65, respectively. Another brother, William Wellesley-Pole, as Master of the Mint and member of Cabinet, would serve Wellington's interest in other ways. This is discussed below in part three, ch. 6.

6. See Charles J. Esdaile, *The Duke of Wellington and the Command of the Spanish Army 1812–14* (New York: St. Martin's Press, 1990), pp. 1–26; Muir, pp. 32–59; & Severn, in Gash, pp. 34–36.

7. Muir, pp. 62–63, 118; Sherwig, pp. 222–224; & S. G. P. Ward, *Wellington's Headquarters. A Study of the Administrative Problems in the Peninsula 1813–1814* (Oxford: Oxford University Press, 1957), ch. III, "The Maintenance of the Army in the Peninsula," pp. 66–101, passim. See also supra, part two, ch. 3.

8. Muir, pp. 84–95, especially, p. 95; Severn, in Gash, pp. 42–43; & Sherwig, pp. 216–223.

9. Quoted in Sherwig, p. 224.

10. Muir, pp. 116–118; & Sherwig, pp. 226–232, especially p. 232, n. 48.

11. See Sherwig, pp. 233–238.

12. W Fuente Guinaldo to H W, 28 April 1812, *WD* IX, 96. See also W Fuente Guinaldo, to Gen. Don Carlos de Espana, 29 April 1812, *WD* IX, 98.

13. W Fuente Guinaldo to L Lon. 6 May 1812, *WD* IX, 125.

14. In 1813, it rose to 70 percent and, in 1814, to more than 80 percent. In 1813, the Portuguese Council of Regency received only about 25 percent of the subsidy in cash and, in 1814, only seven percent. Sherwig, pp. 246–247, 251–53 & 264; & W Fuente Guinaldo to HW 14 May 1812, *WD* IX, 145–149.

15. W Rueda to B Lon. 4 July 1812, *WD* IX, 270. See also B Lon. to W 23 July 1812, *BP* vol 60, & W Cuellar to B Lon. 3 August 1812, *WD* IX, 329. For Bathurst, see Thompson. My thanks to Professor Thompson for consulting with me about manuscript sources.

16. W Flores de Avila to B Lon. 24 July 1812, *WD* IX, 308.

17. B Lon. to W 6 & 16 August 1812, *WSD* VII, 374 & 383.

18. W Madrid to B Lon. 18 August 1812, *WD* IX, 369–370.

19. B Lon. to W 31 August & 9 September 1812, *WSD* VII, 412 & 415, respectively. See also Kelly, p. 96.

20. B Lon. to W 10 September 1812, *WSD* VII, 418. See also Kelly, p. 96.

21. Earl of Harrowby Sandon to B Lon. 17 September 1812. *Report*, pp. 214 & xiv.

22. B Lon. to W 22 September 1812, *WP* 1/350.

23. L Lon. to W 7 October 1812, *WSD* VII, 445; & see B Lon. to W 8 & 13 October 1812, *WSD* VII, 447 & 457, respectively. See also Kelly, pp. 96–97.

24. Sherwig, pp. 256–257; W Ciudad Rodrigo to L Lon. 23 November 1812, *WD* IX, 570–574.

25. T. Sydenham, Villa Toro, near Burgos, to HW 28 September 1812, *WSD* VII, 430.

26. B Lon. to W 12 November 1812, *BP* vol. 60.

27. B Lon. to W 17 February 1813, *WSD* VII, 554 & *BP* vol. 61.

28. B Lon. to W 6 March 1813, *WSD* VII, 578, & *BP* vol. 61. Italics are mine. See also Kelly, p. 99.

29. B Lon. to W 20 & 28 April & 19 May 1813, *BP* vol. 61 & see *WP* 1/368, f. 9.

30. L Walmer Castle to B Lon. 16 & 17 August 1812, *Report*, pp. 195–196 & 196–197, respectively; & Muir, p. 265.

31. Muir, pp. 264–267 et seq. & Sherwig, p. 261.

32. B Lon. to W 16 August & 25 September 1813, *BP* vol. 61 & *WSD* VIII, 277, respectively.

33. "Memorandum from Mr. Herries for Lord Liverpool & Mr. Vansittart 12 June 1816," *HP* BLAddMss. 57367, ff. 12, 16–17; & H Lon. to L & V 12 June 1816, Appendix C, H *Mem.* I, 244–245 & I, 84–85.

34. H Lon. & JmD Lon. to Mint Office, Lon. 10 September & 16 October 1813, PRO Mint 13/184 & 157, respectively.

35. "Minute," August 12, 1813: "Regulations in respect to the Weight and Fineness of the Hanoverian Gold monies to be coined at the Mint, as agreed with Mr. Herries the Commissary in Chief," PRO Mint 13/162.

36. "Memorandum on the Mode in which it is proposed to carry out effect— the Hanoverian Coinage" (dated 18 August [1813]), *HP* BLAddMss. 57396, ff. 51–52.

37. See "Minute," August 12, 1813, "Regulations in respect to the Weight and Fineness of the Hanoverian Gold monies to be coined at the Mint, as agreed with Mr. Herries the Commissary in Chief," PRO Mint 13/162; H Lon. to WH Lon. c.1 November & to Hill Lon. c.3 November 1813, *HP* BLAddMss. 57434 [Letter Book], ff. 35 & 39, respectively; Mint Office Papers, 20 August–1 September 1813, PRO Mint 1/17, pp. 304, 306–310 & "Monthly Reports of the Importations of Bullion into His Majesty's Mint, and the Coinage and Deliveries thereof," PRO Mint 1/17, pp. 325–328; "An Account of the Hanoverian Gold Monies Coined at His Majesty's Mint, and also of The Pieces deposited in the Pix, From the 15th September, 1813, to the 24th May, 1815, inclusive, During the Masterships of The Earl of Clancarty, and the Right Honourable W Wellesley Pole," dated 25th October 1820, Mint-Office, PRO Mint 13/164; "The Account of the Master & Worker of H. M. Mint for the Charge of Coinage of Hanoverian V Thaler Gold Pieces,"14 January 1814, PRO Mint 13/163; "Master's Gold Journal. January 1812 to December 1813, PRO Mint

9/222; "An Account of private Coinage (or Coinage not of the Realm, carried on at The Mint, for whom & under what authority the same were executed.)," PRO Mint 13/2; "References to Currencies of Colonies and Foreign Countries in the Record Books of the Mint," PRO Mint 13/15; *HP* BLAddMss. 57396, ff. 51–52; & Craig, pp. 276, 390–391.

38. H Lon. to The Commissioners for Auditing Public Accounts, 16 January, & to GH Lon. 18 January 1815, PRO T1/1440–1441/No. 823, encl. A, B & C. Italics mine.

39. W St. Jean de Luz, to B 21 November 1813, *WD* XI, 302–303. See W St. Jean de Luz to B 24 November, & 22 December 1813, *WD* XI, 316 & 389, respectively.

40. W St. Jean de Luz to B 21 November 1813, *WD* XI, 303–307 & *VP* BLAddMss. 38255, ff. 55–58.

41. W St. Jean de Luz to B 8 December 1813, *WD* XI, 356.

42. W St. Jean de Luz to B 21 December 1813, *WD* XI, 384–387. At the end of the year, Bathurst sent Wellington another specie shipment of £150,000. B Lon. to W 31 December 1813, *WSD* VIII, 452. The amount of money that passed through Wellington's military chest to fund the Portuguese and Spanish campaigns during the year 1813 came to slightly more than £2,500,000. W St. Jean de Luz to B 8 January 1814, *WD* XI, 427.

43. W St. Jean de Luz to B 8 January 1814, *WD* XI, 425–427.

44. H Lon. to NMR Lon. 4 January 1814, *HP* BLAddMss. 57434 [Letter Book], f. 63.

45. "A Report of the Progress Made by the Commissary in Chief in the execution of the Service intrusted to him by the Lords of the Treasury by their Letter of [*blank*]," *HP* BLAddMss. 57396, ff. 26–27, 30–33; V to H Lon. & H Lon. to NMR Lon. 11 January 1814, RAL xi/38/59A [RAL xi/52/30]; & H Lon. to NMR Lon.11 January 1814, *HP* BLAddMss. 57434 [Letter Book], ff. 63–67.

46. Cf. Ferguson, pp. 85–88. Edward Herries added no new knowledge on this point in his *Memoir* of his father's career. H *Mem.* I, 85–86.

47. *Omnium*: "The aggregate amount of the parcels of different stocks and other considerations, formerly offered by the Government in raising a loan, for each unit of capital (= £100) subscribed." *The Oxford Universal Dictionary on Historical Principles* (3rd. Ed. Rev. Oxford: Clarendon Press, 1955), p. 1368.

48. "A Report of the Progress Made by the Commissary in Chief in the execution of the Service intrusted to him by the Lords of the Treasury by their Letter of [*blank*]," *HP*. BLAddMss. 57396, ff. 26–27, 30–33, passim.

49. See Baring's remarks in the House of Commons on 10 November 1813, *The Parliamentary Debates from the Year 1803 to the Present Time* (London: T. C. Hansard, 1814), XXVII (1813–1814), 70–74 & his letter to Herries in which he defends alleged criticism of the Commissariat. *HP* BLAddMss. 57415, ff. 187–188 (16 November 1814).

50. John Borlaise Warren, Halifax, Nova Scotia, to L Lon. 16 November 1813, *LP* BLAddMss. 38255, f. 43.

51. A. Baring Lon. to H Lon. 14 November 1814, *HP* BLAddMss. 57415, f. 188. Their early estrangement appears to have continued throughout their public lives.

This is the sense conveyed by Lord Brougham's specific references to Alexander Baring's opinion of Herries, which Edward Herries quoted in H *Mem.* I, 220, note. 3 (c. 1828) & II, 277 (29 August 1853).

52. For example, see "Statement of Specie Sent to Holland consigned to Ferrier & Co. of Rottm. and Braunsberg & Co. of Amst. as the Agents of Messrs. Reid Irving & Reid [*sic*]," *HP* BLAddMss. 57394, ff. 15–16.

53. "A Report of the Progress Made by the Commissary in Chief in the execution of the Service intrusted to him by the Lords of the Treasury by their Letter of [*blank*]," *HP* BLAddMss. 57396, f. 33.

54. See *MPG & S: 1811–1813 & 1813–1814.*

55. See James Mayer Rothschild's 1813 correspondence, RAL xi/85/0, passim.

56. Anthony Cox, agent for His Majesty's packets, Harwich to NMR Lon. 9 & 20 June, 1813 & receipts from September–October 1813, RAL xi/112/32B; & receipts from Heseltine & Billingsley, Harwich to NMR Lon. 24–25 & 28 December 1813, RAL xi/112/2.

57. B Lon. to W 22 September 1812, *WP* 1/350.

58. See J. M. Jantzon's correspondence, RAL xi/112/2.

59. See Stieglitz & Co.'s correspondence, RAL xi/112/2, and Stieglitz & Co. StP to NMR Lon. 6 March 1814, RAL xi/112/71; and B V Anan'ich, *Bankirskie doma v Rossii 1860–1914gg.* (Leningrad: Nauka, 1991).

60. Quotes from Buist, pp. 220 & 511.

61. M & B StP to NMR Lon. 16, 20, 23 & 30 May, 3 & 10 June 1813; King StP. to NMR Lon. 1 June 1813, "Captain William King of the Rover His Ship's Account," 23 June 1813; & "Account of Sales of a Cargo of Sundry Merchandize, received on Board the Rover," 9 June 1813, RAL xi/112/2. In May, Nathan Rothschild sent 1280 pieces of Austrian ducats to J. M. Jantzon and later sent him bags of silver coins. J. M. Jantzon StP. to NMR Lon. 23 May, 5, 16, 19, 26 & 30 September 1813, RAL xi/112/2.

62. Meyer & Bruxner correspondence, RAL xi/112/2, passim; &, especially, M & B StP. to NMR Lon. 24 June, 11 July, 10 & 21 October & 11 November 1813, RAL xi/112/2.

63. B. A. Goldschmidt & Co. Lon. to NMR Lon. 29 October, 5, 9, 13, 16 & 23 November & 1 December 1813, RAL xi/112/32B; & M & B StP. to NMR. Lon. 2, 5 & 16 December 1813, RAL xi/112/2. On 16 September 1813, Baruch A. Goldschmidt died and was succeeded by his brother Lion Abraham Goldschmidt. See circular letter dated 1 January 1814, RAL xi/112/72.

64. Meyer & Bruxner correspondence, RAL xi/112/2, passim; &, especially, M & B StP. to NMR Lon. 22 & 29 July, 8, 12, 15, 22, 26 & 29 August, 23 September, 3 & 7 October 1813, RAL xi/112/2.

65. See Michael B. Cullen, *The Cullen's Family Association with the de Rothschilds.* Copyrighted typescript, 1989, deposited in RAL T66. The sons who participated in Nathan Rothschild's operations were: James (1780–1814); John (1782–1814); Hunt (1785–1841); Thomas (1790–1860); and William (1793–1837).

66. The port of Hellevoetsluis, in the province of Zuid-Holland, is located to the west of Rotterdam. Hellevoetsluis is the current Dutch spelling but varies in early nineteenth century sources.

67. V to H Lon. & H Lon. to NMR Lon. 11 January 1814, RAL xi/38/59A (RAL xi/52/30); & see H Lon. to NMR Lon. 11 January 1814, *HP* BLAddMss. 57434 [Letter Book], ff. 63–67.

68. See Castlereagh's recommendation for salary increases for Foreign Office personnel, WH Lon. to Arbuthnot. Lon. 22 May 1815, PRO T1/1467/No. 7635.

69. See "A Statement of payments made by J. Ch. Herries Esq. under the directions of the Lords Commissioners of His Majesty's Treasury in the Year 1815 and 1816 in discharge of Subsidies of Foreign Powers &c included in separate Accounts for those Years rendered by him to the Auditors of Public Accounts," PRO AO 3/1088/2.

70. See correspondence of D[aniel] Crommelin & Sn. & Braunsberg & Co. Ams. for January & February 1814, RAL ix/112/74A, RAL xi/38/55B, & RAL xi/38/59B, respectively. See also Jonker, pp.193–196.

71. MD Harw. to NMR Lon. 13–14 & 20 January 1814, RAL xi/112/72, & RAL xi/T(A) 35 [trans. of RAL xi/38/81a/4], respectively. In 1816, he would become Nathan Rothschild's brother-in-law by his marriage to Levy Barent Cohen's daughter, Jessy (1795–1869).

72. JmD Lon. to NMR Lon. 14 January 1814, RAL xi/112/72. For Nathan Rothschild's receipts of sales and purchases of Omnium and other securities transacted by his brother-in-law Moses Montefiore, see RAL xi/38/60, passim.

73. *HP* BLAddMss. 57416, ff.10–11 (correct date c. April 1814, not 1815).

74. NMR Lon. to MD Ams. 14 January 1814, RAL xi/82/7/3/1. Nathan Rothschild directed deposits and withdrawals from several accounts bearing initials and he maintained those accounts in London and Frankfurt.

75. NMR Lon. to MD Ams. 18 January 1814, RAL xi/82/7/3/2.

76. B Lon. to W 12 January 1814, *WSD* VIII, 508.

77. B Lon. to W St. Jean de Luz 20 January & 2 February 1814, *WSD*, VIII, 524 & 557, respectively; "Specie which has arrived at Head Quarters in the Year 1814," *HP* BLAddMss. 57394, f. 10; & W St. Jean de Luz to B Lon.16 January 1814, *WD*, XI, 458–459. See also Kelly, p. 103.

78. V Lon. to Clancarty n.p. 27 January 1814, *VP* BLAddMss. 31,231, f.14.

79. MD Ams. to NMR Lon. 25 January 1814, RAL xi/T(A)36 [trans. of RAL xi/38/81a/5]; & see Crom Ams. to NMR Lon. 25 January, & HC Hel. to NMR Lon. 26 January, 1814, RAL xi/112/74A; "Account of French & Other Coins purchased at Amsterdam," RAL xi/38/60; *HP* BLAddMss. 57383, ff. 3–4; "Amount of Sundry Coins Purchased by Mr. J M Rothschild & Mr. Davidson through the medium of Sundry Houses in Amsterdam," *HP* BLAddMss 57378, ff. 106–107; & NMR Lon. to JMR Ams. 21, 25 & 28 January 1814, RAL xi/82/7/3/3–5, respectively.

80. MD Ams. to NMR Lon. c. 26 January 1814, RAL xi/T(A)37.

81. MD Ams. to NMR Lon. 28 January 1814, xi/T(A)38 [trans. of RAL xi/38/81a/6] & RAL xi/112/72; & see MD Ams. to NMR Lon. 1 February 1814, RAL xi/ T(A)39

[trans. of RAL xi/38/81a/7]. Benjamin Cohen wrote James Rothschild that he was sending thirty bars of gold to Davidson for sale. BC Lon. to JMR Ams. 8 February 1814, RAL xi/112/74A.

82. H Lon. to NMR Lon. 28 January 1814, *HP* BLAddMss. 57434 [Letter Book], f. 75.

83. Clancarty Hague to V Lon. 12 February 1814, *VP* BLAddMss 31,231, ff. 17–20, passim; & HC Hel. to NMR Lon. 2 & 9 February 1814, RAL xi/112/74A.

84. Clancarty Hague to V Lon. 5 February 1814, *VP* BLAddMss 31,231, f. 15.

85. MD Hel. to NMR Lon. 16 February 1814, RAL xi/112/72. See also HC Hel. to NMR Lon. 20 February 1814, RAL xi/112/74A; & "Specie which has arrived at Head Quarters in the Year 1814" & "Statement of Funds provided for the Public Service," 17 February 1814, *HP* BLAddMss. 57394, ff. 10 & 20–21, respectively.

86. MD Hel. to NMR Lon. 16 February 1814, RAL xi/112/72. See MD Ams. to NMR Lon. 22 February 1814, RAL xi/112/72.

87. MD Ams. to NMR Lon. 25 February 1814, RAL xi/T(A) 41 [trans. of RAL xi/38/81a/9]. See MD Ams. to NMR Lon. 22 February 1814, RAL xi/112/72, & Limburger Fft. to H Lon. 2 March 1814, *HP* BLAddMss. 57378, ff. 3–4.

88. See 1814 correspondence of D. Crommelin & Sn., RAL xi/112/74, passim, and especially, 28 January, 1, 8, 11, 14–16, 18–19, 22 & 25 February & 3, 5, 7–9, 11–12, 14–15 March 1814, RAL xi/112/74A. In March, Nathan sent Davidson and James another £175,000 in bills of exchange to pay for specie purchases. See Nathan Rothschild's correspondence for March 1814, RAL xi/82/7/3/1–58, passim.

89. BB Ams. to NMR Lon. 22 & 25 February, 1, 4, 10–11 & 15 March 1814, RAL xi/38/55B

For Nathan's private transactions of specie and bullion, see JR Harwich to NMR Lon. 31 March 1814, RAL xi/112/71 & NMR Lon. to JMR Ams. 8 & 15 April 1814, RAL xi/82/7/3/24 & 25, respectively; HC Hel. to NMR Lon. 14 March 1814, RAL xi/112/74A. Braunsberg & Co. transacted a minimum of £66,000 and £107,000 in specie and bullion for the private accounts of Nathan and M. A. Rothschild & Sons in March and April, respectively. See Braunsberg & Co.'s 1814 correspondence, RAL xi/38/55B & RAL xi/112/75A, in particular, 10–11, 21–23, 25 & 29 March & 1, 5, 8, 13–16 & 21–22 April 1814.

90. MD Ams. to NMR Lon. 8, 11, 26 March & 5 April 1814, RAL xi/112/72 & *HP* BLAddMss. 57394, f. 4, respectively; Dickens HMS Comus, to NMR Lon. 4 & 10 March 1814, RAL xi/112/72; BB Ams. to NMR Lon. 8 March 1814, RAL xi/38/55B; JmD Lon. to Bunbury, n. p. 9 March 1814, *WSD* VIII, 631; HC Hel. to NMR Lon.14 March 1814, RAL xi/112/74A; Eveir Hel. to NMR Lon. 23 March 1814, RAL xi/112/71; B Lon. to W 9 April 1814, *WSD*, VIII, 735; & "Specie which has arrived at Head Quarters in the Year 1814" & "Statement of Funds provided for the Public Service," 26 March & 25 April 1814, *HP* BLAddMss. 57394, ff.10 & 20–21, respectively.

91. Muir, pp. 304–305, 322–324.

92. The HM Gun Brig Earnest delivered £101,850 on 17 February; the HMS Comus delivered £235,283 on 26 March; and the HMS Thais delivered £215,202 on

25 April. "Statement of Funds provided for the Public Service," & "Specie which has arrived at Head Quarters in the Year 1814," *HP* BLAddMss. 57394, ff. 20–21 & f.10, respectively.

93. GH Lon. to Bunbury, n. p. 26 April 1814, *HP* BLAddMss. 57415, ff. 160–161.

94. Nathan Rothschild received his commission for at least another two years. Herries wrote commissary officials on the Continent: "If you should have any means of discounting these Bills without the intervention of any Agent you will of course make use of them; but if not, Mr. Rothschild will receive your Instructions for that Service which he will execute without any charge in consideration of the commissions which he receives on the general transactions confided to him by the British Government." H Lon. to TD Paris 17 September 1815, RAL xi/38/59A.

95. "Memorandum from Mr. Herries for Lord Liverpool & Mr. Vansittart 12 June 1816," *HP* BLAddMss. 57367, ff. 18–19.

PART THREE

British Subsidies to the
Allied Powers: 1814–1816

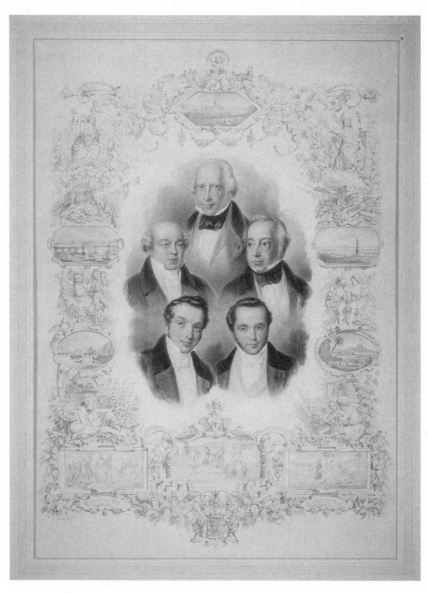

Five Rothschild Brothers by Hermann Raunheim with watercolor portraits and vignettes by Moritz Daniel Oppenheim, Paris, 1852. Reproduced with the permission of The Rothschild Archive.

FIVE

Herries, the Rothschilds, and the Russian

> Count Nesselrode, here, can decide nothing; M. Gervais who is said to have full powers runs away without deciding anything, but protesting that he is only *subordonné*; Count Lieven refers to M. Gervais and in the meantime they draw in all directions and knock down all the exchanges with Money at more advantageous rates at their Command. There is something rotten in this depend upon it.
>
> —JOHN CHARLES HERRIES *to* JAMES DRUMMOND. *22 May 1814.*[1]

> You have transacted a good piece of business with the Russian. That friend, "bribery money," is a great help.
>
> —CARL ROTHSCHILD *to* JAMES ROTHSCHILD. *26 June 1814.*[2]

The wars provoked by Revolutionary France and Napoleon prompted Great Britain and other powers in Europe to form coalitions to defend themselves and it was not until 1813 that they were prepared to go on the offensive. This took enormous amounts of money. For its part, Great Britain formulated policies to supply substantial subsidies in matériel, cash, and credit to its principal allies, Prussia, Russia, and Austria.

The British government's policy of subsidizing Prussia and Russia had evolved from its early position in 1813—whereby it intended to pay Prussia and Russia with "federative paper," a credit instrument that would be redeemed in London after the war—to its final position in 1814, whereby it would pay them in specie on the Continent.[3]

Although the federative paper scheme was referenced in the set of treaties signed by Great Britain, Russia, and Prussia on 14–15 June in Reichenbach, Germany, its details were spelled out in a convention signed on 30 September 1813 in London.[4] Great Britain agreed to subsidize Russia and Prussia with £2,500,000 (15 million Prussian *thalers*) in bills of credit, in fifteen monthly installments, calculated from the signing of the Reichenbach treaties, to be redeemed one month after a general armistice. A three-power commission would be set up in Amsterdam to handle the monthly distribution of the bills. In effect, the bills of credit became a "substitute for the 'federative paper,' which itself was a substitute for British subsidy money." The execution of the federative paper scheme became extraordinarily complicated and, ultimately, Prussia, Russia, and Great Britain agreed in May 1814 that the phantom bills of credit should be replaced by debentures bearing 6 percent interest, but neither the bills of credit nor the 6 percent debentures were ever put into circulation.[5]

Before the war came to an end with Napoleon's abdication in April 1814, the British government had added to its subsidy burden through a new alliance signed in March at Chaumont, France, by which it committed £5 million to be divided equally among Austria, Prussia, and Russia, in return for each power to maintain 150,000 troops in the field. Monthly payments would be made in London, retroactive to 1 January 1814, to the end of the month in which the peace treaty was signed. To cover the cost of demobilization, each power would receive "return money"—Austria and Prussia two additional months of subsidy and Russia, because of the distance to be traveled, four months. The allied powers also agreed to a twenty-year defense pact whereby, in the event that France attacked any of them, each power would commit 60,000 troops in the field. Great Britain had the option of providing 60,000 troops or paying the attacked power an annual subsidy of £1,300,000. Moreover, at the end of June, each allied power agreed to maintain 75,000 troops during the course of the Congress of Vienna but because Great Britain could not fulfill its quota, it would pay £355,333 to Prussia to add 22,000 troops to its contingent.[6]

When Sir George Burgmann, the British commissioner to the federative paper commission, arrived in Amsterdam in January 1814, the British government discovered how challenging it would be to execute its complicated subsidy plan. Burgmann reported to George Harrison, assistant-secretary at the Treasury, that there was no hope of raising money on the bills of credit without a significant discount.[7]

In February, the Russian commissioner to the federative paper commission, Councilor of State de Gervais, a stepson of the prominent St. Petersburg merchant Amburger,[8] arrived in Amsterdam and immediately set about searching for money to support Russia's advancing army. Burgmann had no money to give him and "perceived" that Gervais wanted "at once the whole amount due to Russia" so he could convert the "Bills of Credit" into specie and send it to Russian army headquarters.[9]

Gervais also approached Hope & Co., the prestigious Amsterdam merchant-banking house, which by 1798 had facilitated loans to Russia totaling ƒ.88.3 million Dutch guilders (a little more than £8 million pounds sterling). In June 1812, after Napoleon's invasion, Russia suspended interest payments. By February 1814, Russia needed a great deal more money but Hope & Co. could supply only a half million guilders and enlisted Harman & Co. (London), Russia's agent, to collect subsidy payments from Great Britain and to ship gold to Hellevoetsluis. But only about 750,000 guilders (about £80,000) in Napoléon d'Or, English guineas, and Hanoverian George d'Or were made available to Gervais.[10]

The British government had lost touch with the reality of the Amsterdam marketplace, and it complicated matters by the instructions it provided Burgmann. It had originally limited Burgmann to a discount of 2½ percent on the "Bills of Credit" and an additional ½ percent for brokerage fees. However, if the Russian and Prussian commissioners demanded delivery of the bills of credit and the market discount rate was greater than the above-mentioned limit, Burgmann could offer an advance of up to 75 percent on them.[11] Because bankers repeatedly told Burgmann that the bills of credit could not circulate at less than a discount of 20 percent, he decided to act.[12] On 22 February, he authorized Melvil & Co., Gervais's agent in Amsterdam, to draw £300,000 on Reid, Irving & Co.[13] But Burgmann did not know at the time that Harman & Co. had already requested from the Treasury £325,833 in specie for subsidy payments owing to Russia.[14]

This confusion was not an isolated incident. When Barthold Niebuhr, classicist, historian, and Prussian privy councilor, arrived in Amsterdam in early March to take up his position as the Prussian commissioner to the federative paper commission, he reaffirmed what Burgmann and Gervais already knew: that the bills of credit could only be circulated at a significant discount. Because this would be unacceptable to his court, he joined with Gervais to press Burgmann for the delivery of the specie or the bills of credit. To placate Gervais, in early April, Burgmann gave Gervais bills of exchange that

Herries had sent him.[15] Later that month, Baron Hardenberg, the chancellor of Prussia, declared "the urgent necessity" for Britain to provide his government with an "immediate advance of one hundred thousand pounds sterling, either in cash or bullion."[16] Burgmann subsequently authorized Melvil & Co., now also Niebuhr's agent in Amsterdam, to receive payments for Prussia,[17] and Herries arranged to pay £100,000 in either gold coin or bars to Prussia.[18] In early May, Gervais and Niebuhr presented a joint memorial requesting immediate delivery of bills of credit,[19] which Herries believed would be circulated and have a "most mischievous effect to our Credit upon the Continent."[20] On 26 May, Herries wrote Harrison that he had already paid Prussia a total of £237,500 in French gold coins and bills of exchange. But he also stated that the King of Prussia's agents in London, facilitated by Harman & Co., had already drawn £316,666 against the British subsidy obligation of £416,666 for the first three months of 1814. Thus, the British government had in fact paid Prussia £554,166, that is, an overpayment of £137,500, and Herries wanted to be reimbursed.[21]

A frustrated Herries had already anticipated some of these problems and, on 24 April, he recommended to the Earl of Liverpool, the prime minister, and Nicholas Vansittart, the chancellor of Exchequer, that the administration of British financial outlays on the Continent be restructured. First, the scheme of the federative paper, as it had originally been formulated, could not work, and another mechanism had to be found to pay the British subsidies to the allied powers. Second, as long as the army of Wellington remained in France, a more regular and direct means of funding it had to replace "the present circuitous mode of shipments from Holland." Paris had to become "the centre of exchange operations," where Great Britain could raise "much larger sums without materially influencing the exchanges" and "by prudent management to discharge the current subsidies payable abroad more easily." Third, the "presence of a person confidentially entrusted with power to make arrangements to this effect, would be necessary for a short time only at Paris." Fourth, once in Paris, that person would give Gervais £200,000 (from an unpaid British subsidy of 1805), pursuant to the arrangement made by the Russian ambassador in London. Finally, to thwart the competition from several different agents selling paper on London that would depress the exchanges against England, it was necessary to have: "The operations of an exchange agent of great power and extensive connexion, collecting funds regularly, and with constant regard to the interest of England through all the principal exchanges of Europe." This was classic arbitrage and the model "exchange agent" to execute it was Nathan Rothschild.[22]

Vansittart and Liverpool not only approved the proposal but also sent Herries to Paris to implement it. Vansittart wrote to Viscount Castlereagh, the foreign secretary, about Herries's mission and was particularly laudatory of the Rothschilds.

> We have of late, however, been able to procure very large sums of money in Cash & Bills, with comparatively little effect upon the Exchange by means of a Jew House of very extensive connections on the Continent of the name of Rothschild. Through his channel we have actually received near £1,500,000 in the course of the present year 1814. . . . As the Rothschilds have a House at Paris, I have no doubt Herries will be able by their Agency to procure for you any Sums you may have occasion to raise, & it is one of the principal objects of his mission to receive your directions on that subject. . . . I have not met with any [one] capable of executing any operation on a great scale except those to whom I have referred.[23]

The contributions the Rothschilds made to a victorious British policy on the Continent were, when examined closely, actually far greater than the myths that have grown up about them. Even before Nathan had concluded his contract to supply Wellington with specie in March–April 1814, Herries asked him to execute several other separate and secret commissary services. In each operation, Nathan demonstrated his financial acumen and it is not surprising that the British government would later turn to him to manage the payment of its subsidy obligations to the allied powers.

These operations reveal not only how astute Herries was in managing money and people but also how dependent he was on the services of the Rothschilds. Some operations were complicated and took longer to complete than others. For example, in November 1813, the British government shipped 87,164 Hanoverian pistoles (five thaler gold pieces) to Gothenburg intended for Russia and Prussia. The money was conveyed across the Baltic and in January 1814 it was in the possession of the British consul at Rostock. Subsequently, it was decided that the coins should be diverted to Amsterdam to aid the military chest in Holland. In March—while the cargo was already en route to agents of Reid, Irving & Co.[24]—Herries decided to sell them to Nathan for his private account at a rate of 10 guilders 1 stiuver for each piece delivered to M A Rothschild & Sons, in Frankfurt. Herries wrote the Treasury "that the Army price fixed for these Pistoles is 10 Guilders only, which under all circumstances is the fair value of it *in Holland*, where it is not a Current Coin." He thus valued the 87,164 pistoles in Dutch currency at *875,998 guilders* and, at the army exchange rate of 11 guilders to the pound sterling, this amounted to £79,636. When they were delivered to Frankfurt, Nathan would pay that amount to the commissary in Amsterdam.[25] The coins reached Frankfurt at the end of May and James R. Drummond, Herries's assistant, informed Nathan that, according to the current price of gold, he valued the coins at £95,880.[26] This meant that Nathan's profit over two months amounted to about £16,000. Much of this transaction came full circle in June, when M A Rothschild & Sons sold Herries 50,000 pistoles and sent them to Dresden to make a subsidy payment due Russia.[27]

Herries prided himself on knowing the value of money. In March 1814, he informed Harrison at the Treasury that he had conducted a successful "Experiment upon the price of Bullion." Although the Bank of England had ceased purchasing bullion, "their brokers have continued to quote the price at 108/ the ounce for foreign Bar." But, since Nathan Rothschild offered to sell the government £50,000 of bullion at 104 shillings per ounce, "I intend to purchase it (quietly without the Bank knowing any thing of the matter)," Herries wrote, "at that price it will make as good a remittance, coined into Hanoverian pistols, as Bills purchased on Holland, & will by so much diminish our pressure upon the Exchange." Because Jeremiah Harman, a director of the Bank of England, was actually purchasing gold for coinage at 108/6, Harrison was not to mention this transaction to "the Bank people."[28]

A more delicate matter arose when Herries asked Harrison, in March, to approve his authorization for Nathan to purchase privately and confidentially £300,000 in bills of exchange on Holland and Frankfurt, which Herries would remit to Burgmann to give to Gervais.[29] Herries's intercession was undoubtedly meant to replace Burgmann's 22 February authorization to Melvil & Co. to draw on Reid, Irving & Co. with one now involving Nathan.

When Herries informed Burgmann about this transaction, he also informed him—contrary to Vansittart's original prohibition—about the secret agreement the British government had with Nathan to provide Wellington with French specie. "He has managed that business in a very quiet & faithful manner, & from the experience we have already had of him, I am led to believe that great reliance may be placed upon him & his connexions (all Jews I think) both with regard to their powers, & their dexterity in the application of them. His business is quite *secret*. No person employed in other pecuniary supplies know anything of it." Herries further stated that he had declined Nathan's "offer to undertake the whole management of this matter," because "I am naturally anxious not to be too much in his power."[30]

Instead, Herries ordered Nathan to buy the bills on Amsterdam in the name of Augustus Schmidchen, the deputy commissary-general, and the Frankfurt bills in the name Chevalier Christian de Limburger, an old friend from Leipzig, who was already known to the Rothschilds. Both men would subsequently turn over the bills to Burgmann.[31] Herries wrote Harrison that Limburger was "A Gentleman of Character & integrity known personally to me," and explained why he had chosen him. "My object in selecting this Gentleman for the Service, was that he might act as a Check upon Messrs. Rothschild in that part of the transaction concerning Bills on Franckfort [sic] in German Money" in order to prevent them from "reimbursing themselves" by manipulating the exchange rates. "I conceive their Lordships would not be satisfied that the Public should be entirely in the Hands of any one party in such an operation, however respectable the Character of the persons might be."[32] Limburger effectively did what Herries wanted him to do by periodically reporting on Rothschild activities and transactions. He frequented the Rothschild house in Frankfurt enough for Carl Rothschild to write sarcastically later in the year: "Limburger is here. He is making himself at home like a palace cat."[33]

After Napoleon abdicated, Herries made greater use of Nathan as facilitator and paymaster. First, he was to deliver to Acting Commissary-General Thomas Dunmore at Breda cf. 500,000 (about £45,000) in specie.[34] Second, he was to deliver to Drummond fr.1,100,000 in bills of exchange (about £58,000) made out to John Roworth (who clerked for Nathan in Manchester and in London), that were intended "for a Secret Special" service under Bathurst.[35] Third, Roworth was to be sent to Amsterdam with secret instructions for James Rothschild to pay cf.315,000 (£29,000) to Edward Thornton, the British ambassador to Sweden, who was in Brussels with the crown prince of Sweden. Thornton was to use the money to settle a British subsidy obligation he had made to Denmark in January 1814.[36]

Nathan's resources were called upon to support the return of King Louis XVIII to France. On 14 April, Drummond asked him: "Can you immediately send to London the Value of £20,000 in french [sic] gold or silver Coin?"[37] About a week later, the £20,000 in French specie was delivered to Le Comte de Blacas d'Aulys, the king's agent, who was then in Calais.[38] Nathan also arranged for an additional £50,000 in gold so Herries could deliver it to Le Comte de Blacas d'Aulys in Paris.[39]

Herries's confidence in Nathan strengthened as these operations unfolded and he became more acquainted with him during their frequent meetings at his office in Great George Street, and at his residence at 21 Cadogan Place. He wrote Burgmann that "Rothschild of this place, has executed the various Services lately entrusted to him in this line admirably well, and though a Jew we place a good deal of confidence in him." But he was uncomfortable about James, whom he had met but once in London. "Of his brother I know nothing," he let Burgmann know, "& I think you do well to keep him out of a knowledge of those transactions which do not concern him."[40]

But soon after his arrival in Paris, on 1 May, Herries changed his attitude about the young Rothschild, not yet 22 years old, and he quickly learned how effortlessly his orders could be executed when working with him. Herries was asked to supply the British forces in the south of France with emergency funding and he requested that James, who was then in Paris, send £130,000 in French specie to Bordeaux.[41] One week later, Davidson reported that James had gone to The Hague to arrange with Clancarty for a ship to collect the specie at Hellevoetsluis and concluded that "no time shall be lost, in executing that order."[42]

In response to worrisome letters from Drummond in London about making advance payments to Nathan, Herries informed his assistant that the Rothschilds had placed £200,000 in specie at his disposal in Paris and "You may therefore issue Money liberally to R. There can be no risque in paying him £200,000 immediately and in order to prevent any inconvenience to him, which would recoil upon ourselves."[43] He also detailed £630,000 in expenditures "for which Rothschild is entitled to payment without delay. . . . You may now therefore make a very large payment to Rothschild without the least risk or without even infringing the instructions of the Treasury." The Rothschilds "are now serving us to a very extraordinary extent by their credit and if we fail to supply [them] with funds to meet these engagements the weight is greater than any individual, however rich, could be expected to support."[44]

Herries came to depend more and more on the Rothschilds and, at times, to a greater extent than on his own people. For example, Herries lost respect for Burgmann, when he learned how he would manage the £200,000 intended for Gervais. "Burgmann's difficulties are really ludicrous," he wrote Drummond, "His present establishment of doing nothing is a subject of amusement at Amsterdam & his proposal to have 4 or 5 Clerks to receive & pay £200,000 is preposterous. Spearman & myself have already received &

paid over £150,000 in Gold, and we should want no further assistance to pay ten times that amount." In contrast, Herries praised James: "Rothschild who holds the Money at Amsterdam has only one Clerk to assist him! and prefers paying the Money himself rather than thro' the Bank or any Bankers, because we thereby save a charge for Commission." Herries subsequently turned over to James the responsibility of paying Gervais the £200,000.[45]

The more he worked with James, the more Herries admired the way he conducted his business. "The brother here is doing the business remarkably well and seems capable of supplying me with money to any extent. I have stopped him at £300,000. . . . My payments are made without the intervention of bankers the coin being brought in carriages from the House of R. either to me or to the parties with whom it is to be lodged. This quiet mode of executing the service is the best." Regarding an operation involving Spanish dollars, he wrote Drummond that, if the Bank of England was reluctant to purchase them, "Rothschild could do it."[46]

The Rothschilds in Amsterdam, Frankfurt, London, and Paris became Herries's paymasters without portfolio. When he received a distressing report from Sir Robert Hugh Kennedy, the commissary-general with Wellington's forces, Herries ordered 100,000 Napoléon d'Or sent to Bordeaux with John Roworth from Paris.[47] Because Reid, Irving & Co. could not provide Acting Commissary-General Thomas Dunmore in Brussels with the funds he needed, Herries instructed M A Rothschild & Sons to send him 50,000 Napoléon d'Or from Frankfurt and another 50,000 from Paris.[48] Moreover, Dunmore reported that he had received from the Royal Mint in London £50,000 in Hanoverian gold coins but could only dispose of them in Flanders at a depreciated rate, and, therefore, he sent them to Frankfurt, where "under the careful management of Messrs. Rothschild" they would sell at a premium.[49]

Vansittart's respect for the Rothschilds appreciated the more he witnessed their contributions to the execution of British policy on the Continent and he became disenchanted with other merchant-banking houses for not doing the same:

> Messrs. Reid Irving, Hope & Baring had concerted to make a joint offer to take the Bills of Credit, and it appeared to be extremely desirable to deal with so powerful an Association, or, at least, to know their intentions more distinctly.—I this morning saw Mr. Reid, who appeared to have no digested or specific proposition to make, but who talked in general terms of the parties whom I have mentioned acting in conjunction. I therefore desired, without

entering into particulars, that they would propose their Plan to the Ministers of the Allied Powers at Paris, after conferring with you on the subject. It is to be regretted that Baring, while he was at Paris, did not bring the question under consideration, as it might probably have led to a conclusion satisfactory to all parties.[50]

The failure of these houses to facilitate the redemption of the British bills of credit created an extraordinary opportunity for the Rothschilds. Vansittart decided that they should be employed to liquidate the British subsidy to the allied powers. "With respect to your negotiations with Rothschild," he wrote Herries at the end of May, "we have only to congratulate you on their success; & I think it will be important to make some Arrangement with that House, for the Supply of the Funds which will become successively necessary for the repayment of the Bills of Credit as they become due."[51]

But paying the promised subsidies to the allied powers was more complicated than the authors of that policy had imagined. After he arrived in Paris, Herries reached an understanding with the Austrian and Prussian envoys whereby their courts would accept, in lieu of bills of credit, debentures at 6 percent interest, which they promised not to circulate.[52] Herries believed he had achieved the same understanding with Gervais. Instead, soon after he arrived in Paris, Gervais abruptly informed Herries that he had to return to Amsterdam because "advices have *just been received* from Petersburg" that the minister of finance wanted to draw on the subsidy from England, and he, therefore, could not accept either the £200,000 or the bills of credit.[53]

This startled Herries but he refused to admit defeat and once again turned to the Rothschilds for help. He asked Salomon Rothschild, who managed the Rothschilds' affairs in Paris, to send two letters by courier to Amsterdam, one for James and the other for Gervais. He hoped that James would be able to persuade Gervais to accept the £200,000.[54]

However, Herries's gambit did not work because on 30 May the Treaty of Paris was signed, which triggered the subsidy payment provisions of previous treaties. Accordingly, in July, the allied powers would be entitled to redeem the bills of credit, even though Great Britain had not yet issued them. Austria, Prussia, and Russia were each to receive £138,888 per month for the period January–May 1814. The British subsidy allocations (inclusive of "return money") projected beyond July amounted to £972,222 each for Austria and Prussia and £1,250,000 for Russia.[55] And, pursuant to the Treaty of Teplitz, which had been signed in October 1813, Austria would receive an additional £1,000,000.[56]

But Russian policy underwent another sudden turn. Gervais informed Burgmann that he had a "very urgent Want of a large Sum of Money for the Service of the Russian Armies" and "would be desirous of receiving whatever Sums in Cash or in Bills" he had to give him. When Burgmann told him that he did not have any money to give him,[57] Gervais approached Pierre César Labouchère of Hope & Co. for an advance against seven monthly installments of matured "Russian Bills of Credit." He wanted the money delivered to him at Hamburg, Berlin, and Frankfurt or Leipzig, and, if he could provide the whole sum by 1 July, he would give Labouchère a commission of 2 percent. This Labouchère could not do, given the difficult and unclear financial circumstances in which Hope & Co. found itself at that time, although he would agree to cover a one-month's installment of the subsidy and provide Gervais credit for an additional one million guilders on Hope & Co. For this, Labouchère wanted a commission of 2 percent. This was not what Gervais had hoped to achieve and on 17 June he wrote Labouchère that he had contracted with another merchant bank for the first six months of matured bills of credit.[58]

The other merchant bank was M A Rothschild & Sons, represented by James in Amsterdam and Salomon in Paris. Gervais was undoubtedly encouraged to deal with the Rothschilds because Niebuhr had already contracted James to facilitate three monthly subsidy payments to Prussia, which amounted to one million Prussian thalers, and Niebuhr hinted that another three months might be forthcoming.[59] According to the subsidy convention, the British would pay the subsidy in Amsterdam but Niebuhr wanted the money closer to his court and to have it deposited with M A Rothschild & Sons in Frankfurt. Niebuhr refused James's request for a commission of 2 percent because it was too high and both men agreed to leave that decision to *Seehandlung* in Berlin which would, from time to time, draw specific currencies from the Rothschild house in Frankfurt.[60]

The Prussian account was promising but James focused his immediate attention on his "Russian," as he liked to refer to Gervais. Soon after his return to Amsterdam, Gervais approached James to facilitate the redemption of the Russian bills of credit. James dutifully reported this to Nathan in early June and sought his advice.[61] Nathan wrote to Salomon insisting in the strongest manner that he go to Amsterdam: "And now, dearest brother, follow my advice and if you can, go to Amsterdam for a few days, for the business is too important. . . . I need to tell you that Herries departs on Saturday . . . because you will be needed in Amsterdam." In a postscript, he reiterated his plea: "Dear Salomon, you must go to Amsterdam because I am certain that if you do not go then the whole business is not worth a 'shilling.'" He wanted Salomon to take charge of the negotiation with Gervais because he did not trust in the ability of either James or Mayer Davidson and rudely remarked that they were "two barking dogs who cannot get anything done. They are stupid young men. . . . not businessmen but rascals."[62]

James anxiously awaited the arrival of Herries and Salomon in Amsterdam. He visited with Gervais, who was impatient to obtain an advance on the first installment of the British subsidy payment that was due in July. "I gave him my word of honour, Salomon will be here and I will definitely do business with him," James reported on 14 June to Nathan, "The Russian is giving me indigestion."[63]

On 15 June, Herries and Salomon arrived in Amsterdam and, within days, Salomon concluded two separate contracts, one with Gervais and the other with Herries.[64] However, Herries did not have the prior authority of the British government to enter into such an agreement. He disingenuously wrote to Drummond that the original purpose of his trip was to meet an old friend in Utrecht and *only* after he arrived in Amsterdam did he learn of Gervais's proposal.

> These (the two brothers) communicated their negotiations to me, and represented the advantage of suffering them to accept the Terms offered by Mr Gervais and to authorise them to perform the engagement for the British Government upon a Commission to themselves: *they were limited to that morning for their answer to Mr G—* and I was therefore obliged to decide upon their proposal to me without referring the matter for the previous Determination of the Treasury.—If the advantage had been trifling or doubtful I should have declined the Business on that account; but after fairly weighing it, I have had no hesitation in agreeing to underwrite it.[65]

By his contract with Salomon, Gervais promised to exchange four million Prussian thalers worth of Russian bills of credit, representing six months of the British subsidy due Russia, for specie he urgently needed to cover the expenses of the Russian armies in Central and western Europe. He was so anxious to execute the contract that he immediately deposited the bills of credit with Burgmann for Salomon, who in turn gave them to Herries.[66] For his part, Salomon promised to deliver specie to Gervais—where he wanted it and when he wanted it—for which Gervais willingly paid a premium and also a commission on the entire transaction.

The Convention of 30 September 1813 stipulated that the bills of credit be redeemed in Amsterdam but a payment elsewhere could be arranged, provided it was not less than one million Prussian thalers. If payment were made in Germany, Prussian thalers or their equivalent in other coins would be acceptable; for example, the Hanoverian George d'Or at 5⅓ and the Dutch ducat at 2¾ Prussian thalers.[67] Gervais, however, offered the rate at Berlin between 8 and 12 June, which valued the George d'Or at 5½ and Dutch ducat at 3½ Prussian thalers. To further sweeten the deal, he declined the interest payment of 6 percent per annum on the installments and also agreed to pay the insurance for the transport of the money.[68]

The specie was to be delivered as shown in Table 5.1.

Salomon could not undertake the execution of his contract with Gervais on his own account because, as he put it, he was "coadjutor of my Brother Mr. N. M. Rothschild." He, therefore, asked Herries for permission to execute his transaction on behalf of the British government for a commission of 2 percent on the four million Prussian thalers. In return for the Russian bills of credit, the British government would supply the specie or the funds to purchase the specie that would be delivered to Gervais.[69] Herries authorized Salomon to proceed but he would pay him only 1½ percent on the amount of specie that would be transported from Amsterdam to Hamburg, Dresden, and Warsaw. Herries added that "the payments at Amsterdam would be covered by the General Commission to be allowed Mr. N. M. Rothschild for the whole Service, who will charge the actual expences which may attend the coining of Ducats or the negotiation of Bills for the execution of it."[70] Salomon's contract with Herries was dated 17 June, in Amsterdam

TABLE 5.1[a]

Specie Delivery to Gervais July–September 1814

Immediately	=	Hamburg	500,000 Prussian Thalers
20 July	=	Hamburg	500,000
22 July	=	Dresden	750,000
6 August	=	Hamburg	750,000
1 September	=	Warsaw	500,000
5 September	=	Warsaw	500,000
30 September	=	Amsterdam	500,000
			4,000,000 Prussian Thalers[a]

[a]SMR Ams. to H Ams. 17 June 1814, RAL xi/38/59B; MD Ams. to NMR Lon. 18 June 1814, RAL xi/109/0/1/30, Tape 2, Letter 4; SMR Ams. to NMR Lon. 19 June 1814, RAL xi/87/0A; H Ams. to JmD Lon. 17 June 1814, *HP* BLAddMss. 57436 [Letter Book], ff. 18-22; & "From Notebook of Herries in his own hand," c. 17 June 1814, *HP* BLAddMss. 57397, f. 1.

and in London, undoubtedly to signify not only when they had reached their agreement but also when specific initiatives had commenced.[71] Bills of exchange on the Treasury, dated 17 June, were made out to Nathan for £650,000 so he could arrange for the delivery of specie to Gervais.[72]

The Rothschilds had put together a deal from which Herries claimed significant advantages. He wrote Drummond that the British government would save at least 460,000 Prussian thalers (£76,667) from reduced interest payments and from the profit on gold, because Gervais was paying more than the price stipulated in the 30 September 1813 Convention. Herries also believed the contract was a way of "Keeping the Russians out of the Hands of some great Mercantile Houses here who would immediately have begun to operate upon the Exchange in competition with us." Finally, he expected that "When these specific and contingent advantages are taken into consideration I hope I shall receive some Credit for the Conclusion of this arrangement."[73]

In closing this breakthrough deal, Salomon proved himself a pivotal negotiator for not only Nathan but also Herries, who, on the eve of his departure for Amsterdam, praised him to Nathan: "Public Service has derived essential benefit from the prudent & skillful management with which he has conducted the Exchange operation which I have had occasion to direct at Paris."[74] Herries did not exaggerate because Salomon's Paris operation, exclusive of the Russian account, raised and transferred about £685,000 for the British government.[75]

Salomon fancied himself a practitioner of sleight of hand. He apparently persuaded Herries that Gervais did not know that Herries had "any thing to do with this matter"—at least, that is what Salomon and Mayer Davidson wrote to Nathan and even what Herries wrote to Drummond.[76] Salomon also intended, at first, to keep Herries in the dark about the commission Gervais had promised him but later changed his mind "otherwise we could get into difficulties." Thus, he confessed to Herries that the commission from Gervais would cover the cost of insurance in transporting the specie to Hamburg, Dresden, and "particularly, Warsaw, in Poland, where one really must earn something to justify the risk." James and Mayer Davidson viewed this near-truth-telling as "masterful."[77]

Salomon did not reveal to Herries that in one contract he signed with Gervais a commission of 5 percent was stipulated but in another, secretly agreed upon, the commission was marked down to 4 percent. James explained this subterfuge to Nathan: "4% will be for us, God willing and 1% for the Russian himself as a *bribe.*" And, Herries would not know "about the 4% because the contract he will be shown does not say anything about the commission and the Russian, who is getting 1%, has . . . drawn up a separate contract for the commission which no one will ever find out about." James calculated how much money the Russian commission would earn for the Rothschilds. "We are getting 4% on 4 million making 160,000 or £32,000 [*sic*]," and "there are a number of small things because we are supposed to be buying gold here at 13% and we will certainly get it for 12½ and your commission of 2% is £20,000 [*sic*], God willing."[78]

There are problems with James's arithmetic because his estimate is too generous. He calculated an exchange rate at 5.0 Prussian thalers, not 6.0 to the pound sterling, as the British had stipulated in the 30 September 1813 Convention. On 14 June, the Berlin market exchange rate was 5.4 Prussian thalers to the pound sterling[79] and, while the rate would fall to 5.19 Prussian thalers in September–October 1814 on the Berlin market, when the contract would be completed,[80] James did not explain why, on 17 June, he used 5.0 Prussian thalers to the pound sterling as the exchange rate. It would be more sensible to use the exchange rate of 6.0 Prussian thalers to the pound sterling to estimate the *minimum* commission that James and Salomon would receive from their transaction with Gervais. That would amount to, at most, £26,667 (not £32,000).

Herries intended to pay Salomon a commission of 1½ percent on the transfer of 3,500,000 Prussian thalers in specie from Amsterdam to Hamburg, Dresden, and Warsaw. Again, using 6.0 Prussian thalers per pound sterling, the estimated *minimum* commission would amount to £8,750. Moreover, Salomon expected expense money from Herries, who "will reimburse me for an extra 1½ [percent] for my expenses. . . . Thank G-d my expenses don't even amount to ½ [percent] which leaves us with a clear profit."[81]

Finally, the customary commission of 2 percent that Nathan would receive on the approximate £650,000 in Treasury bills for the purchase of bullion and specie would produce about £13,000 (not £20,000). Thus, the estimated *minimum* commission the Rothschilds could anticipate from the Russian operation would amount to more than £48,000 and, while much less than what James had calculated, was by any contemporary standard a healthy sum of money.

The correspondence of the Rothschild brothers reveals how they coped with the pressure of collecting and shipping Hanoverian George d'Or from the Royal Mint in London to Amsterdam, and of striking Dutch ducats at the Utrecht Mint for their punctual delivery to Hamburg, Dresden, and Warsaw. At first, James was optimistic: "It is not difficult for us here to supply the first million" but he did not want to be left in the "lurch" and he asked Nathan on 17 June to apply his customary energy and speed in sending bullion and specie to Amsterdam.[82] A few days later, however, he expressed considerable concern: "for goodness sake, to send as much gold as possible here . . . we have no time to lose with the whole 4 million, for this will go piece by piece." Davidson echoed his plea to Nathan for more money: "The main thing is now to get hard money sent here in order to build up a good reserve of ducats, for time is very short and Salomon wants very much to remain honourable in his dealings with the Russian who is certainly not a man to be trifled with."[83] The express letter from Frankfurt advising that Amschel and Carl Rothschild had purchased 600,000 Prussian thalers worth of gold lifted James's and Davidson's spirits somewhat.[84]

But stinging letters from Nathan, which arrived in Amsterdam on 24 June, exacerbated an already tense situation. It is hard to imagine what kind of temperamental condition possessed Nathan that would provoke him to such emotional outbursts, especially at a time when he benefited generously from the tireless efforts his brothers and Mayer Davidson. As so often was the case, Nathan's letters were insulting but this time he also attacked his brothers' character, integrity, and honesty. James, Salomon, and Davidson were undoubtedly physically and emotionally fatigued from their marathon negotiations with Gervais and Herries, and their responses are extraordinarily revealing of how much hurt Nathan caused them.

James reacted defensively and incoherently to Nathan's caustic charges of his being a "stupid young man;" a "barking dog;" that he and Davidson were "not businessmen but rascals;" and that "Amschel writes . . . as though Jacob were the only one involved with the business."[85] James refuted Nathan's "accusation about losing £8,000. . . . You say we took your money. . . . This much is certain, what we buy here must be paid for and so we would have had to draw on you. . . . Above all, dear Nathan, write and tell us how you actually get money from the government. . . . For heaven's sake, you must write down the monies which you receive on the 4 million and always notify us precisely of both the purchases as well as the deliveries of the monies."[86]

Salomon's lengthy reply of 24 June to Nathan was heart-wrenching and bordered on being tragic. It is the most important personal letter written from one brother to another during the period under discussion, and reveals, as no other letter, the torment suffered by one brother at the pen of another. It is impossible to misread the pain Salomon felt that morning and the contempt he had for Nathan, who denied him love and respect: "I would gladly have written to you myself . . . however, my dear brother Nathan . . . I feel a little weak . . . so I am dictating this letter to our good Davidson."

> My very dear brother Nathan, your letters make one sick. . . . I cannot accept . . . that if my name is Nathan then all four brothers are stupid boys and only I am the one who has any intelligence. . . .
> I know the situation only too well, my dear Nathan. Of all the people who surround you there is not one who has the strength of character to oppose you. . . .
> My dear Nathan, we are not drunk and we are not some stupid young boys, nor are we asses. We do something which you in London do not do and that is, my dear Nathan, we keep our books in proper order. . . .
> My dear brother . . . Who of us is omnipotent? Is it possible, when dealing with such large scale deals, to know in advance how matters will actually turn out? . . . one can't, therefore, lay any more blame at the feet of our Nathan than at those of any of the other four brothers. Aren't you the one who can't moderate his behaviour? . . .

In an expressive postscript, Salomon wrote in his own hand:

> You cannot begin to imagine how much pain these letters cause me. They depress my heart. I often think *what good is it to me even if I were to be richer by £10,000 and then, within one year, I am no longer alive, G-D forbid, and leave behind a widowed young wife and children.* I don't have your strong nerves and we all have to work and toil more than you. You are, of course, by G-D the King amongst us. However, you are also a very jealous man. . . . Where is your intelligence? Where is your common sense? . . . You write that you are a hot-headed man. Well, aren't we all? Don't we all, my dear Nathan, have the same feelings that you have? . . . You make everyone miserable and you tear their heart apart. Is this what you call brotherly and humane behaviour? You think that you behave very charitably, if you help one of our in-laws by giving him several thousand pounds whilst, at the same time, you bring your very own brothers, your partners and all those that are nearest to you, to an early grave. Where is your common sense? You always keep on twisting. First, you want this and then you want the other. You constantly keep on shutting the door in our face. . . . I could write these few lines which I am now penning to you, with my weeping tears rather than with the aid of ink if only my tears were black and not white.[87]

Mayer Davidson had the maturity and the courage to reprimand Nathan for his destructive and deplorable behavior and cautioned him that he was putting at risk the future unity of the family Rothschild:

> Cullen finally arrived here this morning at 6 o'clock and delivered your letter. . . . Salomon, who was still in bed . . . immediately came down but he had such a sad demeanor and was so dejected that I was extremely shocked and asked him for the cause thereof, whereupon he answered "you should read our letters from Nathan which . . . contain nothing but crude and insulting reproaches and abuses of our whole family." He showed me the letters and I have to admit to you, quite candidly, dear Mr. Rothschild, that I felt embarrassed for your own brother, when I saw the numerous insults in your letters. Honestly, you call your brothers nothing but asses and stupid boys. This, dear Mr. Rothschild, is quite frankly, totally uncalled for and, when brothers are engaged in large scale business deals, can be extremely harmful. It totally confuses your brothers and makes them very sad and can lead to the most disagreeable consequences.
>
> However, having had the pleasure over here of getting to know Salomon, I am very surprised that you don't use a calmer tone, when writing to your brothers. I can tell you, he is a businessman who understands everything and ponders over every move. A businessman, who arranged everything so skillfully with Herries in Paris that, when Herries came here and James went with me to see him, his first words were I am very pleased with your brother. . . . Herries, too, appreciated that this calm and thoughtful man be shown respect. I am very surprised, esteemed Mr. Rothschild, that you don't show any greater respect for your brother, that you send him such letters for him to read and then to forward on to Frankfurt. . . . I swear to you that, by G-D, it pains me to see such a man hurt even for only one moment, a man who has no concerns and works for nothing else in this world other than you and your family's interests. . . . I can't defend you. . . . You should undertake, dear Mr. Rothschild, never to do so again.[88]

There is no evidence that Nathan Rothschild responded to these letters nor did he change his ways, as will be shown in what follows.

Nathan and Herries tapped every monetary source available to them in order to fund both the Russian operation and British military forces on the Continent. Herries lost no time in collecting and shipping tens of thousands of English-minted Hanoverian George d'Or coins, foreign specie, and bullion to Amsterdam.[89] Immediately after the contracts were signed, he sent a courier to Drummond with orders that the gold arriving from India and all the bullion he could find should be sent to the Rothschilds "so that [Dutch] ducats can be minted as quickly as possible."[90] The Utrecht Mint was capable of striking more than 50,000 coins per week and he authorized the Rothschilds to purchase about £60 to £70,000 in gold to keep the Utrecht Mint occupied until Drummond's shipment arrived. Although the price of gold had dipped in Amsterdam, Herries calculated he would still gain 12 percent in coining Dutch ducats at the Utrecht Mint than George d'Or at the Royal Mint in London,[91] which in July coined nearly 250,000 pieces of the Hanoverian gold coin (a 26 percent increase over the previous ten weeks).[92]

Nathan aggressively attacked the market and bought gold for £100,000 and £200,000 in single daily transactions.[93] The 50,000 Dutch ducats, which James had purchased for Wellington, Herries now applied to the Russian account but he, nonetheless, intended to honor his promise to send Wellington £400,000 in specie, and the Rothschilds were instructed to ship him Spanish dollars and French specie from Amsterdam, Frankfurt, and Paris.[94] In July, when Morel in Dunkerque informed Nathan that the French government again permitted the exportation of gold from France, he purchased a large quantity of French coins from Morel for delivery to Commissary General Dunmore in Brussels.[95] That summer, Nathan's specie transactions with Dunmore amounted to £400,000.[96] A credit for £60,000 was opened at M A Rothschild & Sons for Edward Thornton, the British ambassador to the court of Sweden, so he could draw Prussian Friedrich d'Or to cover the expenses of the Russian German Legion.[97] When Sir Robert Kennedy, commissary-general to the British troops in the south of France, informed Herries he did not need, at that time, additional funds, Herries ordered the cargo of gold specie, which had already sailed from Hellevoetsluis for Bordeaux on board the HMS Esk, returned to Amsterdam: "the Spanish Dollars only should go forward, and that the whole of the Gold coin (whether Napoleons or Louis d'Ors [sic]) should be unloaded," melted and minted into Dutch ducats and paid "to the Russian Government on Account of the Bills of Credit delivered over by Mr. Gervais."[98]

Letters among the Rothschild brothers crossed and created the impression that delivery deadlines might not be met. Carl appeared panicky: "You are aware that we in Frankfurt have no money, we are not rich and so are in debt to others," he wrote James on 24 June. He explained that he had resorted to "fraud" by creating "fictitious credit letters everywhere." For him to deliver 750,000 Prussian thalers in specie to Dresden by 22 July, he said the money had to be in his hands by 6 July, when his courier was scheduled to depart for Dresden: "I wish that for once we should not as usual have to use fraud here."[99]

On 27 June, Salomon and James together wrote anxiously to Nathan and Solomon Cohen, who was now handling some of his brother-in-law's business affairs. James claimed he had "almost covered" the specie for the first 500,000 Prussian thalers due in Hamburg on 1 July, and that Frankfurt was supplying the 750,000 Prussian thalers in specie due in Dresden on 22 July.[100] Two days later, Carl wrote his brother Salomon that, although he had amassed about 500,000 Prussian thalers in specie, he still needed another 243,000 Prussian thalers. "We have paid out more than a million of the fraudulent letters of credit."[101] On 30 June, he confessed to his brother that "People here are very angry."[102]

The Rothschild brothers experienced considerable stress and they quarreled with each other more and more about large and small matters. At first, James reacted to Nathan's outrageous behavior in a business-like manner. "As for your screaming that you have not received any money back for the remittances and gold which you sent, you will find herewith [bills] on yourself so that everything is balanced out, for we have used your money to buy Napoleons and have therefore remitted you at rates which prevailed on the day of purchase which balance these operations."[103]

But the bickering continued and James could no longer contain his anger and he struck out in all directions. "[Y]ou think and do what you can on your own and finally we get to know about it," he wrote Nathan. "Sadly you do not take this seriously and regard everyone as an ass[104] and that causes us great embarrassment. . . . Now you write in your last letter, 'I have bought £200,000 gold from the Jamaica fleet.' Dear God! And when this arrives on the same day as payment is due you write saying 'I have despatched this much gold to you.'" James had words, as well, about Herries. "The fact that your Herries is not happy with the business transacted is his fault not ours."[105]

Salomon—depressed and ill—wrote emotionally and attacked Solomon Cohen who he sensed had gained more and more of Nathan's trust. "Your Solomon Cohen is not to be a General any more," he wrote to Nathan, regarding the arbitrage transactions for the Prussian account. "He does not understand anything. When I come over there, I will show you that one is wrong. . . . Solomon Cohen . . . must answer me about this."[106]

Salomon Rothschild, in particular, was not about to relinquish his close—albeit ambivalent—relationship with Nathan to anyone, even to Solomon

Cohen, with whom he continued to do battle. He repeatedly sought to put Solomon Cohen in his place vis-à-vis Nathan, and wrote him a few choice words, which other writers have quoted, paraphrased, or embellished for a different purpose:[107]

> My brother in London is General [? in Chief] and I am his Marshal. I must therefore do my duty as Marshal and give my General [? in Chief] my opinion on everything and present all the information in a slightly more urgent light so as not to sound frivolous. But, my friend, my good friend. . . . I shall not lose my head, praise God . . . because as you know I can apply and use it very well, *with God's help*.[108]

Salomon Rothschild was relentless in his pursuit of Solomon Cohen. He criticized him for contradicting himself from one letter to the next and for not really understanding how exchange rates worked. He patronized him:

> But, my dear Mr Cohen, with regard to what you wrote about not getting cross over quarrelsome letters. . . . I wish for nothing more than for we brothers to be together for a hundred years, exchanging quarrelsome letters from time to time, while remaining on good terms with each other as brothers, except that the accounts have to be done before quarrelling. Well now, *The Day of Atonement* is fast approaching. I wish both you, my dear friend, and your whole, dear family a *happy and prosperous New Year* and if I can be of service to you here at all, then please give your orders to one who is pleased to be of service to my Mr. Cohen.[109]

Salomon also let Nathan know how unhappy he was.

> You can see for yourself what quarrelsome letters you are getting. . . . I must say, the whole business holds no pleasure for me any more. . . . I am sure that in two weeks time those wretched, quarrelsome letters will be arriving from you again. . . . I am too upset. Your Salomon Cohen also writes sheer and utter *nonsense. I am embarrassed* by your General. . . . I have already handed Herries all of the four million thaler bills because the Russian entrusted them to me for payment. Russia, therefore, has more confidence in me than the English have in you. . . . I must say, I am a little melancholic today because I have such bad pains in my back and my limbs. I have had too much upset over your wretched correspondence which is taking its toll on my health and my sanity. This, my dear Nathan, all comes . . . from all this *God damn* letter writing and carrying on this kind of correspondence. One doesn't write like that to one's family and brothers and *business partners*. . . . I am unfortunately not entirely well and neither is Kalman [Carl] and Meyer Davidson. . . . I have too much pain in my limbs today.[110]

While Salomon and his brothers may have argued with Nathan, none ever truly challenged his dominant position in their "partnership," which would be formalized in writing for the first time in March 1815.[111] They recognized that his forceful and frequently unpleasant personality brought to them their most lucrative contracts. One can only speculate as to what their merchant-banking careers might have become, had the British government not chosen to employ Nathan. And they jealously guarded their personal and business relationship with him.

The celebration of the Jewish New Year also celebrated a most prosperous year for the Rothschilds. It signified not only the execution of one contract with Gervais but also the initiation of yet another, their most lucrative. From 1 July to 26 September, the Rothschilds had successfully delivered specie to him in six installments. More than 1 million gold coins changed hands (335,200 pieces of Hanoverian George d'Or and 675,417 Dutch ducats).[112] This was about the same number of coins they had shipped to Wellington earlier in the year.[113] During the first nine months of 1814, the Rothschilds had become experts in crisscrossing the frontiers of Europe buying, selling, and transporting millions of coins.

The Rothschilds also assisted the British government in reducing its subsidy obligations to the allied powers. Castlereagh, Herries, and British envoys had paid Austria £1,466,666 in bills and specie; that is, about three quarters of the promised subsidy, and Herries had opened a line of credit for Austria for an additional £100,000 with M A Rothschild & Sons.[114] Herries and the Rothschilds had paid nearly all of the subsidy that Great Britain owed Prussia.[115] Finally, the Rothschilds had not only facilitated payments to Gervais for at least £666,667, but together with the British government, they had made additional payments to the Russian government amounting to £555,555, which essentially liquidated Great Britain's subsidy obligation of £1,250,000.[116] By contributing to the British government's liquidation of its subsidy obligation to the allied powers, the Rothschilds had learned a great deal more about arbitrage and had gained considerable hands-on experience dealing with government bureaucrats.

The Rothschilds were now well prepared and positioned to undertake yet another operation with Russia. Nathan did not neglect trading in commodities, textiles, specie, and bullion on his own account,[117] and he became more and more interested in the Russian market centered in St. Petersburg where he traded with Meyer & Bruxner & Co. and Stieglitz & Co.[118] Moreover, the Rothschilds ingratiated themselves with Gervais by arranging for his carriage to be shipped from London to Amsterdam,[119] and by James establishing a liaison with his relatives, Amburger & Sons, a prominent merchant house in St. Petersburg.[120] All this augured well for the Rothschilds' future presence in Russia.

In August 1814, the Russian government petitioned the British government for more subsidy money. Russia's ambassador in London authorized Harman & Co. to collect it in London.[121] At the same time, Gervais in Amsterdam asked Burgmann to surrender the bills of credit for the last eight months of subsidy owed to Russia so he could liquidate them. Burgmann reported to the Treasury: "I know that the Negociation to which Mr. de Gervais alludes is with Mr. Rothschild."[122]

Indeed it was, and by early September, talks were well underway among Gervais, James, and Salomon, who had come up from Paris. The reports to Nathan reflected the day-by-day conversations James and Salomon had with Gervais. According to James, Gervais wanted as soon as possible one million Dutch ducats and, as an incentive, he offered the Rothschilds the transaction on a £300,000 credit the Russian government had with Harman & Co. He also asked the Rothschilds to facilitate the redemption of four million Prussian thalers worth of Russian bills of credit.[123]

James wrote excitedly to Nathan about the proposal. He suggested several ways in which the operation could be executed. He surmised that Herries would want to assume the same role in this operation as he had in the previous one, and he calculated that the British government could save from 4 to 5 percent owing to the consolidation of the interest due on the bills of credit. Yet, if Herries chose not to participate, the Rothschilds should devise a plan to undertake the whole operation themselves. He calculated that the operation could return a profit of £80,000 to the Rothschilds.[124]

After meeting with Gervais another eight times in the course of one day, James wrote again to Nathan that, while the general tenor of the negotiation remained essentially the same, some new details made the proposal more complex. Gervais had significantly increased the value of the bills of credit to be redeemed from 4 million to 5.3 million Prussian thalers. This led James to speculate that the execution of the operation would require separate transactions. The first required the delivery of one million Dutch ducats in coin or its equivalent in coin and bills on Berlin, Dresden, Hamburg, or Leipzig to Gervais; the second involved the £300,000 Russian credit on Harman & Co.; and, finally, the Rothschilds would have to raise huge amounts of specie and bullion to cover the redemption of 5.3 million Prussian thalers worth of bills of credit. In his excitement, James increased the amount of profit to the Rothschilds to £100,000.[125]

Salomon, however, provided a sober and detailed analysis of the proposal. Gervais would receive eight monthly installments, from February to September 1815, of 666,666⅔ Prussian thalers for a total of 5,333,333⅓ Prussian thalers in bills of credit. These bills would be discounted by 8 percent; Gervais would receive a bribe of 2 percent; and the Rothschilds would receive a commission of 2 percent (c.£17,778). The feasibility of Gervais's proposal depended on several contingencies being met, and it was evident that the best way of resolving all the issues would be for James to go to London to discuss the operation with Nathan.[126]

On 21 September, Nathan wrote Herries that James was in London with a proposal that would be "an advantageous bargain for this Government." He detailed how much the British government would have to pay to liquidate the Russian bills of credit. These bills carried an interest of 6 percent, which amounted to 373,333 Prussian thalers for the eight months. Taken together, the principal and interest amounted to 5,706,667 Prussian thalers. Added to this sum, was an estimated 142,666 Prussian thalers (about 2½ percent) to cover the costs of remittance, risk, transport, and a commission, making for a total 5,849,333 Prussian thalers. At the rate of 6.0 Prussian thalers to the pound sterling, the total amount would be £974,889.[127]

However, by employing the Rothschilds to liquidate the Russian bills of credit, the British government would save a tidy sum of money. First, the Rothschilds would charge *only* 1½ percent for procuring and transporting the money to Berlin. Second, the British government would pay Nathan in bills on the Treasury, with interest at only 5 percent, for the principal amount of the bills of credit because Gervais would waive Russia's claim to the accrued interest. Third, the Treasury bills would be due at ninety days sight and, "if required on their maturity," Nathan would negotiate a similar amount at ninety days sight, but he ultimately would receive cash for them at redemption. The total sum the British government would pay Nathan would be £912,963 and the British government would save £61,926.[128]

While these negotiations proceeded in London, a worried Salomon reported from Amsterdam that Gervais had become anxious to conclude the deal: "'Dear Rothschild, make sure that your brother is here by next week at the latest. It could be that another courier will arrive, *God forbid*, and the whole business is called off. Afterwards I will not be able to do anything, not at any price. I cannot alter the date to make it look as though it was settled sooner. I cannot and may not do such a thing. . . . I shall be very nervous, my dear Rothschild, until your brother is here because, as you know, the finance minister dreams up something new to do every day.'" Salomon tried his best to speed up the negotiation and wrote his brothers that Gervais was "an *intelligent man* and has understood us" and that "any time lost is a great deal lost." If James did not want to be at sea on the Day of Atonement he should hire a private boat "even if it costs £100." Salomon related what Gervais had told him at dinner the evening before: "'So now, Mr Rothschild, if the operation in London does not proceed, your brother will not bring me my stocks. . . . Dear Rothschild, I don't like to throw away a profit of £20,000, however, if in the meantime orders come from higher up then I cannot help it and I cannot get myself sent to Siberia for the sake of more profit.'" A few days later, a "trembling" Gervais appeared before Salomon: "'dear Rothschild, I'm afraid that another *estafette* will arrive and that then we are done for on this business.'"[129]

On 23 September, Herries restated to Vansittart the Rothschild proposal and he accepted it.[130] Within the week, James and Gervais set in motion its execution. Burgmann gave Salomon and James a "Declaration" certifying that the debentures, in lieu of the bills of credit valued at 5,333,333⅓ Prussian thalers due to Russia, would be held at Nathan's disposal. On 30 September, James sent these documents to Nathan who, in turn, credited M A Rothschild & Sons with £899,999.[131]

When in May 1815 Nathan provided Herries with an accounting of this Gervais–Russian operation, he commented: "From these Statements, you will, I doubt not, do me the Justice to say, that the Business I have had the Honour of transacting, for Government, has been executed most advantageously."[132] Nathan and his brothers had every reason to be proud of themselves.

Notes

1. H Paris to JmD Lon. 22 May 1814, *HP* BLAddMss. 57435 [Letter Book], f. 91.

2. CMR Fft. to JMR [Ams.] 26 June 1814, RAL xi/109/0/2/14, Tape 4/Letter 7; & Tape 125/Letter 9.

3. Sherwig, pp. 289–290.

4. During the intervening months, Great Britain provided Prussia with £100,000 in bills of exchange; promised Russia £500,000 per annum to maintain its seized ships, which were ready for use by the British; dispatched nearly £300,000 in specie and £300,000 in bills of exchange for the use of Prussia and Russia; and agreed to maintain the Russian German Legion (the Germans in Napoleon's army

captured by the Russians). See PROT 1/1390/No.11,678 (in No. 6033); WH Lon. to GH Lon. 18 March 1814, PROT 1/1382/No. 3814; H *Mem.* I, 96–97, n. 8; & Sherwig, pp. 288–301, passim & p. 315, n.1.

5. In October 1813 at Teplitz, Great Britain agreed to pay Austria £1,000,000 to field 150,000 troops against France. See Sherwig, pp. 301–307, 317, & H *Mem.* I, 92.

6. Sherwig, pp. 318–319 & 326.

7. Burg Ams. to GH Lon. Nos. 3, 10 & 13. 22 January, 15 & 18 February 1814, PROT 1/1379/Nos. 3125–3127, respectively.

8. Amburger & fils StP. to NMR Lon. 11 September 1814, RAL xi/112/2.

9. Burg Ams. to GH Lon. Nos.11 & 16. 15 & 22 February 1814, PROT 1/1377/No. 2368 & 1379/No. 3129, respectively.

10. Buist, pp. 259–262; Buist, "Russia's Entry on the Dutch Capital Market, 1770–1815," *Fifth International Conference of Economic History, Leningrad 1970*, vols. IV–V, edited by Herman Van der Wee, Vladimir A. Vinogradov and Grigorii G. Kotovsky (The Hague: Mouton Publishers, 1970), pp. 51–164, passim; & Boris V. Anan'ich & Sergei K. Lebedev, "Russian Finance during the French Revolution and the Napoleonic Wars," in Erik Aerts & François Crouzet, eds. *Economic Effects of the French Revolutionary and Napoleonic Wars*. Session B-1, Proceedings Tenth International Economic History Congress Leuven, August 1990 (Leuven: Leuven University Press, 1990), pp. 38–47. See also Gervais's correspondence with Hope & Co., GAA 735/203–204 & 209.

11. See GH Lon. to Burg Ams. 17 May 1814, *HP* BLAddMss. 57415, ff. 172–174.

12. Burg Ams. to GH Lon. Nos. 13 & 16. 18 & 22 February 1814, PROT 1/1379/Nos. 3127 & 3129, respectively.

13. Burg Ams. to GH Lon. Nos. 12, 17, 19–20 & 22. 18, 22, 24 & 25 February 1814, PROT 1/1379/Nos. 3128, 3130, 3132–3133 & 3135, respectively; Burg Ams. to GH Lon. No. 21. 25 February 1814, PROT 1/1390/No. 3134; & Burg Ams. to GH Lon. No.35. 7 March 1814, PROT 1/1381/No. 3586. Robert Melvil was Hope & Co.'s agent in St. Petersburg in 1808–1809. See Buist, Ch. 7, "'Les Traites Du Nord' and Operation R. M."

14. Har Lon. to GH Lon. 8 February 1814, PROT 1/1390/No.1847 (in No. 6033); & Burg Ams. to GH Lon. No. 99. 3 June 1814, PROT 1/1398/No. 8237.

15. Burg Ams. to GH Lon. Nos. 35 & 74. 7 March &12 April 1814, PROT 1/1381/No. 3586 & PROT 1/1388/No. 5411, respectively.

16. C Paris to Treasury, Lon. 20 April 1814, *Correspondence*, IX, 483–484.

17. Burg Ams. to GH Lon. No. 90 & enclosures from Niebuhr & Melvil & Co., 3 May 1814, PROT 1/1392/No. 6460.

18. H Lon. to Baron Jacobi Kloest 28 April 1814, *HP* BLAddMss. 57435 [Letter Book], f. 36. See H Paris to GH Lon. 15 May 1814 & "Note of the arrangements made by Mr. Herries with persons to receive the Subsidies due to the Russian & Prussian Governments for the Year 1814," 17 May 1814, *HP* BLAddMss. 57435 [Letter Book], ff. 64 & 72, respectively.

19. See GH Lon. to Burg Ams. 17 May 1814, *HP* BLAddMss. 57415, ff. 175–176.

20. H Paris to V Lon. 14 May 1814, *HP* BLAddMss. 57435 [*Letter Book*], ff. 58–59. See also C Paris to Treasury, Lon. 19 May 1814 & enclosure "Count Nesselrode to Viscount Castlereagh dated Paris 14 May 1814," PROT 1/1395/No. 7508.

21. H Paris to GH Lon. 26 May 1814, PROT 1/1396/No. 7776 & *HP* BLAddMss. 57435 [*Letter Book*], ff. 103–104; H Paris to V Lon. circa 12 May 1814, *HP* BLAddMss. 57435 [*Letter Book*], ff. 55–56; & Burg Ams. to GH Lon. No.150. 19 September 1814, PROT 1/1420/No.14786 & *HP* BLAddMss. 57374, f. 104.

22. *"Note for Lord Liverpool and Mr. Vansittart, on the subject of procuring all Supplies of Specie Abroad through one Agent,"* 24 April 1814, in *Correspondence*, IX, 495–497, passim, especially, p. 496. See also Lieven Lon. to V Lon. 10 April 1814, PROT 1/1389/No. 5732; "Mr. Hamilton With Copy of note from Count Lieven resptg a Balance of £206900 . . . claimed to be still due to the Russian Government on acct of the Treaty of Subsidy of 11 April 1805 between this Country and Russia," PROT 1/1388/No. 5459; H Lon. to Lieven Lon. 19 & 25 April 1814, *HP* BLAddMss. 57435 [*Letter Book*], ff. 22 & 30, respectively; H Lon. to V Lon. 20 April 1814, *HP* BLAddMss. 57435 [*Letter Book*], f. 23; & GH Lon. to H Lon. & WH Lon. 26 April 1814, *HP* BLAddMss. 57372, ff. 21–22 & *HP* BLAddMss. 57415, ff.162–163, respectively.

23. V Lon. to C Paris 28 April 1814, *VP* BLAddMss. 31,231, ff. 56–58, passim. It is surprising that in a printed edition of Vansittart's letter to Castlereagh all mention of the Rothschilds is omitted. See *Correspondence*, IX, 520–522.

24. "Invoice." 13 November 1813, RAL xi/38/59B; WH Lon. to GH Lon. 10 January 1814, PROT 1/1370–1371/Nos. 373 & 381; & JmD Lon. to GH Lon. 20 January 1814, PROT 1/1372/No. 931.

25. H Lon. to GH Lon. 14 March 1814, PROT 1/1381/No. 3530, & JmD Lon. to NMR Lon. 10 March 1814, *HP* BLAddMss. 57434 [*Letter Book*], f. 107.

26. GH Lon. to H Lon. 9 April 1814, *HP* BLAddMss. 57392, ff. 17 & 19; JmD Lon. to Deputy Commissary at Deal, 23 May & to NMR Lon. 24 May 1814, RAL xi/38/59B; & NMR Lon. to JMR Ams. 23 & 24 May 1814, RAL xi/82/7/3/46–47, respectively. Italics mine.

27. "Account Sales and disposal of the following Hanoverian Pistoles received from Mr. N M Rothschild for account of J C Herries Esq. Commissary in Chief Viz." dated at Frankfort, 16 June 1814, & signed M A Rothschild & Sons, RAL xi/38/59A. Italics mine.

28. H Lon. to GH Lon. 29 March 1814, *HP* BLAddMss. 57434 [*Letter Book*], ff. 126–127.

Nathan Rothschild had, in effect, undercut the market price by one or more shillings per ounce of gold. See *MPG & S: 1813–1814* & *MPG & S: 1814–1815*. During April and May, he delivered thousands of ounces of gold bullion and Portuguese gold coin at 103 shillings per ounce to Herries and charged him a commission of 6 pence per ounce. "Invoices" in *HP* BLAddMss. 57383, ff. 6–8, 10–14 & 22.

29. H Lon. to GH Lon. 17 March 1814, PROT 1/1459/No. 5508 & *HP* BLAddMss. 57434 [*Letter Book*], ff. 110–111.

30. H Lon. to Burg Ams. 17 March 1814, *HP* BLAddMss. 57434 [Letter Book] ff. 111–112. Italics mine.

31. H Lon. to Burg Ams. 17 March 1814, *HP* BLAddMss. 57434 [Letter Book] f. 113. See H Lon. to NMR Lon. 28 January 1814, *HP* BLAddMss. 57434 [Letter Book], f. 76; & Limburger, Fft. to H Lon. 16 February 1814, *HP* BLAddMss. 57378, ff. 1–2.

32. H Lon. to GH Lon. 26 March 1814, PROT 1/1385/No. 4250. See A. Schmidchen "Receipt," *HP* BLAddMss. 57394, f. 9; Burg Ams. No. 77. to GH Lon. 15 April 1814, PROT 1/1388/No. 5413; & NMR Lon. to JMR Ams. RAL xi/82/7/3/34.

33. CMR Fft. to NMR & SMR Lon. 26 August 1814, RAL xi/82/1. Herries would continue to employ Limburger to handle certain financial transactions for Great Britain in Central Europe, almost always in conjunction with, and through, M A Rothschild & Sons. Limburger is mentioned passim in the Rothschild correspondence and there is a file under his name in *HP* BLAddMss. 57378. 1. Baron Limburger d'Ehrenfels 1814–1816, ff. 1–105.

34. JmD Lon. to NMR Lon. 12 April 1814, *HP* BLAddMss. 57435 [Letter Book], f. 18.

A discrepancy exists between the amount requested and the ƒ.800,000 (about £89,000) Davidson delivered. See MD Ams. to BC & NMR Lon. 7 & 17 May 1814, RAL xi/112/72, respectively.

35. JmD Lon. to V. Lon. 13 April 1814, *HP* BLAddMss. 57435 [Letter Book], f. 19.

36. JmD Lon. to NMR Lon. 14 April 1814, RAL xi/112/72; NMR Lon. to JMR Ams. 15 April 1814, RAL xi/82/7/3/31; Thornton to SMR Ams. 30 April 1814, *HP* BLAddMss. 57415, f. 167; NMR Lon. to MD Ams. 20 May 1814, RAL xi/82/7/3/44; & "Mr. N M Rothschild in account with J M Rothschild for payment to E. Thornton Esq." *HP* BLAddMss. 57383, ff. 16–17.

37. JmD Lon. to NMR Lon. 14 April 1814, RAL xi/112/72.

38. R. Chinnery, Calais-Boulougne-Abbeville, to H Lon. 25–27 April 1814, *HP* BLAddMss. 57415, ff. 154–159; H Lon. to R. Chinnery & to Le Comte de Blacas, n.p. 22 April & 9 May 1814, *HP* BLAddMss. 57435 [Letter Book], ff. 28–29 & 42–43, respectively.

39. H Paris to JmD Lon. 10 May 1814, *HP* BLAddMss. 57435 [Letter Book], ff. 48–50; & "Receipts," *HP* BLAddMss. 57394, ff. 22–23 (24 & 30 May 1814).

40. H Lon. to Burg Ams. 19 April 1814, *HP* BLAddMss. 57435 [Letter Book], f. 20.

41. H Paris to JMR Paris 10 May & to Clancarty, Hague 11 May 1814, *HP* BLAddMss. 57435 [Letter Book], f. 54; & JMR Ams. to NMR Lon. 20 May 1814, RAL xi/109/0, Tape 79.

42. MD Ams. to NMR Lon. 17 May 1814, RAL xi/112/72.

43. H Paris to JmD Lon. 10 May 1814, *HP* BLAddMss. 57435 [Letter Book], ff. 48–50.

44. H Paris to JmD Lon. 15 May 1814, *HP* BLAddMss. 57435 [Letter Book], ff. 65–67.

45. H Paris to JmD Lon. 17 May 1814, *HP* BLAddMss. 57435 [Letter Book], ff. 76–77.

Both Davidson and James reported that when gold coins were deposited at a bank in Amsterdam a charge of ⅛ percent would be levied for three months and another ⅛ for the next three months. MD Ams. to NMR Lon. 17 May 1814, RAL xi/112/72, & JMR Ams. to NMR Lon. 20 May 1814, RAL xi/109/0, Tape 79.

46. H Paris to JmD Lon. 15 & 17 May 1814, *HP* BLAddMss. 57435 [Letter Book], ff. 65–67 & 78, respectively.

47. H Paris to Kennedy Toulouse & to JR Paris 25 May 1814, *HP* BLAddMss. 57435 [Letter Book], ff.100–101 & 102, respectively; H Paris to GH Lon. 3 June 1814, PROT 1/1406/No.10096; H Paris to GH Lon. 8 June 1814, *HP* BLAddMss. 57436 [Letter Book], ff. 15–16; *HP* BLAddMss. 57378, ff.127, 129–130–132 (circa 13 June 1814); & Dale Bordeaux to NMR Lon. 1 July 1814, RAL xi/112/73B.

48. H Paris to Messrs Rothschild, Paris to TD Bru. & to JmD Lon. 28 May 1814, RAL xi/38/59A, & *HP* BLAddMss. 57435 [Letter Book], ff.105–107, respectively.

49. H Paris to GH Lon. 3 June 1814, PROT 1/1406/No. 10096; & "Account Sales of 43304 Hanoverian Pistoles received from Commissary General Dunmore for account of J H Herries Esq. Commissary in Chief….," signed M A Rothschild & Sons Fft. 21 July 1814, RAL xi/38/59A.

50. V Lon. to H Paris 25 May 1814, *HP* BLAddMss. 57415, ff. 180–183 (Private & Duplicate, variation in spelling). See "Note"(dated 18 May) containing a proposal for paying the subsidy, from Mr. Irving (Reid, Irving & Co.) to Herries, who sent it to GH Lon. (22 May 1814), in *HP* BLAddMss. 57435 [Letter Book], ff. 92–93. Although Reid, Irving & Co. would continue to provide financial services to the British government on the Continent, it frequently disappointed Herries. Thus, whenever the opportunity allowed, he excluded Reid, Irving & Co. from transactions. In April, he had 21,075 Hanoverian five thaler pieces for the military chest in Holland but he chose to sell them to Nathan at 10 guilder 1 stiuver each, in return for his bills of exchange on Amsterdam. He wrote Harrison that he had transmitted these bills directly to Dunmore "not conceiving it necessary that this transaction should pass thro' Messrs. Reid & Irving [*sic*] or be subject to further charge against the Public." H Lon. to GH Lon. 2 April 1814, PROT 1/1385/No. 4689.

51. V Lon. to H Paris 25 May 1814, *HP* BLAddMss. 57415, ff. 180–183 (Private & Duplicate, variation in spelling).

52. See GH Lon. to WH Lon. 26 May 1814, *HP* BLAddMss. 57415, ff. 184–185; & "Bills of Credit Prussia," *HP* BLAddMss. 57389, f. 17.

53. H Paris, to GH, JmD, V. Lon. & "Note of the arrangements made by Mr. Herries with persons to receive the Subsidies due to the Russian & Prussian Governments for the Year 1814," 15, 17 & 19 May 1814, *HP* BLAddMss. 57435 [Letter Book], ff. 61–62, 65–67, 72–73, 79–80 & 85, respectively; & H Lon. to GH Lon. 1 July 1814, in Appendix A. "Report from Mr. Herries on the results of his Mission to Paris," H *Mem.* II, 239.

54. See H Paris to V Lon. 19 May 1814, *VP* BLAddMss. 31,231, ff. 64–65; H Paris to SMR Paris, JMR & Gervais Ams. 20 May 1814, *HP* BLAddMss. 57435 [Letter Book], ff. 86–88, respectively; JMR Ams. to NMR Lon. 20 May 1814, RAL xi/109/0, Tape 79; H Paris to JmD Lon. 22 & 30 May & JMR Ams. 30 May 1814,

HP BLAddMss. 57435 [Letter Book], ff. 91, 109–110 & RAL xi/38/59A (xi/52/30), respectively.

55. "A Statement of the Sums paid & remaining to be paid on account of Subsidies under the Treaty of the 1st March 1814 by Great Britain to Austria [to Prussia; to Russia]," 3 August 1814, *VP* BLAddMss. 31,231, ff.114, 117 & 120, respectively; & "From Notebook of Herries in his own hand," *HP* BLAddMss. 57397, f. 2.

56. "Memorandum respecting Austrian Subsidies." circa 21 September 1814, *VP* BLAddMss. 31,231, f. 159. See also, Sherwig, pp. 301–307, 317, & H *Mem.* I, 92.

57. Burg Ams. to GH Lon. No. 95. 31 May 1814, PROT 1/1398/No. 8093. Gervais also needed to redeem the paper *assignats* that the advancing Russian armies had introduced into the German states. Buist, p. 263.

58. Buist, pp. 263–265. See also Burg Ams. to Hope & Co. Ams. 25 & 28 July & 9 August 1814, GAA 735/187; Gervais Ams. to Hope & Co. Ams. No. 387. 23 July 1814, GAA 735/201; Burg Ams. to GH Lon. No. 159. 14 October 1814, PROT 1/1425/No. 15111; & Lushington, Treasury Chambers, Lon. to H Lon. 19 October 1814, *HP* BLAddMss. 57374, f. 102.

59. See Burg Ams. to GH Lon. 14, 21 & 23–24 June, 1, 5 & 8 July 1814, PROT 1/1401/No. 8855, 1403/No. 9173, 1404/No. 9478, 1406/No.10137, 1411–1412/Nos. 11787 & 12132, respectively; JmD Lon. to GH Lon. 6 August 1814, PROT 1/1411–1412/No. 12037; & NMR Lon. to JMR Ams. 28 June 1814, RAL xi/82/7/3/58.

60. JMR Ams. to NMR Lon. 14 June 1814, RAL xi/109/0/1/26, Tape 1 & RAL xi/109/0, Tape 80; & see also, CMR Fft. to SMR Paris & to JMR Ams. 2 June 1814, RAL xi/109/0/2/9, Tape 4/Letter 2. *Seehandlung*'s full name is *Seehandlungssozietät*, a Prussian society of merchants and capitalists, founded by Royal patent, in 1772, and granted the monopoly on trade in sea salt and wax, under the supervision of the Prussian finance ministry. For this, my thanks to Dr. Rainer Liedtke.

61. See NMR Lon. to JMR Ams. 3 June 1814, RAL xi/82/7/3/51A; JMR Ams. to NMR Lon. 7 June 1814, RAL xi/109/0/1/22, Tape 1/Letter 3 & RAL xi/109/0, Tape 79/Letter 6; & NMR Lon. to JMR & to MD Ams. 7 June 1814, RAL xi/82/7/3, f. 61, Tape 249/Letter 3. For these, my thanks to Mordichae Zucker and Dr. Rainer Liedtke.

62. NMR Lon. to SMR Paris 7 June 1814, RAL xi/109/0/1/21, Tape 1/Letter 2 & Tape 241/Letter 10; & see SMR Paris to NMR Lon. 8 June 1814, RAL xi/87/0A.

63. JMR Ams. to NMR Lon. 14 June 1814, RAL xi/109/0/1/26, Tape 1 & RAL xi/109/0, Tape 80.

64. JMR Ams. to NMR Lon. 17 June 1814, RAL xi/109/0/1/24, Tape 1/Letter 5, & RAL xi/109/0, Tape 80; & MD Ams. to NMR Lon. 18 June 1814, RAL xi/109/0/1/30, Tape 2/Letter 4.

65. H Ams. to JmD Lon. 17 June 1814, *HP* BLAddMss. 57436 [Letter Book], ff. 17–18.

66. MD Ams. to NMR Lon. 21 June 1814, RAL xi/109/0/27, Tape 3/Letter 4 & SMR Ams. to NMR Lon. 28 June 1814, RAL xi/109/0/3/2; & SMR & JMR Ams. to NMR Lon. 28 June 1814, RAL xi/109/0, Tape 170/Letter 2.

67. GH Lon to WH Lon. 26 May 1814, *HP* BLAddMss. 57415, ff. 184–185.

68. JMR Ams. to NMR Lon. 17 June 1814, RAL xi/109/0/1/24, Tape 1/Letter 5 & RAL xi/109/0, Tape 80; MD Ams. to NMR Lon. 18 & 21 June 1814, RAL xi/109/0/1/30, Tape 2/Letter 4 & RAL xi/109/0/2/7, Tape 3/Letter 4, respectively; H Ams. to JmD Lon. 17 June 1814, *HP* BLAddMss. 57436 [Letter Book], ff. 18–22. Please note that James Rothschild and Mayer Davidson frequently confused George d'Or with Louis d'Or. See JMR Ams. to NMR 7 June 1814, RAL xi/109/0/1/22, Tape 1/Letter 3 & RAL xi/109/0, Tape 79/Letter 6 & JMR Ams. to NMR Lon. 14 June 1814, RAL xi/109/0/1/26, Tape 1 & RAL xi/109/0, Tape 80.

69. SMR Ams. to H Ams. 17 & 20 June 1814, RAL xi/38/59B.

70. H Ams. to SMR Ams. 17 June 1814, *HP* BLAddMss. 57436 [Letter Book], f. 109; & see SMR dictated to MD Ams. to NMR Lon. 21 June 1814, RAL xi/109/0/2/7, Tape 3/Letter 4.

71. Spearman, n.p. to NMR Lon. circa 17–20 June 1814, RAL xi/38/59B.

72. H Ams. to GH Lon. 17 June 1814, PROT 1/1459/Nos. 11737 & 14096; *VP* BLAddMss. 31,231, f. 130 (17 June 1814); & H Lon. to GH Lon. 28 September 1814, PROT 1/1459/No. 15012.

73. H Ams. to JmD Lon. 17 June 1814, *HP* BLAddMss. 57436 [Letter Book], ff. 18–20, passim.

74. H Paris to NMR Lon. 8 June 1814, *HP* BLAddMss. 57435 [Letter Book], f. 133.

75. "Memorandum of the monies raised in Paris through M. Rothschild," H Ams. to JmD Lon. circa 17 June 1814, *HP* BLAddMss. 57436 [Letter Book], f. 24 & "Statement of Sums Paid to N M Rothschild by J C Herries, Commissary in Chief," *HP* BLAddMss. 57390, f. 7.

76. SMR Ams. to NMR Lon. 19 June 1814, RAL xi/87/0A; MD Ams. to NMR Lon. 18 June 1814, RAL xi/109/0/1/30, Tape 2/Letter 4; & H Ams. to JmD Lon. 17 June 1814, *HP* BLAddMss. 57436 [Letter Book], f. 21.

77. JMR & MD Ams. to NMR Lon. 20 June 1814, RAL xi/109/0/2/6 & SMR Ams. to NMR Lon. 24 June 1814, RAL xi/109/0/2/11; & MD Ams. to NMR Lon. 21 June 1814, RAL xi/109/0/2/7, Tape 3/Letter 4.

78. JMR Ams. to NMR Lon. 17 June 1814, RAL xi/109/0/1/24, Tape 1/Letter 5 & RAL xi/109/0, Tape 80. See also, MD Ams. to NMR, Lon. 18 & 21 June 1814, RAL xi/109/0/1/30, Tape 2/Letter 4 & RAL xi/109/0/2/7, Tape 3/Letter 4, respectively. Italics mine.

79. "Wechsel und Geld Cours, Berlin 14 Juny 1814," *HP* BLAddMss. 57394, f. 1.

80. For a discussion of these rates, see NMR Lon. to H Lon. 21 September 1814, PROT 1/1420/No.14748 & SMR Ams. to NMR Lon. 18 October 1814, RAL xi/109/1, Tape 172/Letter 8.

81. SMR Ams. to NMR Lon. 24 June 1814, RAL xi/109/0/2/11; & see MD Ams. to NMR Lon. 21 June 1814, RAL xi/109/0/2/7, Tape 3/Letter 4.

82. JMR Ams. to NMR Lon. 17 June 1814, RAL xi/109/0/1/24, Tape 1/Letter 5 & RAL xi/109/0, Tape 80.

83. MD Ams. postscript to JMR Ams. to NMR Lon. 20 June 1814, RAL xi/109/0/2/6, Tape 3/Letter 3.

84. JMR Ams. to NMR Lon. 20 June 1814, RAL xi/109/0/2/6, Tape 3/Letter 3 &
RAL xi/109/0, Tape 80.

85. NMR Lon. to SMR Paris 7 June 1814, RAL xi/109/0/1/21, Tape 1/Letter 2.

86. James confessed he had lied to Herries about purchasing 250,000 Dutch
ducats and, instead, "concluded another piece of business with the Russian," to
whom he sold the Dutch ducats that were destined for Dresden. JMR Ams. to NMR
Lon. 24 June 1814, RAL xi/109/0/2/12, Tape 4/Letter 5 & RAL xi/109/0, Tape 80.

87. SMR Ams. to NMR Lon. 24 June 1814, RAL xi/109/0/2/11. My thanks to
Mordichae Zucker for his translation of these letters; punctuation changes are mine.

88. MD Ams. postscript to SMR Ams. to NMR Lon. 24 June 1814, RAL xi/109/
0/2/11. My thanks to Mordichae Zucker for his translation of these letters; punctuation changes are mine.

89. NMR Lon. to JMR Ams. 28 June 1814 (RAL xi/82/7/3/58), 1, 8, 12, 15, 22 &
29 July, 5, 9, 12, 16, 18–19, 26 & 30 August, 2 & 6 September 1814, RAL xi/82/7/4/1,
4–7, 9, 12, 14–17, 19, 21, 25–26, 29–30; JMR Ams. to NMR Lon. 22 July & 30 August 1814, RAL xi/85/0; MD Ams. to NMR Lon. 1, 8, 15, 22, 26 & 29 July, 12, 16, 23
& 26 August, 2 & 6 September 1814, RAL xi/112/72; H Lon. to SMR Ams. 30 June
1814, *HP* BLAddMss. 57436, ff. 32–33, & H Lon. to NMR Lon. 22 July 1814, RAL
xi/38/59B; "Invoice" of gold delivered to H Lon. 30 June 1814, *HP* BLAddMss.
57383, ff. 24–25; "Invoice of Hanoverian Pistoles delivered to Mr N M Rothschild,"
6 & 15 July 1814, RAL xi/38/59B; Heseltine & Billingsby, Harw. to NMR Lon. 8 July
1814, RAL xi/109/0/3/22; HC, Hel. to JMR Ams. 7 & 21 August, & John Cullen
Hel. to MD Ams. 18 & 25 July 1814, RAL xi/112/74A; Anderson Spithead to NMR
Lon. 9, 19 & 21 August 1814, RAL xi/112/2; & Hudig Blokhuyzen & Van der Eb,
Rot. to JMR Ams. & NMR Lon. 8–9 August 1814, RAL xi/112/75B.

90. Quoted in JMR Ams. to NMR Lon. 17 June 1814, RAL xi/109/0/1/24, Tape 1/
Letter 5 & RAL xi/109/0, Tape 80.

91. H Ams. to JmD Lon. 17 June & to Burg Ams. 19 June 1814, *HP* BLAddMss.
57436 [Letter Book], ff. 16–22 & 24–27, respectively.

92. See "Monthly Account of Bullion Imported into His Majesty's Mint, with
the Coinage & delivery thereof, for July 1814," Royal Mint Record Book. 1814–1815,
PRO Mint 1/8, p. 21; & "An Account of the Hanoverian Gold Monies Coined at
His Majesty's Mint, and also of The Pieces deposited in the Pix, From the 15th September, 1813, to the 24th May, 1815, inclusive, During the Masterships of The Earl of
Clancarty, and the Right Honourable W. Wellesley Pole," dated 25th October 1820,
Mint-Office, PRO Mint 13/164. See also "Invoice of Hanoverian Pistoles delivered
to Mr N M Rothschild," 15 July 1814, RAL xi/38/59B & NMR Lon. to JMR Ams. 15
& 29 July 1814, RAL xi/82/7/4/7 & 12, respectively.

93. In early June, Nathan sent James 10,000 ounces of gold (circa £50,000) and
purchased £80,000 of gold with intentions to buy another £350,000. NMR Lon. to
JMR Ams. 3 & 4 June 1814, RAL xi/82/7/3/51A & B, Tape 263/Letters 5 & 6, respectively. JMR Ams. to NMR Lon. 8 July 1814, RAL xi/109/0, Tape 81 & NMR
Lon. to JMR Ams. 9 August 1814, RAL xi/82/7/4/15.

94. H Ams. to JmD Lon.17 June 1814, *HP* BLAddMss. 57436 [Letter Book], ff.16–24; &, among others, "Account Sales of Dollars," 3, 11 August 1814, RAL xi/38/59B.

95. "Mr. N M Rothschild in Account Current with Mr Rothschild for Russian Bills of Credit & payment to Commissary GenDunmore," RAL xi/112/15; NMR Lon. to JMR Ams. 19 July 1814, RAL xi/82/7/4/8 & encl. B1, in "Mr N M Rothschild in Account Current with S M Rothschild for the Payment of 4,000,000 Thalers Russian Bills of Credit to Monsr. De Gervais," Ams. 14 October 1814, RAL xi/82/7/2/4; "Invoice of Specie consisting of French Gold Coin . . . " 25 July 1814, RAL xi/38/60; *HP* BLAddMss. 57378, f. 119; TD Bru. to MAR Fft. 1 & 15 July 1814, RAL xi/112/72; H Lon. to NMR Lon. 20, 22 & 28 July 1814, RAL xi/38/59A & B, respectively; HC Bru. to MD Ams. 2 August 1814, RAL xi/112/72A; & MD Ams. to NMR Lon. 26 August 1814, RAL xi/112/72.

96. See "Schedule of Bills," 19 August 1814, "Abstract of Money," 12 May–24 August 1814, "Abstract of Payments," 16 June–24 August 1814 & *HP* BLAddMss. 57394, ff. 36–37, 38–39 & 40, respectively; & TD Bru. to GH Lon. 23 August & JmD Lon. to GH Lon. 27 August 1814, PROT 1/1459/Nos.13273 & 13137, respectively.

97. H Lon. to NMR Lon. & NMR Lon. to JMR Ams. 4 October 1814, RAL xi/38/59A & B & RAL xi/82/7/4/39, respectively; & Thornton, Stockholm, to MAR Fft. 24 October 1814, RAL xi/38/59A.

98. H Lon. to NMR Lon. 5 July 1814, RAL xi/38/59A; H Lon. to NMR Lon. 9 & 22 July 1814, RAL xi/38/59A & B, respectively; *HP* BLAddMss. 57394, f. 34; MD Hel. to NMR Lon. 10 July 1814, RAL xi/112/72; & H Lon. to NMR Lon. 4 November 1814, RAL xi/38/59A (xi/52/30). Nathan cautioned his brothers to handle only "full weight" Dutch ducats because "the Russian" might purchase "light ones" from someone else and claim the Rothschilds had shorted him. JR for NMR Lon. to SMR, JMR, & MD Ams. 16 September 1814, RAL xi/82/7/4/33.

99. CMR Fft. to JMR Paris 24 June 1814, RAL xi/109/0/2/13.

100. JMR & SMR Ams. to NMR & SC Lon. 27 June 1814, RAL xi/109/0/2/15, Tape 4/Letter 8 & RAL xi/109/0, Tape 80; & JMR Ams. postscript to NMR Lon. 28 June 1814, RAL xi/109/0/3/2.

101. CMR Fft. to SMR Paris 29 June 1814, RAL xi/109/0/3/4, Tape 5.

102. CMR Fft. to SMR Paris 30 June 1814, RAL xi/109/0/3/7, Tape 6.

103. JMR's postscript to SMR & JMR Ams. to NMR Lon. 28 June 1814, RAL xi/109/0/3/2, Tape 5 & RAL xi/109/0, Tape 170/Letter 2.

104. My thanks to Dr. Rainer Liedke, who verified that in the original letter the crossed out blotched word was probably "Esel," not uncommon to the Rothschilds' vocabulary.

105. JMR Ams. to NMR Lon. 8 July 1814, RAL xi/109/0, Tape 81. See also, JMR Ams. to NMR & SMR Lon. 19 July 1814, RAL xi/109/0, Tape 81.

106. SMR & JMR Ams. to NMR Lon. circa 28 June 1814, RAL xi/109/0, Tape 170/Letter 3. See also, JMR & SMR Ams. to NMR & SC Lon. 27 June 1814, RAL xi/109/0/2/15, Tape 4/Letter 8 & RAL xi/109/0, Tape 80.

107. Cf. Ferguson's epigraph, *"My brother in London is the commanding general, I am his field marshal,"* to his ch. three, *"The Commanding General,"* pp. 83 & 498 (and cited incorrectly as RAL T29/159, XI/109/0/6/11).

108. SMR Paris to NMR & SC Lon. 17 August 1814, RAL xi/109/0/6/12, Tape 170/Letter 7.

109. SMR Ams. to SC Lon. 20 September 1814, RAL xi/109/1/2/16, Tape 172/Letter 2.

110. SMR & JMR Ams. to NMR Lon. 28 June 1814, RAL xi/109/0/3/2, Tape 5 & RAL xi/109/0, Tape 170/Letter 2.

111. The details of which are found in the following chapter.

112. "Mr N M Rothschild in Account Current with S M Rothschild for the Payment of 4,000,000 Thalers Russian Bills of Credit to Monsr. De Gervais," with enclosures, A–G, signed S M Rothschild, Ams. 14 October 1814, RAL xi/82/7/2/1–9.

113. "Statement of Funds provided for Public Service," *HP* BLAddMss. 57394, ff. 20–21.

114. "Memorandum respecting Austrian Subsidies," *VP* BLAddMss. 31,231, f. 159; WH Lon. to GH Lon. 21 September 1814, PROT 1/1420/No.14604; H Lon. to GH Lon. 24 September 1814, PROT 1/1420/No.14739; & H Lon. to NMR Lon. 28 September 1814, RAL xi/38/59A.

115. "A Statement of the Sums paid & remaining to be paid on account of Subsidies under the Treaty of the 1st March 1814 by Great Britain to Prussia," *VP* BLAddMss. 31,231, f. 117; H Lon. to GH Lon. 5 September 1814, PROT 1/1417/No.13552; NMR Lon. to JMR Ams. 9 September 1814, RAL xi/82/7/4/31; Burg Ams. Nos.122, 125, 131–132. 8, 19, 25–26 July 1814, PROT 1/14092/Nos.10172, 10940, 11298–11299, respectively; & PROT 1/1420/No.14647.

116. "A Statement of the Sums paid & remaining to be paid on account of Subsidies under the Treaty of the 1st March 1814 by Great Britain to Russia," *VP* BLAddMss. 31,231, f. 120. The interest payment on the Russian debentures held by Hope & Co. was due on 11 October. See Burg Ams. to GH Lon. 19 September & 14 October 1814, Nos.150 & 159, PROT 1/1420/No.14786 & 1425/No.15111, respectively; & *HP* BLAddMss. 57374, f.104.

117. See RAL xi/112/ 71, 72 & 74A, passim. Nathan added to his staff and now had three Cohens assisting him: Benjamin, Isaac, and Solomon. Among others, see MD Ams. to BC Lon. 29 July & 5 September 1814, RAL xi/112/72; BC Lon. to JMR Ams. 30 August 1814, RAL xi/112/74A; & Hinton for NMR Lon. to JMR Ams. 16 & 23 September 1814, RAL xi/82/7/4/34 & 36, respectively.

118. See RAL xi/38/55B; RAL xi/112/71, 72, 74A & 75B; & RAL xi/82/7/3/49, 52–57, passim.

119. See MD Ams. to NMR Lon. 27 September & 7 October 1814, RAL xi/112/ 72 & NMR Lon. to JMR Ams. 14 October 1814, RAL xi/82/7/4/42.

120. Amburger et fils StP. to NMR Lon. 11 September 1814, RAL xi/112/2. For the Amburger family, see Erik Amburger, *Deutsche in Staat, Wirtschaft und Gesellschaft Russlands. Die Familie Amburger in St. Petersburg 1770–1920* (Wiesbaden: Otto Harrassowitz, 1986).

121. Lieven Lon. to V Lon. 16 August 1814, *VP* BLAddMss. 31,231, f. 123; Har Lon. to GH Lon. 26 August 1814, PROT 1/1415/No.13052; & Treasury Chambers. Lon. to H Lon. dated 5 & 6 September 1814, *HP* BLAddMss. 57372, ff. 23–24.

122. Burg Ams. to GH Lon. No. 148. 13 September 1814 (enclosures, Gervais Ams. to Burg Ams. 12 September & Burg Ams. to Gervais Ams. 13 September 1814), PROT 1/1419/No.14282. See Burg Ams. to GH Lon. 16 September 1814, No. 149, PROT 1/1419/No.14458.

123. JMR Ams. to NMR Lon. 5 & 6 September 1814, RAL xi/85/0.

124. JMR Ams. to NMR Lon. 5 & 6 September 1814, RAL xi/85/0. See NMR Lon. to JMR Ams. 13 September 1814, RAL xi/82/7/4/32.

125. JMR Ams. to NMR Lon. 6 September 1814, RAL xi/85/0.

126. SMR Ams. to NMR Lon. 9 September 1814, RAL xi/109/1/1/19, Tape 172/ Letter 1.

127. NMR Lon. to H Lon. 21 September 1814, PROT 1/1420/No. 14748; *HP* BLAddMss. 57379, ff. 1–2; & H Lon. to GH Lon. 10 October, PROT 1/1423/No. 15625.

128. NMR Lon. to H Lon. 21 September 1814, PROT 1/1420/No. 14748; *HP* BLAddMss. 57379, ff. 1–2; & H Lon. to GH Lon. 10 October 1814, PROT 1/1423/ No. 15625.

129. SMR Ams. to NMR & JMR Lon. 20 September 1814, RAL xi/109/1/2/19, Tape 172/Letter 3.

130. H Lon. to NMR & V Lon. 23 September 1814, RAL xi/38/59B.

131. Burg Ams. to GH Lon. No.153. 30 September 1814, PROT 1/1421–1422/No. 15199, PROT 1/1423/No. 15625 (& encl: H Lon. to GH Lon. 10 October 1814; NMR Lon. to H Lon. 5 October 1814; & "Schedule of Bills."); JMR Ams. to NMR Lon. 30 September 1814, RAL xi/87/0A; NMR Lon. to JMR Ams. 4, 11 & 14 October 1814, RAL xi/82/7/4/39, 41–42, respectively; H Lon. to NMR Lon.11 October 1814, RAL xi/38/59; & MD Ams. to NMR Lon.14 October 1814, RAL xi/112/72.

132. NMR Lon. to H Lon. 11 May 1815, RAL xi/38/59A (xi/52/30).

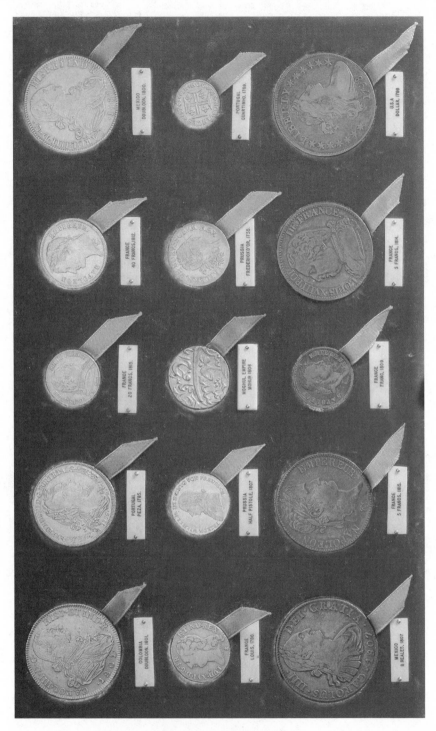

Commemorative case of coins labeled "An Account of Bullion specie furnished by Mr N M Rothschild to J C Herries Esq. Commissary in Chief April–October 1815," n.d. Reproduced with the permission of The Rothschild Archive.

Herries, the Rothschilds, and the Royal Mint

> I have given in my proposals relative to the manner of
> Payment of the new Subsidies to Russia Austria & Prussia,
> which appear to have met with a very favourable reception
> on the part of this Gov't . . . and should a war Commence
> I have no doubt but I shall get the Commission to pay
> the whole of the subsidies to the abovementioned three
> powers. I shall then have occasion to draw on you and
> other places, probably a million Stlg on each place.
>
> —NATHAN ROTHSCHILD *to*
> JAMES ROTHSCHILD. *7 April 1815.*[1]

> I have written to you a thousand times that we do our
> business by *miracles* or *luck* . . . we get nothing written
> down clearly. . . . There is unfortunately no order in
> this important business. . . . I don't know what you
> mean . . . I don't know what account is meant . . . or
> what you want. If no clear and detailed letters are written,
> then it is impossible to manage such important business
> as this. . . . It causes *a great deal of grief,* so that one
> *really* curses.
>
> —SALOMON ROTHSCHILD *to*
> NATHAN ROTHSCHILD. *4 October 1815.*[2]

Great Britain's war against France formally ended on 30 May 1814, when it signed the Treaty of Paris. Subsequently it began paying the subsidies it had promised to those powers that had contributed to Napoleon's defeat. In this, and in making payments to British military forces on the Continent under Wellington's command, the Rothschilds became indispensable to the British government in transacting, collecting, and delivering huge sums of monies across frontiers.

It took a long time before Great Britain could liquidate its subsidy obligations to Portugal and Spain because the three powers could not agree on the value of the matériel Britain had delivered to those countries during the war. This "battle of the bookkeepers" was not resolved until 1822.[3] In the meantime, in October 1814, the Portuguese and Spanish governments demanded more subsidy payments, and Herries asked the Rothschilds to purchase £250,000 in Spanish dollars, doubloons, and bills of exchange on Cadiz, Lisbon, Madrid, and Oporto. He ordered the HMS Daphne to sail to Hellevoetsluis and Dunkerque to receive the money destined for Commissary General John Murray in Lisbon.[4] By early November, James and Salomon reported that they had executed these orders.[5]

However, no sooner had this operation been completed than Murray wrote again for much more money and, once again, Herries turned to the Rothschilds to expedite the payment.[6] But this time Herries recognized that ad hoc responses could not meet the ongoing challenges from the Peninsula and, in December, after discussing the situation with Nathan, he formulated a long-term strategy. He requested that Nathan purchase in Amsterdam, Hamburg, and Paris the equivalent of 445,000 Spanish dollars per month, in Spanish dollars, doubloons (at 16 dollars per doubloon) and bills on Bilbao, Cadiz, Gibraltar, Lisbon, Madrid, and Oporto. Within the limits Herries stipulated on exchange rates, the cost of transport and commission, the British government would expend about £113,000 per month. Because of the precarious winter weather conditions in the North Sea, Herries wanted the specie transported overland to Dunkerque. To save on the cost of transport, he preferred the purchase of doubloons over dollars and bills of exchange over specie. As in previous operations, British ships of war would collect and convey the specie and bills to Lisbon.[7]

In October 1814, Herries deposited with Carl Rothschild two million Prussian thalers to pay the subsidies Great Britain owed Prussia in five installments.[8] He also instructed Salomon to redeem the one-month Russian bills of credit, which Hope & Co. had held since June 1814. The British government owed Hope & Co. nearly 700,000 Prussian thalers or its equivalent in Spanish dollars[9] but Hope & Co. wanted to be paid in Dutch guilders.[10] However, in January 1815, when Salomon offered to pay 1,175,527 Dutch guilders to Pierre César Labouchère of Hope & Co.,[11] Labouchère complained about the unfavorable exchange rate that Rothschild offered him.[12]

Perturbed, Salomon wrote Nathan that Labouchère was "a great *hater of the Jews*" and did "not favour a *Jew* with business and wanted to use every mean trick in the book, but it has not helped him."[13] Labouchère grudgingly accepted the money and protested to the Russian finance minister but there was no hope that he would prevail.[14] At that time, Russia, Great Britain, and Holland were negotiating the settlement of Russia's debt to Holland in return for Russia's acceptance of the union of Belgium and Holland. In the end, Hope & Co. benefited from this agreement because Russia subsequently resumed payment of the principal and interest on its outstanding loans to Dutch bondholders.[15]

In early February 1815, Herries discovered that he needed much more money to liquidate Great Britain's subsidy obligations and maintain its military presence abroad. He, therefore, proposed to Nicholas Vansittart, the chancellor of Exchequer, that the British government raise a significant sum of money on the Continent. He calculated that, given the current price of gold in France, Holland, and Germany, when coupled with the exchange rate, the British government could make (after deducting 1½ percent for expenses) from 12 to 13 percent profit by selling English gold in those countries and by buying bills of exchange on London. Herries wrote: "the Cheapest mode & the most favorable for the Exchanges, appears to be that of taking from the Bank the Sum required in Guineas"—from £400,000 to £500,000—and "under *our engagement* to replace it in the same Coin within six or Eight Months."[16]

Herries's decision could not have been more timely. At the end of February, Napoleon escaped from Elba and landed in the south of France on 1 March. He took Paris on 20 March, the day after King Louis XVIII fled to Ghent, where he was effectively cut off from the French mint.[17]

These events caused the market price of foreign gold in London to increase significantly: Portugal gold coins rose from £4. 6s. 6d. per ounce in early January to £4. 9s. in late February. On 21 March, the price spiked to £4. 14s. and on 31 March to £5. 7s. The market price of Spanish dollars also increased. In February through the first half of March, Spanish dollars sold at 5 shillings 10 pence per ounce; on 23 March, the price rose to 6 shillings 3 pence per ounce, and on 31 March to 6 shillings 9 pence per ounce. During the same period, the exchange rates at Hamburg and Paris on London fell about 11 and nearly 15 percent, respectively.[18]

The Duke of Wellington learned of Napoleon's escape in Vienna, where he had replaced Viscount Castlereagh at the Congress.[19] The allied powers appointed Wellington to command the combined forces in Flanders and, on 25 March, they renewed the essential provisions of the Treaty of Chaumont (March 1814). Thus, Austria, Great Britain, Prussia, and Russia each agreed to field 150,000 troops. Because there were only about 50,000 British and Hanoverian troops in Flanders, Great Britain was permitted to hire another 100,000.[20]

Upon his arrival at headquarters in Brussels on 4 April,[21] Wellington immediately complained to Bathurst, the secretary-at-war: "It appears to me that you have not taken in England a clear view of your situation, that you do not think war certain, and that a great effort must be made. . . . how we are to make out 150,000 men, or even the 60,000 of the defensive part of the treaty of Chaumont, appears not to have been considered. . . . Without these equipments, military operations are out of the question."[22]

The war clouds hovering over Europe could not have provided a better business climate for Nathan and his brothers. One striking feature of the success the Rothschilds enjoyed during the past several years was their ability to collect and move money across frontiers in a timely fashion. The threat of a resumption of a war against Napoleon meant that Great Britain and its allies would require once again enormous amounts of money to pay for it. And once again, the skills and the energies of the Rothschilds would be mobilized. Leading this effort, of course, would be Nathan but he would do this within a more formal context. On 21 March 1815, the five Rothschild brothers for the first time entered into a written partnership comprising Nathan's firm in London, the firm in Paris headed by Salomon and James, and Mayer Amschel Rothschild & Sons in Frankfurt. The *Articles of Agreement* spelled out the value of each brother's share of the capital and testified to Nathan's dominant position in the partnership: Amschel and Salomon each with £18,000; Carl and James each with £5,000; and Nathan with £90,000.[23]

At first, Nathan's reaction to the "unpleasant News" about Napoleon's return was subdued and woven into a routine business letter in which he wrote about the "stagnation" in bill transactions at the Exchange.[24] But as soon as Herries took decisive action, so did he. On 17 March, Herries informed the Treasury that he had authorized the collection of £500,000 in gold specie in Paris or Frankfurt for the military chest in Belgium.[25] That same day, Nathan wrote James in Hamburg requesting that he not only continue buying Spanish dollars to send Murray in Lisbon but also Prussian, French, and Dutch gold specie.[26] He also wanted James to send him between £50,000 and £100,000 of bar silver for the East India Company, presumably to pay for gold imports.[27] He sent Carl, who was then in Amsterdam, about £215,000 in Portuguese specie, bars of gold, and remittances for the British government account G.[28] He wrote again to James that "my order is to purchase plenty of Gold for the Armies, I beg you will not permit any to Slip through your fingers . . . if you can make yourself an accommodation for 100 or 150,000£ & get gold for it; it can not fail proving highly advantageous to send to the army but first always keep our Brother Amschel supplied."[29]

In the first week of April, Herries and Nathan devised a plan to subsidize Austria, Prussia, and Russia.[30] This prompted Nathan to write excitedly to his brothers: "should a war Commence I have no doubt but I shall get the Commission to pay the whole of the subsidies to the abovementioned three powers;" "The amount of Gold and Silver that I should be able to procure here is immense;" "there is plenty of Gold to be got here;" "[t]he present price of Gold brings very large sums to Market. . . . indeed there is more in the Market than I can readily find money to purchase," however, "our resources here are like Lions, equal if not superior to all & every demand." But, he added: "we must not however reckon our chickens before they are hatched."[31]

Yet that was exactly what he did. Nathan purchased tens of thousands of ounces of gold on the London,[32] Cadiz,[33] and Rio de Janeiro markets[34] and prepared to send James and Carl £150,000 in foreign gold coin, 300,000 Spanish dollars, nearly £200,000 in good bills of exchange and "abt 100,000 Guinea Gold."[35] Deputy Commissary General Anderson facilitated most of Nathan's transactions at the Royal Mint and, in return for the delivery of bullion and specie, Anderson gave him an equivalent value in English-minted George d'Or and Louis d'Or coins. In April, Nathan's transactions at the Royal Mint amounted to almost £355,000.[36]

Vansittart approved and forwarded the subsidy plan formulated by Herries and Nathan to Lord Harrowby, the Lord President of the Council, who the Cabinet had sent to Brussels with William Wellesley-Pole (Master of the Mint, member of the Cabinet, and Wellington's brother) to determine the duke's military and financial needs.[37] In his letter of 7 April to Harrowby, Vansittart complimented both Herries and the Rothschilds: "I enclose a plan of Herries's, who, with his Jew friends, will be our principal instruments in the management, & who have, indeed done wonders for us."[38] He also included a valuable piece of information about Herries's subsidy plan—"in substance, I should think it likely to be carried into effect with advantage, *especially if we obtain leave to coin Louis d'Ors at the mint.*"[39]

Vansittart's wish became a reality—and much sooner than scholars have hitherto believed. This is so because recently discovered sources reveal that the activities of both Herries and Nathan contradict the received official version on the subject. According to the latter, soon after King Louis XVIII fled Paris to Ghent and was deprived of access to the French mint, the British government sought and received his permission to strike Louis d'Or 20 franc pieces at the Royal Mint, provided their fineness and weight conformed to French mint standards. The British government intended to use the Louis d'Or to support Wellington's army in France. Wellesley-Pole informed the House of Commons that "the object of coining Louis d'Or was for the convenience of transmitting for the pay of the army when it first entered France a coin which would pass current in that country."[40] Herries affirmed this intention "for the facility of paying the British Troops under His Grace the Duke of Wellington."[41]

There is *prima facie* evidence that officially documents the British-coining of Louis d'Or. On 10 May, an Order in Council instructed the Royal Mint to coin into Louis d'Or all such gold delivered to the Mint for that purpose by the commissary-in-chief. On 11 May, Herries requested the preparation of the dies; on 23 May, Herries delivered the first gold ingots to the Royal Mint; and, on 27 May, discussions took place on the dies or trial pieces. On 7 June, the first British-struck Louis d'Or was delivered to the commissary-in-chief and, in July, the coins were in circulation in Paris. However, the French government subsequently claimed that the Royal Mint's coinage was illegal and, by year's end, they were denied circulation in France and also in The Netherlands.[42]

There are problems with this "official" narrative. When, at the end of the year, the French government challenged the "legality" of the British-coined Louis d'Or, Vansittart offered his recollection as to how he had gained the authority to strike the coins: "I accordingly applied to Comte de la Chatre [*sic*] who readily saw the Utility of the Plan and accordingly signified the Consent of H. M. C. M. . . . We have therefore a right to consider this Coinage as executed under the Special Authority of the French King, as much so as if he had directed a Coinage at Ghent under his own immediate Inspection." However, he conceded that "It may be . . . the Comte de la Chatre acted probably on his own judgement, and without Instructions."[43]

Vansittart also remarked that "The Coinage commenced in the Middle of May."[44] By this, he presumably meant the issuance of the Order in Council on 10 May. But he failed to mention that he and Herries had much earlier discussed their intention to have French coins struck at the Royal Mint, that is, prior to 10 May. On 21 February, Herries had ordered the Mint to conduct experiments "to ascertain the average Weight of old and new French Silver Coins," which he wrote would be "received & accounted for" abroad.[45] On 29 March, he informed Vansittart that he had "given directions to the Die Maker at the Mint to prepare *secretly* a Die for striking Louis d'or, according to the recent Coinage in France; *not doubting but that you will readily obtain the Kings permission to strike this Coin*; & conceiving that it may be very useful to avail ourselves of it in the course of the Campaign." He added: "If Lord Liverpool & yourself should not approve of this, there will be no harm done by the new preparation of the Die."[46]

There is no record that these two gentlemen disapproved of Herries's action. Given the imminent threat that Napoleon's return to Paris posed to Great Britain's security, the proactive Herries did not wait for an Order in Council and acted once again in the name of national security. In essence, this was not different from his previous circumvention, in arrangement with the Bank of England, of the law prohibiting the exportation of English guineas to Wellington. Although the extant sources may not be a perfect record of all that transpired in this matter, it is clear that Herries intended a deception by writing one thing in his private letters and another thing in his pro-forma official letters. On 29 March, he wrote privately to Thomas Wyon, Jr., the die maker at the Royal Mint: "I have to request that you will immediately prepare a die for striking *Louis* according to the last French Coinage: you will receive in the course of the Evening six Specimens." Wyon was to report to him "as soon as possible" and was to consider this "*as quite Secret.*"[47] On 5 May, Herries wrote again to Wyon urging him "lose no time in Completing the *Dies* for the French Louis, and in preparing it for coinage,"[48] even though many such coins had already been delivered to Nathan Rothschild. Finally on 11 May, the day after the Order in Council was issued, as if he had never before addressed this subject, Herries wrote to he master of the Mint: "I have now the honor of requesting that you will issue authority to the Officers of the Mint to prepare the necessary dies in Communication with me for this purpose, and further to proceed in the Coinage of Louis d'Or with such Gold as I may deliver to them for that object."[49]

Nathan Rothschild's correspondence overwhelmingly confirms that the Royal Mint had struck and delivered Louis d'Or to him prior to the issuance of the Order in Council on 10 May. On 7 April, Nathan wrote James: "Wednesday or Thursday next I shall have the satisfaction to forward to our

Brother Charles abt 30000 Louis dors." Nathan was not mistaken about the coins he intended to send his brother because he crossed out "& 20000 five dollar pieces" and wrote in its place "Louis dors."[50] On 11 April, he twice mentioned to James that Louis d'Or were "in work" (that is, being struck at the Royal Mint): the first time, in the body of the letter—"I expect by next week to have £300,000 *Louis Dors in work*"—and, the second, in a post script to that letter—"Next Friday I shall send you some Louis Dor's, which will *Come out of the Mint, being the first parcel.*"[51] He also informed Carl that day that he had sent him 756 Louis d'Or.[52] The following week, he wrote to Salomon that he had sent him a box of gold containing 1,828 Louis d'Or.[53] On 25 April, he wrote to Carl: "There is now about *400,000 Louis D'ors in the Work at the Mint, Bullion for the whole of which I have furnished* and have engaged with Mr Drummond to deliver a sufficient quantity by the 15th May to make up that *already delivered One Million Sterling*, and do not doubt in the least but I shall be able to fulfil my engagement. I shall forward in a short time for Act of Frankfort *25,000 Louis* & Naps which you will appropriate as before."[54] On 28 April, Carl wrote Nathan: "*Do you send the Louis d'or which are in the Mint* direct to Ostend to Mr Dunmore or by my medium?"[55]

By the end of June, the Royal Mint had struck 500,000 Louis d'Or, which Nathan promptly shipped to his brothers to be deposited into Wellington's military chest in Brussels. By the end of October, a total of 871,581 pieces had been struck, equivalent in value to about £691,000.[56] Soon after the French government protested their continued circulation, Herries arranged through the Rothschilds to replace the English-minted Louis d'Or on deposit in the military chest with French-minted Louis d'Or.[57]

Herries also ordered the Royal Mint to strike and deliver every week no fewer than 85,000 George d'Or (Hanoverian five-thaler pieces).[58] Nathan sent large quantities of them to James in Hamburg, who was to exchange them one for one for Friedrich d'Or to pay Prussia.[59] By 24 May, 38 percent of the Mint's entire production of George d'Or since 14 September 1813, had been struck with a value of about £433,000.[60] In addition, Nathan transacted for Herries in April at least one million ounces of Spanish dollars for delivery mostly to Malta and the East India Company.[61]

Prime Minister Liverpool was pleased with the report that Lord Harrowby and William Wellesley-Pole submitted on their meeting with Wellington. On 14 April, Liverpool wrote Wellington that he was sending Herries to discuss with him a plan for subsidizing the allied powers and the German states: "I can assure you that I know no person in this country more generally well informed on the subject of our finances and resources and more likely therefore to be able to afford you assistance on the important arrangements which you will have to conclude both with respect to the means of supplying the British army in the ensuing campaign and likewise with regard to the subsidiary engagements to be made with our allies."[62]

That same day, Nathan met with Herries at his residence in 21 Cadogan Place and they crafted a memorandum of understanding. First, once the subsidy operation commenced, Herries guaranteed that Nathan would be paid for all the remittances "on the day preceding the Post day on which he may have to pay for them himself"; second, Nathan would "be put in funds to meet any draft on him for the Public account," as soon as the draft was delivered to the office of commissary-in-chief; third, Nathan would assume the risk on bills transacted "to the extent of £3,000 upon each respectable House" but "beyond that amount the risk to be on account of Government"; and, finally, Herries estimated that Nathan would need "about 250,000, or perhaps 300,000 per Week" to execute his mission.[63]

Nathan wrote his brothers that evening of what promised to be their biggest operation. He instructed Salomon to depart Amsterdam immediately for Brussels to consult with Wellington and Herries "relative to the new Subsidy for Aust Russ & Prussia."[64]

> I have received orders to provide in Bills & Gold one million Stg. per month on account of new Subsidies to Austria Prussia & Russia, it will be necessary for me to remit upon an average £100/m Stg. in Bills every post night, also to purchase £100/m Stg. in Gold & Silver, weekly which will likewise be forwarded from here to the Continent. . . . this is a great undertaking but it will not be attended with any risk on our part as Government guarantees the whole. . . .
>
> I have no doubt whatever but I shall be able to accomplish this order, having received the fullest assurances from Govt that every assistance shall be rendered on their part to facilitate the completion of my engagements; with such a Back you must well know that almost anything may be done.[65]

When reports reached London that Napoleon was marching his troops to the frontier, Herries and Nathan accelerated their timetable for making payments to Wellington and the allied powers.[66] After Wellington wrote on 3 May, that Napoleon was "quitting Paris . . . to attack us,"[67] Castlereagh called on the Treasury to send large sums of money to Austria.[68] Consequently, without waiting for Great Britain to sign subsidy conventions, Herries ordered the Rothschilds to deliver bills of exchange and British-minted Hanoverian George d'Or to Austria and £37,000 to Württemberg.[69]

On 17 May, Great Britain signed a subsidy convention whereby it promised to pay £5,000,000 to the allied powers for their services to 1 April 1816. Austria, Prussia, and Russia would receive equal shares, in monthly installments, through the month when a definitive treaty of peace would be signed with France. In addition, Austria and Prussia would receive the equivalent of two months of subsidy and Russia four months as "return money" for their troops. Parliament later added millions in foreign aid and also budgeted money to pay for the hiring of 100,000 men from German states.[70]

Once again, Great Britain would pay dearly to defeat Napoleon. And, once again, the Rothschilds would become indispensable to the British government, and become even richer because of it. Herries and the Rothschilds were charged with dispensing specie and bills worth millions of English pounds sterling to more than two dozen large and small states and principalities. The Rothschilds focused on buying, collecting, shipping, and delivering bullion and specie, tasks they were very good at executing. In May, Nathan delivered to Anderson at the Royal Mint bullion and specie valued at £526,000—nearly 50 percent more than he had in April—and in June he delivered another £321,000, for which he received an equivalent amount in Louis d'Or and George d'Or coins to be shipped to his brothers on the Continent.[71] The Rothschilds also transacted significant amounts of Spanish dollars in London and on the Continent for the British government account. When the Bank of England could not supply the East India Company with Spanish dollars to be remitted to China, Herries stepped in and asked Nathan to purchase nearly £100,000 in Spanish dollars.[72] The demand on the British government for money was so great that Herries could not meet his obligations with what he had on hand.[73] He therefore authorized Nathan to raise one million pounds sterling through Messrs. Braunsberg & Co. in Amsterdam.[74]

On 18 June 1815, the armies of Wellington and Napoleon engaged at Waterloo, a crucial event that has not only punctuated European history but also has been insinuated into the mythic history of the Rothschilds. Rory Muir recounted the battle in his *Britain and the Defeat of Napoleon* and concluded that "Contemporary accounts of the battle certainly make confusing reading, and it was many years before the now familiar story . . . emerged."

Wellington, near exhaustion, did not complete his report of the battle until the following day and it reached Cabinet members at dinner in London late in the evening of 21 June.[75]

Supposedly this was not the first report on Waterloo to reach London. "A confused Dutch report of a British victory was received by the government on the morning of the 21st through Nathan Rothschild," wrote Neville Thompson in his book on Earl Bathurst.[76] This report—in the Dutch language or emanating from The Netherlands?—has not survived. Muir commented on this matter: "According to the well-known story, the first reports of the great victory to reach London were received by Nathan Rothschild on 20 June. He tried to inform the ministers and is said to have taken advantage of his knowledge on the Stock Exchange, though the size of his profit has always been greatly exaggerated."[77] Muir cautioned his readers: "how slight is the evidence."[78]

Indeed, it has always been that way. Lucien Wolf, a journalist and publicist, who is known for his publications about the Rothschilds, searched in vain for evidence to corroborate Nathan's involvement in the story of the Dutch report and Waterloo. The Public Record Office had been collecting documents for him containing references to Nathan Rothschild and on 30 May 1923 he wrote to a member of the staff about this matter:

> …there are very few letters about the date of Waterloo and I should like the bundles of that period—say the second and third weeks of June, 1815—to be closely scrutinised. There is overwhelming evidence that either Rothschild himself or someone on his behalf took the first news of the victory to the Treasury either late in the evening of the 19th June or on the morning of the 20th. There ought to be something about this in the Treasury papers. I am surprised there is nothing in the Vansittart papers.[79]

Recently, Niall Ferguson, in *The House of Rothschild*, reviewed the story of the Dutch report and Waterloo: "This idea that Nathan profited from the dramatic events of 1815 is central to Rothschild mythology: it has been repeatedly claimed that, by obtaining the first news of Napoleon's defeat at Waterloo—before even the government itself—Nathan was able to make a huge sum of money on the Stock Exchange."[80] According to Ferguson, the Dutch report was "a newspaper version of the fifth and conclusive extraordinary bulletin—issued in Brussels at midnight on June 18—via Dunkirk and Deal to reach New Court on the night of the 19th."[81] But, he added: "The bulletins Nathan received have not been preserved, though a letter confirming the news from a Dutch source based just six miles from the battlefield survives."[82] Unfortunately, Ferguson not only incorrectly cited the file where this letter was supposed to be found but also the letter, in fact, cannot be found.[83] Ferguson further stated that the British government could not believe this report or even a second one arriving from Ghent.[84] Moreover, Ferguson followed Lord Rothschild's account,[85] that, if the Rothschilds purchased government stock immediately after the Waterloo battle, they could not have profited by much more than £10,000: "Indeed, it is possible that a series of miscalculations by the brothers led to losses rather than profits in the critical period before and after Waterloo. On this occasion, it seems, reality is diametrically opposite to myth."[86]

There are no verifiable extant contemporary sources to support the story that Nathan received a Dutch report of the victory and/or that he was the first to communicate it to the British government. In the extant Rothschild archival correspondence there are only rare mentions of Napoleon and Waterloo. If there was a government official with whom Nathan would have first shared such an important report, it most certainly would have been Herries, a member of the Cabinet and someone he met with almost every day. But there is not a trace of such a report in Herries's extant archival correspondence and papers or in Liverpool's or Vansittart's papers that would lend credence to this story.

There also is not a shred of evidence in Nathan's extant correspondence that he enriched himself from information about Wellington's Waterloo victory. Nor is there any contemporary extant evidence that Nathan lost a great deal of money because of Waterloo.[87] There is no indication that he was in the market for a significant number of government securities during the period under discussion. The first mention of investing in securities of any kind is on 30 June, when Nathan asked Carl: "If you can purchase me Bank Stock in Amst." for about £4000.[88] In August, he acknowledged this transaction: "The Bank Stock you purchased in Amsterdam had [sic] been transferred at the Bank into my name, and if you can purchase stock so as to secure a low exchange I would advise you doing it with what spare money you may have."[89] Again, writing to Carl about specific stock purchases and transfers: "Your Power for the navy Stock has been lodged in the Bank & I have not yet received their answer. You hand me Powers of Attorney for the transfer of . . ."—securities in 3 percent Consols, 3½% South Sea Co. and Bank Stock for a total investment of merely £1,895. "Stocks here are going down & I would not advise you to continue purchasing just now as they will be still lower: with what you have hitherto bought I am perfectly satisfied."[90] There is no hint that the Rothschilds had made a killing in government securities.

Waterloo "was certainly a stunning blow," as Thompson commented but, from his reading of Earl Bathurst's letters, he also added that "no one in Britain could be sure that Waterloo marked the end for Napoleon."[91] And, why should anyone, including Nathan Rothschild, have thought otherwise, given that only four months earlier they were confident that they were safe from his territorial ambitions. Allied forces continued to cross into France and Wellington vowed to continue fighting until King Louis XVIII was back on his throne. On 7 July, British and Prussian troops entered Paris and Louis XVIII soon followed, while Napoleon journeyed into exile on St. Helena in the South Atlantic.[92]

Although the fighting had come to an end, a peace settlement was five months away. Until then, Herries was obliged to pay subsidies to Great Britain's allies and to supply Wellington's military chest. In June, he acknowledged that he did not have enough money to do both and also that he did not have the right specie in the right places. He therefore instructed Dunmore to exchange whatever Hanoverian and Prussian gold coins there were in the military chest for French coins, preferably in silver, which the Rothschilds would deliver to him—at first, £20,000 to £30,000 per week but later £100,000 per week.[93] But this shift in money supply could not solve the problem facing Herries, who desperately needed to generate new funds, and in July he went to Frankfurt and commissioned M A Rothschild & Sons to raise £2.61 million against Treasury bills: £1,000,000 in Paris, £500,000 in Hamburg, £510,000 in Amsterdam, and £600,000 in Frankfurt.[94]

Nathan continued purchasing and delivering huge quantities of gold specie and bullion to the Royal Mint—from April to mid-September, his total came to more than £1.76 million—in exchange for English-minted Louis d'Or and George d'Or.[95] He shipped these gold coins and also English guineas—"furnished by Gov't"[96]—to his brothers to supply the military chest and to pay the British subsidies.[97] Moreover, from late August to mid-September, Nathan purchased and delivered 1.2 million ounces of Spanish dollars—£338,000—to the Royal Mint for Herries's account,[98] and purchased £100,000 in Spanish dollars for Gervais for the Russian government.[99] Salomon appreciated this: "A ½ penny commission always gives 3,000 gulden on business like that, *with God's help*."[100]

But not every transaction worked out just the way the Rothschilds wished. At the end of June, James experienced a setback in his negotiation with the Prussian court, when he sought to liquidate two months of subsidy amounting to £277,777 that Britain owed Prussia. During two days of heated discussions, the Prussian government was adamant in protesting what it considered the high and unfair rate of exchange that James had stipulated and refused to grant him the 1 percent commission he had requested. Both sides reluctantly signed the agreement but the Prussian court vowed to press the British government to ameliorate the rate of exchange.[101]

In September, the situation at the Prussian court changed and James opined that "the Prussians are getting clever and not least because they are no longer pressured by a shortage of money. They don't want to sell. We made them an offer . . . and they weren't interested. We should have done a little work for it. . . . What can one do? We must be patient."[102] Later that month, Salomon reported that an agreement had been forged to liquidate a one-month subsidy valued at £138,888 and the Rothschilds would receive a commission of 1 percent. Writing to Nathan, he speculated on the profit the Rothschilds would make: "There will be 2% profit on the ducats *with God's help* so that with the commission and the *profit* on the ducats there will still be something left, *God willing* . . . a few thousand carolines *profit*, not including your commission in London."[103]

Nathan also suffered setbacks. One caused him public embarrassment. In February and March 1815, English Customs arrested and fined Nathan £248 for illegally possessing goods and semiprecious stones and for his attempt to bribe a Customs officer. Nathan petitioned the Treasury to stay the prosecution and provided a complicated explanation for what had transpired. He claimed that the arresting Customs officer had actually seized the goods from his premises two and one half years earlier and that the goods had originally been a gift to one of Hannah's sisters from her husband (both unnamed), who had gone bankrupt, and who was under Nathan's protection until his brother-in-law's affairs were settled. Because the goods were "so trifling" his sister-in-law "did not think it worth the trouble to apply about it." The Treasury perfunctorily forwarded Nathan's petition to Customs but Customs informed the Treasury that it intended to proceed with the prosecution unless the Treasury ordered it to end. It is not known how this affair was resolved because no additional documents have been found.[104]

No one who knew Nathan Rothschild had ever denied that he was man devoid of emotion, the kind that was both volatile and embarrassing to encounter. It was, indeed, a rare moment when he displayed his feelings in a way that challenged this stereotype. In July, the news of the death of his sister, Julie Beyfus, was just such a time. Writing to his brothers, he confessed: "I feel my spirits very depressed indeed and by no means able to attend to business as I could wish. The melancholy communication of the death of my Sister has entirely unhinged my mind."[105]

Nathan sustained yet another disappointment when his vision of establishing a permanent Rothschild merchant-banking enterprise in The Netherlands was clouded by his brothers' lack of enthusiasm for Amsterdam and the Dutch. While Nathan considered Hamburg a wartime expedient operation and agreed to Mayer Davidson's request to leave that city and return to London to marry Hannah's sister, Jessy Cohen,[106] he regarded Amsterdam still a leading financial and commercial entrepôt where he had built a network since 1809. However, none of his brothers wanted to reside in Amsterdam because there was something about the Dutch people and The Netherlands that did not appeal to them. Salomon never had a kind word for either: "You have no idea how sick and tired I am of Holland," he wrote Nathan. He could not reside in Amsterdam because the dampness caused his painful rheumatism to flare up. He complained that there were no "distractions here of any kind. You don't know the Dutch—there is nothing except business. They don't exchange a word and don't visit anyone—deadly dull people."[107] Since Amschel would not leave Frankfurt and Carl said he did not care for the Dutch and that Amsterdam made him melancholy,[108] Salomon's solution was to have James reside in Amsterdam, even though he did not like the place any more than his older brothers. "Now, dearest Nathan, this is between you and me. . . . leave James there because we will need him as the mid point between London . . . Paris and Frankfurt. . . . One has to be where business dictates."[109] Salomon wanted desperately to return to his family in Frankfurt and attend his son's *Bar Mitzvah*—"I have hardly spent three weeks at home in the last three years."[110] "God willing, it will be Adieu, Adieu, Adieu Napoleon. They sing a song like that here. Adieu Holland!"[111]

Nathan was at this time not prepared to give up on Amsterdam just because his brothers found it temperamentally unsuitable. "With respect to what you mention about giving up the Concern in Holland owing to the very great expence attending it," he wrote Carl candidly, "I am of a very different opinion and cannot by any means consent to it, but if you are desirous of leaving that quarter, I shall then (provided you actually do leave) be under the necessity of sending out two persons from here, as it is of consequence to have some one on the spot."[112]

Nathan's bluff did not work. But sound economic reasons most likely contributed to Nathan's decision not to establish a merchant bank in Amsterdam, although the Rothschild correspondence is silent on this matter. Dr. Joost Jonker, an authority on Dutch international trading companies and the Amsterdam money market, has suggested that "there was simply no niche" for the Rothschilds in Amsterdam.

As a mature market, the city had a range of firms like Braunsberg, Crommelin or Hope & Co., engaged in the same services as the Rothschilds and of similar capital means. Competing with them head on in the same market would have been expensive without offering prospects of price cutting being rewarded by increased turnover, if only because during the wars Paris and London had assumed Amsterdam's pivotal functions in the bills and bullion trade for Western Europe. In this respect it is significant that the Jewish bankers who did establish themselves in Amsterdam during the 1810s and 1820s took about twenty years to come to prominence, suggesting a tough struggle which the Rothschilds, having arrived, would have found beneath them.[113]

In early September, Carl provoked Nathan in yet another way. Vansittart personally informed Nathan that Thomas Atkinson, the commissary general in Amsterdam, accused Carl of transacting forged Treasury bills. Atkinson recommended that Melvil & Co. take over the operation and certify that every Treasury bill transacted to be genuine. Nathan was furious with Carl:

I consider the cause to be entirely yours, and unless you adhere to the plans I propose, and comply with my wishes, I find that all my exertions to Keep the business will be fruitless. If I did not possess the greatest confidence with Government, I should never have been made acquainted with the contents of that letter, and thereby have been exposed to the calumny of these Gentlemen, and without doubt have lost the management of this business. It is easy to conceive their intention from the tenor of the letter, and it doubtless was intended to frustrate our operations, and get the concern out of our hands, which I still fear will be the case if you continue to follow your own opinion in preference to mine, I am at a loss to conjecture your reason for wishing to circulate these Bills without your endorsement. . . . If you object still to signing them (which I hope will not be the case) I will endeavour to raise the exchange here and remit you £400/m or £500/m Stg and take the whole of the Treasury Bills on my own account, then you certainly cannot for a moment hesitate signing them. I must impress upon your mind that Mr. Vansittart informed me of the Contents of Comy Atkinsons letter in confidence, therefore you must be careful that not a word is mentioned on this subject.[114]

Neither James or Salomon would defend Carl. "Our brother Carl has failed abysmally with the Treasury bills," James wrote Nathan. "What is there to do? It has happened. He is no merchant and has no courage."[115] While Salomon would later write that Carl was "a little *feeble minded*,"[116] at this time he wanted to calm Nathan: "Our Kalman has really made a big mistake, a howling mistake. . . . But scolding him doesn't do any good. . . . It will only make him more foolish. The letter from you written in red ink made our hearts sink. . . . Herries is coming now and can help you."[117]

Herries rescued the reputation of the Rothschilds by replacing the eight "defective" Treasury bills with good ones.[118] However, he was disappointed that the Rothschilds were taking too long to market the £2.61 million in Treasury bills he had entrusted to them. The brothers defended themselves by claiming that not only did investors find the bills unattractive in price, discount, and commission[119] but also that Nathan's contradictory instructions caused delays in executing their sale. Carl complained to Salomon and James that "the letter I have from our brother Nathan is in Yiddish" and was "not very clearly [written] and in such things clarity is everything;"[120] and he wrote to Nathan: "Write to me clearly in English what I am to do and how I am to behave."[121] Salomon was more direct: "Now, my dear Nathan, your Bills operation with Herries is setting our heads spinning."[122]

What Carl and Salomon meant was that Nathan's letters in Judendeutsch were for the most part almost incomprehensible. They remain a challenge to learned translators.[123] Not only was his meaning unclear or confusing but his references to accounts were imprecise.[124] "[S]o help me God, I cannot quite see from your letter which plan you mean with Gervais," Salomon wrote Nathan, "what Herries['s] plan is and what it is he would like. Let us have a letter in English so that we can show the letter to Gervais, or get Davidson to write a letter in German."[125]

But it was more than just Nathan's difficulty in communicating Judendeutsch that caused problems. Despite his hiring more qualified staff to meet the demands of the British government, Nathan's management style had not changed over the years. The merchant bank N M Rothschild was in essence his personal fiefdom and he was subject only to the rules imposed on him by Herries and Vansittart with whom he acted in a civilized manner. But with his brothers and his staff, he was often imperious. Nathan could change his mind and his instruction from one moment to the next in the expectation that his staff and brothers would act accordingly and quickly. His brothers, unlike his staff in London, were however several days away by courier or post and they could not alter their course of action as swiftly as he would command.

At the end of October, Metternich of Austria and Hardenberg of Prussia told Salomon that they would depart Paris because the Second Treaty of Paris would soon be signed.[126] The treaty would automatically trigger another round of British subsidy payments to the allies and huge amounts of money in several currencies would have to be generated and exchanged quickly. Salomon expected to execute a multitude of arbitrage transactions: "we now have our work cut out," he wrote excitedly to Nathan, "from noon till night there is no time to be at home and one's head is so full that one no longer knows where one is."[127]

Moreover, Great Britain and the allied powers had determined that pursuant to the peace treaty, France would indemnify them for the war. The allies would also occupy key fortresses, secure the frontiers, and sustain the regime of Louis XVIII. The Rothschilds looked to profit from this financial settlement, which they invariably but incorrectly referred to as *contributions*—as if France were actually *contributing* their penalty payment—rather than *Pecuniary Indemnity*, the precise and formal term for the sum of money the allies would exact from France.

Given their long-standing relationship with Herries, the Rothschilds could expect to transact Great Britain's share of the French indemnity. Russia was their next best client and they depended on the favor of Commissary Gervais: "we will not do anything for Russia without Gervais. If Gervais tells me that we must, or should, make a *partnership*," Salomon wrote Nathan, "then we will do so. That is up to Gervais."[128] Indeed, it was and he told James: "I can do what I like with my contributions. . . . You can count on getting three quarters of it [*sic*]. Don't make any partnerships over Russia until I tell you to."[129] For this, the Rothschilds would pay him "a bribe of 2%,"[130] and Salomon asked Nathan to "Buy £5,000 capital stocks in your name for the Russian Minister and send me the account."[131]

It was questionable whether the Rothschilds would handle similar transactions for Prussia or Austria. "There is nothing doing with the Austrians," James wrote Nathan in late September, "They are collecting their own money." But at that time Austria was not aware of how complex that task would become.[132] It also appeared that Prussia wanted to deal with everyone and, according to Salomon, the only way the Rothschilds could transact its Pecuniary Indemnity would be in partnership with other merchant-banks because "Privy councillor Rother is not a good friend of ours and is no *bribe taker*."[133]

But Salomon persevered and found a good bribe-taking friend in Prussian State Councillor Jordan. Salomon asked Nathan to purchase about £1,100 in 3 percent Consols on behalf of Jordan: "he is number one in the Prussian ministry of finance [who] is also involved with Prussian financial operations [and] I should like to send this minister a *handsome bribe.*"[134] Salomon's "handsome" investment paid off handsomely. Mayer Amschel Rothschild & Sons was placed "at the top *in the partnership*" that would handle Prussia's share of the French indemnity. Salomon reported to Nathan that "we have now played the entire Prussian account into your hands and we would be very much obliged if you would attend to the affairs of Prussia because Prussia has promised us that if you manage this affair well for them, we will be given all the business of the Prussian court. . . . we have earned *approximately* £12,000 through them in 24 hours."[135]

On 20 November, the Second Treaty of Paris was signed and France lost all the territory it had acquired since 1790. To safeguard the monarchy and the new frontiers, the allies would garrison seventeen fortresses and maintain an army of occupation of 150,000 soldiers for five years.[136] France agreed to pay the allies a Pecuniary Indemnity of 700 million French francs and another 250 million French francs to cover the cost of the army of occupation.[137]

The administration of these funds was vested in the Special Service Allied Commission headquartered in Paris, about which, until now, little has been known.[138] Two archival sources that provide detailed information on the work of the commission are James Rothschild's letters from Paris, and the reports of James Drummond, Herries's associate, and the British representative on the commission. Drummond's job was to supervise and coordinate with Thomas Dunmore, the commissary in charge of the military chest, the receipt and distribution of French government bonds and warrants—*Bons du trésor Royal* and *Mandats*—in payment for Great Britain's share of the Pecuniary Indemnity (125 million French francs) and for the British army of occupation (30 million French francs). The *Bons du trésor Royal* and *Mandats* originated in Paris and in the *Départements*, respectively, and once deposited into the military chest they would be converted into specie or bills of exchange according to the instructions of the British government.[139]

To facilitate these transactions a banker was needed and, soon after his arrival in Paris at the end of December 1815,[140] Drummond authorized James, Salomon, and Carl to transact 1,750,000 francs of *Bons du trésor Royal.* Drummond spent a lot of time with James, who managed the Paris office after Salomon returned to Frankfurt; he visited James almost daily during James's recuperation after falling off his horse.[141] James considered Drummond a "very good friend" and appreciated his meticulous and deliberative business manner.[142] At the end of the month, Herries authorized the Rothschilds to sell 7 million francs of *Mandats* and requested that 4.5 million be remitted to England and 2.5 million be sent to Lisbon in bills on the City of Oporto.[143]

Other representatives on the commission followed a similar procedure, which encouraged competition among the several bankers who wanted their business. Negotiating commission rates on these transactions was complicated and costly. Gervais contracted the Rothschilds in partnership with another bank "to be the Agent for receiving & paying their Share of the Indemnity, to the Amount of 30 million of Francs" and paid them ½ percent for receiving and paying money at Paris; 2⅜ percent for receiving money in the *Départements* and paying it at Paris; and 2⅞ per cent for receiving the money at Paris and paying it in Germany in bills of exchange where they would receive an additional two months of interest.[144] The Rothschilds expected to make £12,000 in commission on this transaction.[145] Austria at first took charge of transporting its own indemnity collection from Paris to Colmar but found it too risky and subsequently employed the Rothschilds as its agent at 1¼ percent to handle those shipments and accept the risk.[146] Although the contract was not large, the Rothschilds hoped "thereby to be given the whole of the contribution for Austria."[147] The collection and distribution of the Prussian indemnities presented an additional challenge, as James lamented: "Today we shared out 13m Prussian mandates of which we received 3m but all these things give one a headache and require a lot of thought. The minister has instructed us to sell the mandates but there are eight partners and each one wants to be in charge of their own share, whereas the minister wants them all sold together."[148]

To simplify matters and provide the British government with a more predictable rate schedule, Nathan proposed in February 1816 that he "become the Banker either of the Military or the Indemnity Chest" but Herries rejected the idea.[149] However, in March Herries agreed that James should at his own expense and risk take "custody" of the monies or securities arising from the Pecuniary Indemnity or from payments destined to the army of occupation. James would "recover" and "negotiate" the *Bons du trésor Royal* and *Mandats* and every week convey those sums of money in gold and silver coins to the military chest under the command of the Duke of Wellington at Cambrai or elsewhere. In London, Nathan would credit those sums to the account of the commissary-in-chief. Although Drummond told James that "half a per cent was too much,"[150] that was the commission Nathan arranged for his brother to receive on the sum of monies or securities he would recover, transact, and convey. The initial sum Drummond entrusted to James was £200,000. Drummond estimated that during the remainder of the year another 15 million francs would be conveyed to James and in each subsequent year about 34 million francs.[151]

This initial success and the promise of more to come emboldened James to propose to the French government that he, in partnership with other banking houses, buy out France's entire Pecuniary Indemnity obligation. But Baring Brothers & Co. and Hope & Co. were now prepared to take a more active role in continental European finance and they submitted, in partnership with other banking houses, a competitive proposal. The bidding continued for several months with Baring and Hope eventually winning the final round. This defeat chastened the Rothschilds. They recognized that what had worked for them so successfully during wartime could not sustain their advancement during peacetime. In the future, if they hoped to win out against rival merchant-banking institutions, they would have to engage aggressively in areas of international finance that were still unfamiliar to them.[152]

In the meantime, the Rothschilds unexpectedly profited from transactions stemming from the £2.61 million in British Treasury bills, which Herries had in July 1815 contracted them to sell. In February, Nathan informed Herries that the Amsterdam banker B J de Jongh was in London to dispose of £360,000 of these bills to various mercantile houses. Herries and Nathan decided to keep these bills out of circulation and Herries authorized Nathan to accept and discount them, for which Herries issued Nathan Exchequer bills to execute the transaction.[153] Additional Treasury bill redemptions followed and, before he retired from the office of commissary-in-chief (disbanded in October 1816), Herries issued a total of £1,560,000 of Exchequer bills to Nathan, who facilitated their transactions through his brother-in-law's firm, Montefiore Brothers, Brokers.[154]

Nathan further enhanced his credibility with the Treasury, and ingratiated himself with the royal family, when he offered to accept only £148,800 to liquidate the £194,800 debt which the Prince of Wales and the dukes of York and Clarence owed to the Elector of Hesse-Kassel. Nathan was even willing to allow them to postpone payment to him for two or three years at 5 percent interest. The Prince of Wales quickly accepted the offer and directed that Nathan be paid £75,000 immediately along with a 3 percent commission—£4,464—on the full purchase price. The Prince of Wales also promised to pay Nathan £28,000 per annum until the balance of £73,800 (with interest) would be discharged.[155]

Nathan had not acted out of patriotism or pocket. The Rothschilds had negotiated an agreement with the elector whereby he would accept, in return for what the Prince of Wales and the dukes of York and Clarence owed him, 3 percent Consols. Despite their lament about paying the elector's officials significant bribes, the Rothschilds expected to receive a handsome profit from this transaction.[156]

The Rothschilds could also take pride in having provided extraordinary public service to the British government during the previous two years. While Herries took credit "that every step they have taken has been under [my] orders & responsibility," he wrote Liverpool and Vansittart prior to his departure from the commissary "that the greatest credit is due to these Gentlemen for their exertions which have been devoted entirely to the Public Service" and "the remuneration which they will receive for them (amounting upon the smallest scale to an ample fortune) will have been fairly & honorably earned."[157]

How much did the Rothschilds honorably and fairly earn in service to the public? Unfortunately, no definitive answer can be given because there is insufficient extant contemporary information to make a determination. There is no substantive evidence for any of Nathan's brothers or for the firm Mayer Amschel Rothschild & Sons. However, there are archival sources available that allow a minimum estimate to be made of Nathan's earnings based on the 2 percent commission he received on the transactions he handled for Herries from the beginning of January 1814, when he began supplying specie to Wellington, to the end of February 1816, when the Pecuniary Indemnity and army of occupation monies were being collected and transferred to the military chest. In 1814, Nathan delivered bullion to the Royal Mint and paid subsidies to Great Britain's allies amounting to £4.3 million. For this, Nathan would have earned in commission at least £86,000. From January 1815 to just before the Second Treaty of Paris was signed on 20 November 1815, he delivered bullion to the Mint and paid subsidies to the allies amounting to £7.7 million, nearly 90 percent of it from the time Napoleon returned to France in March. Nathan's commission would have been at least £154,000. Moreover, when Herries later reported to the Treasury that his account for the year 1815 showed an increase to nearly £9.8 million, Nathan's earnings most likely increased as well to about £196,000. During the first two months of 1816, Nathan added to his earnings because he delivered on behalf of Herries nearly £466,000 in specie to the East India Company. Thus, it would be fair to say that Nathan earned in commission from January 1814 through February 1816 between £250,000 and £290,000.[158]

Of course, this was only part of what Nathan earned during the two years because he continued to conduct business as a merchant banker on his own account, although there are no existing contemporary accounts current or other documents that would permit a calculation of those transactions. This is true as well for his brothers and for the firm of Mayer Amschel Rothschild & Sons. But the absence of those sources does not preclude a determination of the approximate worth of the Rothschilds because there are two contemporary sources that do contain relevant information.

As briefly mentioned earlier, on 21 March 1815, the five Rothschild brothers for the first time entered into a written partnership comprising Nathan's firm in London, the firm in Paris headed by Salomon and James, and Mayer Amschel Rothschild & Sons in Frankfurt. The *Articles of Agreement* spelled out the value of each brother's share of the capital and testified to Nathan's dominant position in the partnership: Amschel and Salomon each with £18,000; Carl and James each with £5,000; and Nathan with £90,000. Amschel, Salomon, Carl, and James each could draw £2,500 annually for expenses but no limit was placed on Nathan. Furthermore,

> . . . the remainder of the property employed in the said partnership after payment of the said capital belongs to the said parties herein in equal shares and proportions" and "as the greatest portion of the partnership property is in England and under the control of the said Nathan Mayer Rothschild he . . . has given to each of his brothers his promissory note . . . herewith for the sum of fifty thousand pounds payable on demand, but it is hereby expressly declared and agreed that such notes . . . are only to be against the said Nathan Mayer Rothschild so long as he has in his hands sufficient partnership property over and above his own share therein. [159]

The latter provision not only permits an estimate of the minimum value of the property owing to each of Nathan's brothers but it also suggests the magnitude of Nathan's share. His share had to be at least equal to what he had promised each of his brothers—£50,000—but more likely it was twice the total he promised to all of them—£200,000—because his share in the capital of the firm was approximately twice theirs. While this number is astonishing, it is not an exaggeration because Nathan had deposited £400,000 with the British government against James's transactions in Paris,[160] and Salomon had advised Nathan about his investment in omnium stocks, estimated at £450,000.[161]

These are good numbers and they compare favorably with those posted by the long-established London merchant-banking firm of Baring Brothers & Co. Baring's "accepting and other commission income" in 1814 and 1815 amounted to an annual average of about £53,000, that is, about two-thirds of what Nathan Rothschild derived from his 2 percent commission in 1814 and about one-third in 1815. Moreover, although Baring's capital had peaked in 1806 to about £450,000, in 1814 and 1815 it averaged about £348,000. Each year thereafter it increased, reaching a high of nearly £622,000 in 1821.[162] While the latter represented a considerable improvement in the fortunes of Baring Brothers & Co., it was, nevertheless, modest in comparison to what the Rothschilds achieved.

Rothschilds' numbers not only reached higher levels but also did so much earlier. On 2 June 1818, the brothers formed a new partnership of their "joint houses" of London, Paris, and Frankfurt and boasted a capital of £1,772,000 (see Table 6.1).

"Respecting the division of the profits and losses," the brothers further "agreed That as our Brother and partner Nathan Mayer Rothschild is possessed of the largest Capital in our aforesaid three joint Establishments We have ceded to him four eighths of all profits to be realized by our joint Mercantile Establishment in London" and one eighth each to Amschel, Carl, James, and Salomon. Nathan would also receive four sixteenths of the profits at the Frankfurt and Paris houses, while each of his brothers received three sixteenths.[163]

The predominance of Nathan and the London house in the new joint partnership was clear, understandable, and acceptable to each of the brothers. Nathan's achievement was far greater and much different from anything

TABLE 6.1

Capital of 1818 Joint Houses Partnership

N. M. Rothschild of London	= £ 742,000
Mayer Amschel Rothschild & Sons of Frankfurt	= £ 680,000
de Rothschild freres of Paris	= £ 350,000
	£1,772,000

Amschel	= £	324,000
Salomon	= £	324,000
Nathan	= £	500,000
Carl	= £	312,000
James	= £	312,000
	£1,772,000	

his father had accomplished. Mayer Amschel Rothschild had founded a successful merchant-banking house in Frankfurt and he had prepared his sons to succeed to his legacy. However, Nathan's business ability and the opportunities created by the war permitted him to create a formidable financial dynasty in London and on the Continent—in Frankfurt and Paris, and soon in Naples and Vienna. Nathan's success, of course, depended very much on the endeavor and cooperation of his brothers, as Mayer Davidson cogently reminded him:

> As long as a House like yours, as long as you are in unison with your brothers, then there is no House in the whole wide world which can imitate your achievement or cause you any harm or distress, because when your all together, you can undertake and accomplish more than any other House in the world. But if such a family were to split asunder, this will then change the situation entirely.[164]

Despite their internal bickering and disagreements, Nathan's brothers willingly followed his lead, as they had their father's. Where Nathan led them was to the top of the financial institutions in Europe.

Notes

1. NMR Lon. to JMR Ham. 7 April 1815, RAL xi/82/7/5/29.

2. SMR Paris to NMR Lon. 4 October 1815, RAL xi/109/3/1/9, Tape 175/Letter 8 & Tape 17.

3. Sherwig, pp. 324–326, passim.

4. H Lon. to NMR Lon. 4 & 6 October 1814, RAL xi/38/59B; H Lon. to GH Lon. 8 & 14 October 1814, PROT 1/1423/No.15436; JmD Lon. to NMR Lon. 10 October 1814, RAL xi/112/72; NMR Lon. to JMR Ams. 7, 25 & 28 October, 8 & 11 November 1814, RAL xi/82/7/4/40, 46, 48–50, respectively; MD Ams. to NMR Lon. 11 & 18 October 1814, RAL xi/112/72 & RAL xi/85/o; JMR Ams. to NMR Lon. 18 October & 1 November 1814, RAL xi/85/o; Coudere & Brants Ams. to NMR Lon. 31 October–1 November 1814, RAL xi/112/74A; & instructions to Captain Green of the HMS Daphne, 22 October 1814, RAL xi/112/2.

5. "Mr. N M Rothschild in Account Current with J M Rothschild for Dollars and Bills . . . to . . . Murray. . . . ," 10 October 1814–5 January 1815; "Particulars of Remittances made to . . . Murray . . . from Amsterdam [& Paris] by order of N M Rothschild Esq.," 18 October–22 December & 20 October–5 November 1814, respectively, RAL xi/38/59B; JMR Ams. to Murray Lis. 3 November & 23 December 1814, RAL xi/38/189A; H Lon. to NMR Lon. 4 November 1814, RAL xi/38/59A (RAL xi/38/52/30); JMR Ams. to NMR Lon. 4 November 1814 & 27 January 1815, RAL xi/85/o & RAL xi/82/7/5/11, respectively; SMR Ams. to NMR Lon. 28 October, 8–9

& 11 November 1814 & 17 January 1815, RAL xi/109/1, Tape 171/Letter 15 & Tape 172/Letter 9, RAL xi/87/oA, RAL xi/87/OB & RAL xi/109/1, Tape 172/Letter 7, respectively; & HC Hel. to JMR Ams. 18 November 1814, RAL xi/112/74A.

6. H Lon. to GH Lon. 17 November & 6 December 1814, PROT 1/1429/No.17744 & PROT 1/1433/No.18803 & 18807, respectively; WH Lon. to GH Lon. 25 November 1814, PROT 1/1430/No.18178; NMR Lon. to JMR Ams. 25 November 1814, RAL xi/82/7/4/54; & "No. 76. Account of Mr. S M Rothschild for bills Dollars & Doubloons purchased at Paris & forwarded to . . . Murray at Lisbon," 25 November 1814, RAL xi/38/59B, respectively. Herries purchased 100,000 Spanish dollars from Nathan Rothschild at ½ pence per ounce below the Bank of England rate. H Lon. to NMR Lon. 6 December 1814, RAL xi/38/59B.

7. H Lon. to NMR Lon. 14 & 28 December 1814, & 8 February 1815, RAL xi/38/59A (RAL xi/52/30) & RAL xi/38/59B, respectively; NMR Lon. to JMR Ams. 20, 23, 27 & 30 December 1814, 3, 17 & 27 January 1815, RAL xi/82/7/4/58–62 & RAL xi/87/7/5/1, 7 & 11, respectively; NMR Lon. to H Lon. 23 January 1815, *HP* BLAddMss. 57379, f. 8; JMR Ams. to NMR Lon. 23 December 1814, RAL xi/38/189A; HC Hel. to NMR Lon. 24 & 27 December & to JMR Ams. 31 December 1814, RAL xi 112/74A; SMR Ams. to NMR Lon. 20 & 23 December 1814, 3, 10, 13, 17, 20, 24 & 31 January 1815, RAL xi/87/oA & oB & RAL xi/109/1, Tape 173/Letter 7, respectively; "No. 77. Account of Mr. S M Rothschild for bills purchased at Paris & remitted to . . . Murray at Lisbon," 24 December 1814–2 January 1815; "Mr. N M Rothschild in Account . . . with J M Rothschild [with S M Rothschild] for remittances to . . . Murray at Lisbon," 20–30 January [& 1 February–19 March], 1815, RAL xi/38/59B, respectively; "Invoice of Seven Boxes Shiped by . . . Morel & fils.," RAL xi/38/59B; & JmD Lon. to NMR Lon. 24 February 1815, RAL xi/38/59B.

8. The final installment was due on 15 March 1815. Burg Ams. Nos. 155, 157 & 164, to GH Lon. 4, 7 & 25 October 1814, PROT 1/1423/Nos.15484 & 15625 & PROT 1/1425/No.16499, respectively; SMR Ams. to NMR Lon. 22 October 1814, RAL xi/87/oA; JmD Lon. to NMR Lon. 1 November 1814, RAL xi/112/72 & RAL xi/38/59B; & MAR Fft. to NMR Lon. 7 November 1814, No. 92. "Account of Messrs. M A Rothschild & Sons for payment on account of Prussian Subsidy," RAL xi/38/59B. Subsequently, Herries questioned the way in which the interest was paid. H Lon. to NMR Lon. 15 November 1814, RAL xi/38/59A & B; H Lon. to Atkinson Ber. 10 January 1815, RAL xi/38/59A; & NMR Lon. to JMR Ams. 15 November 1814 & 13 January 1815, RAL xi/82/7/4/51 & RAL xi/82/7/5/5, respectively.

9. The principal of 666,666 Prussian thalers and the interest (1 April 1814 to 15 January 1815, at six percent per annum) of 31,666 Prussian thalers amounted to 698,333 Prussian thalers. At the Treaty rate of three Spanish dollars for two Prussian thalers, this converted into 465,555½ Spanish dollars. See H Lon. to NMR Lon. 5 December 1814, RAL xi/38/59B; SMR Ams. to Hope & Co. Ams. 13 December 1814, RAL xi/38/59B, RAL xi/112/71 & GAA 735/204; & Hope & Co. Ams. to SMR Ams. 13 December 1814, GAA 735/1, pp. 616–617.

10. Lushington Lon. to H Lon. 19 October 1814, *HP* BLAddMss. 57374, f. 102; Burg Lon. to Hope & Co. Ams. 13 November 1814, GAA 735/139; H Lon. to NMR

Lon. 5 December 1814, RAL xi/38/59B; NMR Lon. to JMR Ams. 6 December 1814, RAL xi/82/7/4/57; SMR Ams. to NMR Lon. 13, 16 & 20 December 1814, RAL xi/109/1, Tape 173/Letters 5–7, respectively; SMR Ams. to Hope & Co. Ams. 13 December 1814, RAL xi/112/71 & GAA 735/204; Hope & Co. Ams. to SMR Ams. 13 December 1814, GAA 735/1, pp. 616–617; & Hope & Co. Ams. to Gervais Ams. 17 December 1814, GAA 735/1, p. 617. Herries shipped to Hellevoetsluis bullion and Spanish dollars (74,635 ounces of the latter, he purchased from Nathan Rothschild, who charged him a net rate of 5 shillings 7½ pence per ounce, that is, ½ pence per ounce below the price quoted on the London market). H Lon. to GH Lon. 29 December 1814, PROT 1/1437/No. 20012.

11. SMR Ams. to Hope & Co. Ams. 13 January 1815, GAA 735/202; SMR Ams. to NMR Lon. 13 January 1815, RAL xi/109/2–3, Tape 174/Letter 11; & see SMR Ams. to NMR Lon. 6 & 10 January 1815, RAL xi/109/2–3, Tape 174/Letters 9–10, respectively.

12. Hope & Co. Ams. to Har Lon. 30 December 1814, GAA 735/1, pp. 624–626.

13. SMR Ams. to NMR Lon. 13 January 1815, RAL xi/109/2–3, Tape 174/Letter 11. The Yiddish usage is "*rishus*," and is best translated as "*Jew-hatred.*" For this, my thanks to Dr. Rainer Liedtke.

14. Salomon Rothschild paid Hope & Co. through B. J. de Jongh & Sons in Amsterdam. SMR "Receipt" in GAA 735/202; Hope & Co. Ams. to SMR Ams. 16 January 1815, & to Har Lon. 17 January 1815, GAA 735/10, pp. 11 & 15–16, respectively; Guriev StP. No. 60, to Hope & Co. Ams. 20 January 1815, & No.175, 20 February 1815, GAA 735/202, respectively; & NMR Lon. to JMR Ams. 24 January 1815, RAL xi/82/7/5/9.

15. Sherwig, pp. 331–332; Buist, pp. 270–274; & "Memorandum of Subsidiary Engagements By a Convention Concluded at London May 19th 1815, Between His Majesty King of Netherlands and the Emperor of Russia . . . Intervention of Russian Loan by Hope & Co. Amsterdam," *HP* BLAddMss. 57372, ff. 49–53.

16. "Memorandum for the payment of any Sums to the extent of 4 or 500,000£ immediately wanted on the Continent," in H Lon. to V Lon. 8 February 1815, *HP* BLAddMss. 57394, ff. 73–74. Italics mine.

17. Dyer, p. 419; & Craig, p. 390.

18. *MPG & S: 1815–1816.*

19. See W Paris to HW n.p. 24 January 1815, W Vienna to B Lon. 5 February 1815 & W Vienna to C Lon. 12 March 1815, *WD* XII, 259–260 & 266, respectively.

20. See W Vienna to C Lon. 18 & 27 March 1815, *WD* XII, 271–274, 282–283 (copy of Treaty of Alliance signed by the Ministers of Austria, Prussia & Russia), respectively; Sherwig, pp. 334–338; & Thompson, pp. 88–90.

21. W Bru. to C Lon. 5 April 1815, *WD* XII, 287.

22. W Bru. to B Lon. 6 April 1815, *WD* XII, 291–292; & see Thompson, pp. 90–91.

23. "Articles of Partnership," 1815, RAL C/1 [0000089]. Additional important details of the partnership are addressed later in this chapter.

24. NMR Lon. to JMR Ham. 10 March 1815, RAL xi/82/7/5/18.

25. H Lon. to GH Lon. 17 March 1815, PROT 1/1455–1456/No. 4336; & "John Charles Herries Esq. in Account with Mr N M Rothschild for a Sum of French and

Dutch Money to the extent of £500,000 to be placed at the disposal of C G Dunmore at Brussels," *HP* BLAddMss. 57389, f. 6.

26. NMR Lon. to JMR Ham. 17 March 1815, RAL xi/82/7/5/20; & "Statement[s] of Sundry Bills on Lisbon [Oporto, Cadiz, Gibraltar, Seville; & Spain, Portugal & Gibraltar] procured by S M Rothschild Paris and forwarded to John Murray Esq. Lisbon. 19th March 1815," RAL xi/38/59A.

27. NMR Lon. to JMR Ham. 23 March 1815, RAL xi/82/7/5/21. On the arrival of 210,000 Spanish dollars, weighing 181,453 ounces, and 7 barrels of Silver from Hamburg, see NMR Lon. to H Lon. 14 April 1815, *HP* BLAddMss. 57379, f. 30, & Mint office, 17 April 1815, *HP* BLAddMss. 57394, f. 85.

28. NMR Lon. to CMR Ams. 23, 28 & 31 March & 4 April 1815 & to H Lon. 23 March 1815, RAL xi/82/7/5/22–24 & 26–27, respectively. Carl acknowledged receipt of the money sent to him by Nathan, in CMR Ams. to NMR Lon. 4 April 1815, RAL xi/84/0.

29. NMR Lon. to JMR Ham. 31 March 1815, RAL xi/82/7/5/25.

30. See "Given to Lord Liverpool & Mr. Vansittart, as a Memorandum relating to Subsidiary Arrangement—4 April 1815," & "Mem[orandum]," 21 April 1815, *HP* BLAddMss. 57397, ff. 18–20 & 22–23, respectively; & NMR Lon. to JMR 7 April 1815, RAL xi/82/7/5/29.

31. NMR Lon. to JMR Ham. & CMR Ams. 7 & 11 April 1815, RAL xi/82/7/5/ 29–33, respectively & passim.

32. NMR Lon. to JMR Ham. 11 April 1815, RAL xi/82/7/5/32; NMR Lon. to H Lon.14–15, 18 & 21 April 1815, *HP* BLAddMss. 57379, ff. 34, 36–39, 41, 43, & 45, respectively; & Goodbehere & Butt, RAL VII/10A/2, f. 5.

33. "Remitted Wm. Londigan & Co. (Cadiz) for the purchase of Bullion, by order and for account of J C Herries Esq. Commissary in Chief. London," NMR Lon. to H Lon.14 April 1815, *HP* BLAddMss. 57379, ff. 34, 36–38 (28 March, 5 & 12 April 1815); & RAL VII/10A/2, ff. 4,100.

34. "Remitted to Messrs. S. Phillips & Co. on account of the Bullion order for Rio Janeiro," 2–3 May 1815, *HP* BLAddMss. 57383, ff.67, 69 & 71, respectively; & RAL VII/10/A2, f. 61.

35. Nathan had already remitted £500,000 to Carl for Dunmore in Brussels. NMR Lon. to JMR Ham. 7 April 1815, RAL xi/82/7/5/31. See NMR Lon. to CMR Ams. 4 & 7 April 1815, RAL xi/82/7/5/28 & 30, respectively; "Account Sales of Gold received from M. C M Rothschild Amsterdam," 7 April 1815, RAL xi/38/59A; & NMR Lon. to H Lon.1 & 6 April 1815, *HP* BLAddMss. 57379, ff. 24 & 26, respectively.

36. "Statement of Bullion & Specie delivered to Depy Comy GL Anderson at the Mint on Account of J. C. Herries Esq. Commissary in Chief," in NMR Lon. to H Lon. 21 June 1816, *HP* BLAddMss. 57380, ff. 91–92.

37. For this, see C Lon. to W [Bru.] 3 April, Harrowby Bru. to C Lon. 7 April & Memorandum (A) & (B) by Lord Liverpool, Lon. 1 April 1815, *WSD* X, 17, 31–35, 35–37, respectively; L. Fife House to W Bru.14 April 1815, *Report*, pp. 345–346; & Thompson, p. 91.

38. V Lon. to Harrowby Bru. 7 April 1815, *VP* BLAddMss. 31,231, f. 256. Salomon Rothschild, who was in London at the time, journeyed to Brussels with gold for Commisary General Dunmore and the promise of an additional one million French francs. If Salomon did not actively participate in this meeting with Wellington, he certainly made himself available to report on how and when monies would reach his headquarters. See NMR Lon. to JMR Ham. 7 April 1815, RAL xi/82/7/5/31; SMR n.p. to NMR Lon. 9 April 1815, RAL xi/87/oB; CMR Ams. to NMR Lon. 11, 14 & 22 April 1815, RAL xi/84/o; For receipts of specie delivered to Dunmore, see NMR Lon. to CMR Ams. & SMR Antwerp & Bru. 18 & 28 April 1815, RAL xi/82/7/5/37, 39 & 45, respectively; & SMR Bru. to NMR Lon. 18, 23–24 April 1815, RAL xi/87/oB.

39. V Lon. to Harrowby [Bru.] 7 April 1815, *VP* BLAddMss. 31,231, f. 256. Italics mine.

40. Quoted in Dyer, p. 419.

41. H Lon. to the master of the Mint. Lon. 11 May 1815, *HP* BLAddMss. 57437 [Letter Book], f. 47.

42. Dyer, pp. 419–422, & G. P. Dyer, "L'Atelier Royal de Londres et la Frappe de Louis d'Or en 1815," *Revue numismatique* 6e série, XVIII (1976), 136–141, Pl. XIII.; Craig, p. 391; "Reports of the Weight and Fineness of French Monies of Gold and Silver, from Pieces of the date of 1815, procured from the Paris Mint, by The Rt Hon. W. Wellesley Pole Master of H. M.'s Mint, and tried, pursuant to his direction, by Robt. Bingley Esq. the King's Assay Master." "Gold. XX Franc Pieces. Impression of Louis XVIII," PRO Mint 1/18, "Royal Mint Record Book 1814–1815," pp.127–128 & "Regulations of the Weight & Fineness of XX Fr. Louis dors [*sic*], p.129; PRO Mint 9/77; & "Mint Office in Accot. with The Commissary in Chief for Gold," 7 April–6 November 1815, PRO Mint 9/78, pp. 131–132.

43. V Lon. to Charles Stuart Lon. 27 December 1815, *VP* BLAddMss. 31,231, ff. 441–443, passim.

44. V Lon. to Charles Stuart Lon. 27 December 1815, *VP* BLAddMss. 31,231, f. 442.

45. H Lon. to the deputy master of the Mint 21 February 1815, "Experiments made for the Commissary in Chief on French Silver Coins by Order of the Master." Royal Mint Record Book. 1814–1815. PRO Mint 1/18, pp. 95–97.

46. H Lon. to V Lon. 29 March 1815, *HP* BLAddMss. 57437 [Letter Book], f. 35.

47. H Lon. to Thomas Wyon, Jr. Royal Mint. 29 March 1815, *HP* BLAddMss. 57437 [Letter Book], f. 35. Italics mine.

48. H Lon. to Thomas Wyon, Jr., Royal Mint 5 May 1815, *HP* BLAddMss. 57437 [Letter Book], f. 47.

49. H Lon. to the master of the Mint Lon. 11 May 1815, *HP* BLAddMss. 57437 [Letter Book], f. 47.

50. NMR Lon. to JMR Ham. 7 April 1815, RAL xi/82/7/5/31.

51. NMR Lon. to JMR Ham. 11 April 1815, RAL xi/82/7/5/32. Italics mine. In a second letter that day, Nathan Rothschild stated: "I have had a long conference with Mr. Herries respecting the Bills still unpaid on Berlin, I made a proposition for

Gov't to redeem the whole by payments in Bullion viz F'dors L'dors." NMR Lon. to JMR Ham. 11 April 1815, RAL xi/82/7/5/33.

52. NMR Lon. to CMR Ams. 11 April 1815, RAL xi/82/7/5/34.

53. NMR Lon. to SMR Antwerp 18 April 1815, RAL xi/82/7/5/39. See also VII/10A/2, f. 128 (14 April & 5 May 1815).

54. NMR Lon. to CMR Ams. 25 April 1815, RAL xi/82/7/5/42. Italics mine. See also NMR Lon. to JMR Ham. 25 April 1815, RAL xi/82/7/5/43.

55. CMR Ams. to NMR Lon. 28 April 1815, RAL xi/84/0. Italics mine. By the beginning of May, Nathan had received from Salomon receipts for more than 12,500 Louis d'Or he had already sent him. NMR Lon. to SMR Bru. 28 April, & to CMR Ams. 5 May 1815, RAL xi/82/7/5/45 & 49, respectively. In a letter dated 9 June, just two days after the Mint officially made its first delivery of Louis d'Or to Herries, Nathan wrote Carl: "There is a great Quantity of Gold *gone from here last week* and this I believe—about £40/m in L'D'ors." NMR Lon. to CMR Ams. 9 June 1815, RAL xi/82/7/5/75. Italics mine.

56. Dyer, p. 420; Craig, p. 391; & William John Hocking, "Catalogue of the Coins, Tokens, Medals, Dies, and Seals in the Museum of the Royal Mint," *Dies, Medals and Seals* (London: His Majesty's Stationery Office, 1910), II, 139–140.

57. H Lon. to NMR Lon. 16 January & 12 February 1816, RAL xi/38/59C. James Rothschild also exchanged French Louis d'Or for English-minted Louis d'Or that were in Frankfurt. See JMR Paris to NMR Lon. 19 & 21 February 1816, RAL xi/109/2/1/35–36, Tape 244/Letter 12–13.

58. JmD Lon. to J. W. Morrison, Mint Office, 27 April 1815; J. W. Morrison, Mint Office, to JmD 3 May 1815, PRO Mint 1/18, pp. 122–123, respectively.

59. See H Lon. to George Best n.p. 27 March 1815, *HP* BLAddMss. 57437 [Letter Book], f. 33; H Lon. to W. W. Pole Mint Office, 4 April 1815, PRO Mint 1/18, p.114; H Lon. to NMR Lon. 2 May 1815, RAL xi/38/59A; "An Account of 93,573 Hanoverian Five Thaler Pieces delivered to Mr. Rothschild the 16 May 1815," RAL xi/38/60; NMR Lon. to CMR Ams. & JMR Ham. 11 April & 2, 5, 9, 12, 16 & 19 May 1815, RAL xi/82/7/5/34, 47–48, 50, 52–55 & 58, respectively; & NMR Lon. to H Lon. 14 April 1815, *HP* BLAddMss. 57379, ff. 34, 36–37 & 39.

60. "An Account of the Hanoverian Gold Monies Coined at His Majesty's Mint, and also of The Pieces deposited in the Pix, From the 15th September, 1813, to the 24th May, 1815, inclusive, During the Masterships of The Earl of Clancarty, and the Right Honourable W. Wellesley Pole," dated 25th October 1820, Mint Office, PRO Mint 13/164; "An Account of 84300 [&152985] Hanoverian Five Thaler Pieces delivered to Mr. M N Rothschild the 19 [& 29] May 1815," RAL xi/38/60, respectively.

61. NMR Lon. to H Lon 11 & 14 April 1815, *HP* BLAddMss. 57379, ff. 28, 30 & 32, respectively; "Invoice of Spanish Dollars purchased for Account of J C Herries Esq. Commissary-in-Chief," *HP* BLAddMss. 57383, ff. 71–72 & 82; Mint Office, 17 April 1815, *HP* BLAddMss. 57394, f. 85; & Spearman & NMR Lon. n. d. RAL xi/38/59A, respectively.

62. L Fife House to W Bru. 14 April 1815, *Report*, pp. 345–346.

63. "Mr Rothschild is to receive Money immediately for all Bullion delivered to him," signed J. C. Herries, 14 April 1815, *HP* BLAddMss. 57383, ff. 65–66.

64. NMR Lon. to CMR Ams. 14 April 1815, RAL xi/82/7/5/36. See also, CMR Ams. & SMR Bru. to NMR Lon. 18, 21, 23 & 25 April & 5 May 1815, RAL xi/84/0 & RAL xi/87/0B, respectively; NMR Lon. to CMR Ams. 2 May 1815, RAL xi/82/7/5/47; & JmD Lon. to NMR Lon. 2 May 1815, RAL xi/38/59A.

65. NMR Lon. to JMR Ham. 14 April 1815, RAL xi/82/7/5/35; & see NMR Lon. to CMR Ams. 14 & 21 April 1815, RAL xi/82/7/5/36 & RAL xi/84/0, respectively.

66. See NMR Lon. to JMR Ham. & CMR Ams. 2, 5, 9 & 12 May 1815, RAL xi/82/7/5/47–51 & 53, respectively; SMR Bru. to NMR Lon. 18, 23–24 April 1815, RAL xi/87/0B; & CMR Ams. to NMR Lon. 9, 12, 16, 19 & 23 May 1815, RAL xi/84/0. For deliveries made between October 1814 and March 1815, see RAL xi/38/59A & B, passim; & SMR Ams. to NMR Lon. 28 October 1814, 6, 10 & 13 January 1815, RAL xi/109/1, Tape 172/Letter 9 & RAL xi/109/2–3, Tape 174/Letters 9–11, respectively; & "Schedule of Sums paid into the Military Chest by Rothschild & Co. by Authority of Commissary General Dunmore and for Account of J. C. Herries Esq. Commissary in Chief etc etc." (dated 3 April–10 July 1815), RAL xi/38/61.

67. W Bru. to Clancarty Vienna, 3 May 1815, *WD* XII, 346.

68. C Paris to Treasury, 9 & 31 May 1815, *HP* BLAddMss. 57372, ff. 35, 37, 39, 41, respectively, & PROT 1/1465/No. 6897.

69. See H Lon. to NMR Lon. 16 May & 2 June 1815, *HP* BLAddMss.57438 [Letter Book], ff. 16–18 & RAL xi/38/59A, respectively; NMR Lon. to H Lon 11 June 1815, *HP* BLAddMss.57379, f. 53; NMR Lon. to JMR Ham. & CMR Ams.16 May & 2 June 1815, RAL xi/82/7/5/54–55, 70A & 79A respectively; & CMR Ams. to NMR Lon. 26 May 1815, RAL xi/84/0.

70. The rate was £30 per cavalryman and £11. 2s. per soldier for the year. "Memorandum of Subsidiary Engagements entered into by Gt. Britain with Foreign Powers subsequent to the 25th March last," dated 17 May 1815, *HP* BLAddMss. 57372, ff. 29–30, 33–34. See also "A Statement of payments made by J. C. Herries Esq. under the directions of the Lords Commissioners of His Majesty's Treasury in the Years 1815 and 1816 in discharge of Subsidies of Foreign Powers &c. included in separate Accounts for those Years rendered by him to the Auditors of Public Accounts," PRO AO 3/1088/2; *WSD* X, passim; & Sherwig, pp. 334–335.

71. "Statement of Bullion & Specie delivered to Depy Comy GL Anderson at the Mint on Account of J. C. Herries Esq. Commissary in Chief," in NMR Lon. to H Lon. 21 June 1816, *HP* BLAddMss. 57380, ff. 91–92. For details on the flow of money transacted by the Rothschilds, see "Mr N M Rothschild in Account Current with M A Rothschild & Sons for Payments of British Subsidy," RAL xi/38/59A; NMR Lon. to JMR Ham. & CMR Ams. 19, 23 & 26 May, 2, 6 & 9 June 1815, RAL xi/82/7/5/58–59, 61, 63, 65, 67, 69, 70A–72A, 73 & 75, respectively; H Lon. to NMR Lon. 20, 22 & 26 May 1815, *HP* BLAddMss. 57438 [Letter Book], ff. 21–22 & 24, respectively; H Lon. to NMR Lon. 22 & 25 May, 2–3 & 5 June 1815, RAL. xi/38/59A; & *HP* BLAddMss. 57416, ff. 23–25, 28 & 30 (22–23 & 26 May 1815).

72. H Lon. to GH Lon. 12 May 1815, PROT 1/1465/No.7051. NMR Lon. to JMR Ham. 2 & 13 June 1815, RAL xi/82/7/5/71 & 77, respectively; "Invoice[s] . . . Spanish Dollars," 6, 9 & 13 June 1815, *HP* BLAddMss. 57383, ff. 76–78, 80 & 82, respectively; & MD Ham. to NMR Lon. 7 July 1815, RAL xi/85/o.

73. See "Foreign Payments in the Way of Subsidy paid & to be paid in *the Year 1815*," "Given to Mr. Vansittart 7 June 1815," & "An Account of Sums required to Complete Certain Engagements entered into with *Foreign Powers* previous to the Year 1815," "Sent to Mr. Vansittart 16 June 1815," *HP* BLAddMss. ff. 28 & 29, respectively.

74. NMR Lon. to CMR Ams. 13 June 1815, RAL xi/82/7/78–78A & CMR Ams. to NMR Lon. 16 June 1815, RAL xi/84/o.

75. Muir, pp. 357–369, passim; & see Thompson, pp. 96–97.

76. Thompson, p. 97.

77. Muir, p. 364.

78. Ibid, p. 420.

79. I found Wolf's letter tucked within a Treasury paper in PROT 1/1453–1454/No.3519 (8 March 1815).

80. Ferguson, p. 96.

81. Ibid, p. 98.

82. Ferguson, p. 502, n. 133.

83. *RAL T3/41*, cited in Ferguson, p. 502, n. 133, comprises letters from the years 1812–1814, not the letter from *Van der Velde to Carl, June 19, 1815*. An extensive search of the RAL archival files by me and a RAL staff person could not find this letter anywhere. Furthermore, letters to and from Carl and Nathan Rothschild in June 1815 make no mention of this incident and/or this letter. For this, see RAL xi/84/o & RAL xi/82/7/5, respectively.

84. Ferguson, pp. 98–99.

85. Lord Rothschild discusses this matter at length in *The Shadow of a Great Man* (London: New Court, St. Swithins's Lane, 1982), pp. 35–39.

86. Ferguson, p. 96. For Ferguson's additional remarks about Waterloo and other related matters, see Ferguson, "The Fortunes of War," *Financial Times*, 24–25 October 1998.

87. Cf. Ferguson, "The Fortunes of War," *Financial Times*, 24–25 October 1998.

88. NMR Lon. to CMR Ams. 30 June 1815, RAL xi/82/7/5/88–88A. See CMR Ams. to NMR Lon. 4 July 1815, RAL xi/84/o.

89. NMR Lon. to CMR Ams. 4 August 1815, RAL xi/82/7/6/25. See NMR Lon. to CMR Ams. 1 August 1815, RAL xi/82/7/6/23–23A.

90. NMR Lon. to CMR Ams. 15 August 1815, RAL xi/82/7/6/30. In September, Carl Rothschild purchased East India, 3 percent Consols, South Sea, Thames Ship Insurance, and Russian stocks. CMR Ams. to NMR Lon. 13 September 1815, RAL xi/109/2/2/70, Tape 11.

91. Thompson, p. 97.

92. Thompson, pp. 97–103, and Muir, pp.365–369.

93. H Lon. to MAR Fft.& NMR Lon. 20 & 28–29 June 1815, RAL xi/38/59A; NMR Lon. to CMR Ams. & JMR Ham. 9, 20 & 23 June, 4 & 21 July & 1 August

1815, RAL xi/82/7/5/75, 81A, 84–85 & RAL xi/82/7/6/1,15–15A, 23–23A, respectively; CMR Ams. to NMR Lon.13 & 23 June & 8 August 1815, RAL xi/84/0; JmD Lon. to GH Lon. 15 June 1815, *HP* BLAddMss. 57372, ff. 43–48; & JmD Lon. to NMR Lon. 8 July 1815, RAL xi/38/59A.

94. H Lon. to GH Lon. 30 June & 2 July 1815, *HP* BLAddMss. 57438 [Letter Book], ff. 54–55 & *HP* BLAddMss. 47372, ff. 56–57, respectively; H Fft./Lon. to NMR Lon., Limburger Fft. & Atkinson Ams. 18 July & 4 August 1815, *HP* BLAdd-Mss. 57438 [Letter Book], ff. 56–59, 62–63 & 67 & RAL xi/38/59A, respectively; NMR Lon. to CMR Ams. 30 June 1815, RAL xi/82/7/5/88–88A; & "List of Bills on the Lord Commissioners of His Majesty's Treasury drawn by the Commissary in Chief," *HP* BLAddMss. 57395, ff. 61–64.

95. NMR Lon. to H Lon. 21 June 1816, *HP* BLAddMss. 57380, ff. 91–92; And. Lon. to H Lon. 15 & 18 August, 1 & 8 September 1815 & "Statement of Expences," 18 August–1 November 1815, RAL xi/38/59A; "An Account . . . Louis d'or delivered," 15 & 19 August & 1 September 1815, RAL xi/38/60; "Particular Service. The Commissary in Chief in account with the Mint Office for the Coinage of French Gold Monies," 1, 7 & 29 September & 1 November 1815, RAL xi/38/59A; & "An Account of Bullion & Specie purchased by order and for Account of J. C. Herries Esq. Commissary in Chief etc.," RAL xi/38/61.

96. NMR Lon. to CMR Ams. 7 July 1815, RAL xi/82/7/6/5; CMR Ams. to NMR Lon.14 July 1815, RAL xi/84/0; & "Account Sales of Gold [Guineas]," 26 July 1815, RAL xi/38/59A.

97. Hesseltine & Billingsley Harw. to NMR Lon. 6–7 & 15 July, 7 & 9 September 1815, RAL xi/112/21; NMR Lon. to CMR Ams. & JMR Ham. 4, 7, 12, 14, 18, 21, 25 & 28 July, 25, 29 & 30 August, 1, 5, 15, 19 & 22 September–22 December 1815, RAL xi/82/7/6/1, 5, 10–13, 15–15A, 18–19, 21, 34–38 & 40–66, respectively; "Military Chest Office," 12, 14, 17, 22, 24, 28–29 & 31 July, 2 August 2 & 16 September 1815, RAL xi/38/59A & 61, respectively; "Invoice [Doubloons]," 20 July 1815, "Invoice . . . Spanish Dollars," 2 August & "1815 Cash Charge against Mr. NMR," *HP* BLAddMss. 57383, ff. 87, 91 & 104, respectively; "Account . . . Silver Ingots," 28 July 1815, RAL xi/38/59A; "Invoice . . . gold," RAL xi/82/7/6/37; MD Ham. to NMR Lon. 7 & 28 July 1815, RAL xi/85/0; JmD Lon. to H Lon. 8 & 14 July, 2 & 12 September 1815, RAL xi/38/59A, & *HP* BLAddMss. 57375, ff. 165–167, respectively; NMR Lon. to H Lon. 3, 13, 15, 21, 26 & 28 July, 11–12, 19, 22 & 29 August, 22–23, 27 & 30 September, 7, 10–11 & 30 October 1815, *HP* BLAddMss. 57379, ff. 55, 57, 61, 63, 65, 69, 71, 73, 83, 95, 97, 103, 105, 107, 109, 113, 115, 119, 121, 123, & 129, respectively; Bülow Ber. to H Lon.1 July & 4 August 1815, *HP* BLAddMss. 57416, ff. 41–42 & 50–51, respectively; "N M Rothschild . . . Payments to Baron von Bülow," RAL xi/82/7/7/1–5; "Mr N M Rothschild in account current with M A Rothschild & Sons for purchase of coins forwarded to Amsterdam, & Antwerp & Brussels," 31 August 1815, RAL xi/38/59A; Spearman Lon. to Customs Lon. 2 September 1815, PROT 1/1489/No.13777; CMR Ams. to SMR & JMR Paris & NMR Lon. 11–13 September 1815, RAL xi/109/2/2/65–67, 71 & 78, Tapes 11–12, respectively; "An Account of Bullion & Specie purchased . . . for Account of J. C. Herries,"14 September 1815, RAL

xi/38/61; And. Lon. to H Lon. 29 September 1815, RAL xi/38/59A; SMR Paris to NMR Lon. 13 & 23 September 1815, RAL xi/109/2–3, Tape 174/Letter 17 & Tape175/Letter 4, respectively; *HP* BLAddMss. 57374, ff. 121, 123 & 125–126; H Lon. to Atkinson Ams. 6 & 20 October 1815, RAL xi/38/59A, & *HP* BLAddMss. 57438 [Letter Book], f. 110, respectively; H Lon. to NMR Lon. 6 & 10 October 1815, *HP* BLAddMss. 57438 [Letter Book], ff. 97 & 100–101, respectively; H Lon. to GH Lon. 10 October 1815, PROT 1/1495/No.15487; JmD Lon. to GH Lon. 12 October 1815, PROT 1/1495/No.15571; GH Lon. to H Lon. 13 October 1815, *HP* BLAddMss. 57372, ff. 76–77; & Moirer Lon. to GH Lon. 20 October 1815, PROT 1/1496/No.15962.

98. "Invoice of Spanish Dollars, purchased by order & Account of J. C. Herries Esq. Commissary in Chief . . . , delivered to Dept Comy Genl Anderson," *HP* BLAddMss. 57383, ff. 97–98; NMR Lon. to CMR Ams. 22 August 1815, RAL xi/82/7/6/33 & NMR Lon. to H Lon. 23–25 August & 6–14 September 1815, *HP* BLAddMss. 57379, ff. 75, 77, 79 & 85–93, respectively; & And. Lon. to H Lon. 15 September 1815, RAL xi/38/59A.

99. NMR Lon. to H Lon. 26 August 1815, *HP* BLAddMss. 57379, f. 81.

100. SMR Paris to NMR Lon. 10 September 1815, RAL xi/109/2–3, Tape 174/Letter16.

101. "Agreement Berlin 27 June 1815," *HP* BLAddMss. 57416, ff. 78–79, & JMR Ber. to MD n.p. 27 June 1815, RAL xi/109/2/2/46. The payment to the Prussian government would be in Dutch ducats, Friedrich d'Or, and in bills of exchange. See Bülow Ber. to H Lon.1 July & 4 August 1815, *HP* BLAddMss. 57416, ff. 41–42 & 50–51, respectively; "N M Rothschild in Account of Payments to Baron von Bülow at Berlin in the Month of June [et seq.]," RAL xi/82/7/7/1–5; JmD Lon. to NMR Lon.12 July 1815, RAL xi/38/59A; JmD Lon. to H Fft. 14 July 1815, *HP* BLAddMss. 57375, ff. 165–167; NMR Lon. to H Lon. 21 July, 11 & 22 August 1815, *HP* BLAddMss. 57379, ff. 59, 65, 71 & 73, respectively; & NMR Lon. to JMR Ham. 21 June 1815, RAL xi/82/7/5/83, NMR Lon. to H. Lon. 26 August 1815.

102. JMR Paris to NMR Lon. 25 September 1815, RAL xi/109/2/2/107. See also, SMR Paris to NMR Lon. 25 September 1815, RAL xi/109/2/2/109 & RAL xi/109/2–3, Tape 175/Letter 5.

103. SMR Paris to NMR Lon. 30 September 1815, RAL xi/109/2–3, Tape 175/Letter 6. See also NMR Lon. to H Lon. 7 October 1815, *HP* BLAddMss. 57379, f. 117.

104. "N. M. Rothschild for stay of proceeding against him by the Customs," PROT 1/1453–1454/No. 2138 (dated 8 & 11 February & 8 March 1815).

105. NMR Lon. to CMR Ams. & JMR Ham. 7 July 1815, RAL xi/82/7/6/5 & 6. In 1811, Julie Rothschild (1789/1790–1815) married Meyer Levin Beyfus (1790–1860).

106. NMR Lon. to JMR Ham., CMR Ams. & MD Ham. 11, 25 & 28 July, 1 & 8 August 1815, RAL xi/82/7/6/9, 18, 20 & 22, RAL xi/85/0, respectively.

107. SMR Ams. to NMR Lon. 6 January 1815, RAL xi/109/2/1/14, Tape 174/Letter 9 & Tape 244.

108. See SMR Paris to NMR Lon. 13 & 22 November 1815, RAL xi/109/2–3, Tape 176/Letters 4 & 5, respectively.

109. SMR Ams. to NMR Lon. 19 March [?] 1815, RAL xi/109/2/45, Tape 174/Letter 12 & Tape 8.

110. SMR Paris to NMR Lon. 16 December 1815, RAL xi/109/2–3, Tape 176/Letter 13.

111. SMR Ams. to NMR Lon. 10 January 1815, RAL xi/109/2/1/18, Tape 174/Letter 10.

112. NMR Lon. to CMR Ams. 28 July 1815, RAL xi/82/7/6/19.

113. Quoted with Dr. Jonker's permission from his email to me dated 26 March 2002.

114. NMR Lon. to CMR Ams. 8 September 1815, RAL xi/82/7/6/39. He must have written about this earlier but that letter has not survived. Atkinson's letter cannot be found.

115. JMR Paris to NMR Lon. 10 September 1815, RAL xi/109/2–3, Tape 87/Letter 8. My thanks to Dr. Rainer Liedtke for this translation.

116. SMR Paris to NMR Lon. 13 November 1815, RAL xi/109/2–3, Tape 176/Letter 4.

117. SMR Paris to NMR Lon. 10 September 1815, RAL xi/109/2/1/63, Tape 174/Letter 15 & Tape 10.

118. H Lon. to Atkinson Ams. 20 September 1815, *HP* BLAddMss. 57438 [Letter Book], f. 93. See also SMR Paris to NMR Lon. 13 September 1815, RAL xi/109/2–3, Tape 174/Letter 17.

119. CMR Ams. to SMR & JMR Paris 20 September, to MD & NMR Lon. 22/23 September 1815, RAL xi/109/2/2/95, 98 &103, respectively; & SMR Paris to NMR Lon. 4 October 1815, RAL xi/109/2–3, Tape 175/Letter 8.

120. CMR Ams. to SMR & JMR Paris 25 September 1815, RAL xi/109/2/2/108.

121. CMR Ams. to NMR Lon. 26 September 1815, RAL xi/109/2/2/112. See also NMR Lon. to H Lon. 17 October 1815, RAL xi/38/61.

122. SMR Paris to NMR Lon. 2 October 1815, RAL xi/109/3/1/3, Tape 175/Letter 7.

123. Mordichae Zucker, translator at the Rothschild Archive, and Dr. Rainer Liedtke have told me that Nathan's Judendeutsch letters are the most difficult of all the brothers to read and translate.

124. SMR Paris to NMR Lon. 4 October 1815, RAL xi/109/3/1/9, Tape 175/Letter 8 & Tape 17.

125. SMR Paris to NMR Lon. 9 October 1815, RAL xi/109/3/1/19, Tape 175/Letter 10 & Tape 18.

126. See SMR Paris to NMR Lon. 25 & 29 October & 6 November 1815, RAL xi/109/3/1/33 & 36, Tape 175/Letters 13 & 14 & Tape 176/Letter 2, respectively & Tapes 19 & 245.

127. SMR Paris to NMR Lon. 6 November 1815, RAL xi/109/3/1/42, Tape 176/Letter 2 & Tape 20. Receipts for the subsidy payments the Rothschilds made to various states in 1816, see *HP* BLAddMss 57380, passim.

128. SMR Paris to NMR Lon. 18 September 1815, RAL xi/109/2/1/85, Tape 175/Letter 1 & Tape 13.

129. JMR Paris to NMR Lon. 16 September 1815, RAL xi/109/2/2/81, Tape 12. See also SMR Paris to NMR Lon. 20 September 1815, RAL xi/109/2/2/1, Tape 175/Letters 1–2, respectively & Tape 14.

130. SMR Paris to NMR Lon. 22 September 1815, RAL xi/109/2/2/99. See also JMR Paris to NMR Lon. 25 September 1815, RAL xi/109/2/2/107; & SMR Paris to NMR Lon. 2 October 1815, RAL xi/109/2–3, Tape 175/Letter 7.

131. SMR Paris to NMR Lon. 6 November 1815, RAL xi/109/2–3, Tape 176/Letter 2. See also SMR Paris to NMR Lon. 4 November 1815, RAL xi/109/2–3, Tape 89.

132. JMR Paris to NMR Lon. 25 September 1815, RAL xi/109/2/2/107. See also, AMR Fft. to SMR & JMR Paris 26 September 1815, RAL xi/109/2/2/111.

133. SMR Paris to NMR Lon. 11 October 1815, RAL xi/109/2–3, Tape 175/Letter 11. See also SMR Paris to NMR Lon. 4, 7 & 9 October 1815, RAL xi/109/3/1/9, 14, 19, Tape 175/Letters 8–10, respectively & Tapes 17 & 18.

134. SMR Paris to NMR Lon. 23 October 1815, RAL xi/109/3/1/29, Tape 175/Letter 12 & Tape 19.

135. SMR Paris to NMR Lon. 13 November 1815, RAL xi/109/2–3, Tape 176/Letter 4. See also NMR Lon. to H Lon. 9 November 1815, *HP* BLAddMss. 57379, f. 142; & "N M Rothschild in Account of Payments to Baron von Bülow at Berlin in the Month of November," RAL xi/82/7/7/1–5.

136. See Muir, p. 372 and Thompson, p. 107.

137. At circa 24 French francs = £, this amounted to circa £29.2 million and circa £10.4 million, respectively. The principal allied powers would receive nearly 500 million French francs: Austria (113,822,140), Great Britain (125,000,000), Prussia (158,822,140), and Russia (100,000,000); and the remainder would be divided among Bavaria, Denmark, Pays Bas, Portugal, Sardina, Spain, Switzerland, the fortifications de Mayence & the construction of new fortresses on the Rhine. "Répartition des September Cent Million Que la France s'est engagée a payer aux Puissances Alliés comme Indemnité pecuniaire basée sur le hoter le en Suite de Traité de Paix 20 Novmbre 1815. [700,000,000 fr.]," *HP* BMAddMss. 57394, ff. 142–143. Austria, Great Britain, Prussia, and Russia each would supply 30,000 troops; and Bavaria, Denmark, Hanover, Saxony, and Württemberg would provide collectively 30,000 troops. "Partition of the 250 Millions Francs which is to be paid by France to the Allied Powers for the Maintenance of 150/M Men who are to occupy its Frontiers during Five Years also the Monthly proportion which each Power is to receive," *HP* BMAddMss. 57396, ff. 3–4.

138. Cf. Charles P. Kindlelberger, *A Financial History of Western Europe*, 2nd Ed. (New York: Oxford University Press, 1993), pp. 214–215.

139. JmD Paris to H & GH Lon. 4, 8 & 11 January 1816, *HP* BLAddMss. 57372, f.110 & BLAddMss. 57376, ff.1–3, 8–11, respectively; "Statement of Mandats remaining in the Military Chest the 11th January 1816," *HP* BLAddMss. 57395, ff. 4–5; "Statement of Mandates delivered to Mr. Rothschild, on 28 December·1815" [dated 10 January 1816], in *HP* BLAddMss.57376, ff. 18–19; "Copy of Treasury Minute 12

Jany 1816," *HP* BLAddMss. 57376, f. 99; H Lon. to JmD Paris 18 January 1816, *HP* BLAddMss. 57440 [Letter Book], ff. 35–36; & GH Lon. to H Lon. 19 January 1816, *HP* BLAddMss. 57372, f. 106.

140. See SMR Paris to NMR Lon. 16 December 1815, RAL xi/109/3/2/16, Tape 26 & Tape 176; JMR Paris to NMR Lon. 20 & 23 December 1815, RAL xi/109/3/2/24 & 29, Tapes 27 & 90, respectively; & JMR's postscript to SMR Paris to NMR Lon. 30 December 1815, RAL xi/109/3/2/43, Tape 29.

141. JmD Paris No. 6. to GH Lon. 8 January 1816, *HP* BLAddMss. 57372, f.113; GH Lon. to H Lon. 19 January 1816, *HP* BLAddMss. 57372, ff.108 &111; JmD Paris to TD Paris 27 January & to H Lon. 29 January 1816, *HP* BLAddMss. 57376, ff. 43 & 49–50, respectively; TD Paris to H Lon. 20 January & to [Rothschilds], Paris, 23 January 1816, *HP* BLAddMss. 57417, ff.1, 3 & 4, respectively; SMR Paris to NMR Lon. 30 December 1815 & 1 January 1816, RAL xi/109/9, Tape 176/Letter 15, RAL xi/109/4/4/1, Tape 177/Letter 1 & Tape 91; & JMR Paris to NMR Lon. 1, 4, 24, & 27 January 1816, RAL xi/109/4/1/1, 9, 42, 45 & 47, Tapes 91 & 92, respectively.

142. JMR Paris, to NMR Lon. 9 March 1816, RAL xi/109/4/2/42, Tape 93. For an example of Drummond's meticulousness, see his detailed discourse on specie conversion rates, JmD Lon. to GH Lon. 15 June 1815, *HP* BLAddMss. 57372, ff. 43–48.

143. H Lon. to NMR Lon. 18 & 30 January, *HP* BLAddMss. 57440, ff. 34–35 & RAL xi/38/59C, respectively; NMR Lon. to TD Paris 30 January 1816, RAL xi/38/59C; SMR & JMR Paris to NMR Lon. 1 & 4 January 1816, RAL xi/109/4/1/1, RAL xi/109/4/4/1, Tape 177/Letter 1 & Tape 91, respectively; JMR Paris to NMR Lon. 6–7, 10, 12, 14, 19, 21 February 1816, RAL xi/109/2/1/28–29, 31–33, 35–36, Tape 244/Letters 7–13, respectively & 2, 4, 6, 9 & 30 March 1816, RAL xi/109/4/2/31, 33, 36 & RAL xi/109/4/3/24, respectively.

144. JmD Paris to H Lon. 8 January 1816, *HP* BLAddMss. 57376, f. 6. Rothschild's share in the partnership was two-thirds. See SMR Paris to NMR Lon. 16 December 1815, RAL xi/109/2–3, Tape 176/Letter 13.

145. SMR & JMR Paris to NMR Lon. 1, 4 & 6 January 1816, RAL xi/109/4/1/1 & 12 & RAL xi/109/4/4/1, Tape 177/Letters 1 & 3 & Tape 91, respectively. See also JMR Paris to NMR Lon. 9 March 1816, RAL xi/109/4/2/42, Tape 93.

146. JmD Paris to H Lon. 13 January 1816, *HP* BLAddMss. 57376, f. 14. See also JMR Paris to NMR Lon. 29 November 1815, RAL xi/109/2–3, Tape 90.

147. SMR Paris to NMR Lon. 6 January 1816, RAL xi/109/4/1/11, Tape 177/Letter 2 & Tape 91. See JMR Paris to NMR Lon. 13, 16 & 21 March 1816, RAL xi/109/4/2/52 & 56 & RAL xi/109/4/3/4, Tape 93, respectively.

148. JMR Paris to NMR Lon. 23 March 1816, RAL xi/109/4/3/8, Tape 93. See also JMR Paris to NMR Lon. 28 March & 17 April 1816, RAL xi/109/4/3/21 & 52, Tapes 93 & 94, respectively & to CMR & AMR Fft. 9 May 1816, RAL xi/109/4/3/88, Tape 95. The Rothschilds expected additional commissions would be forthcoming to handle the indemnities for lesser German states. See SMR Paris to NMR Lon. 23 December 1815, RAL xi/109/2–3, Tape 176/Letter 14; CMR Fft. to JMR Paris & NMR Lon. 2 February 1816, RAL xi/109/4, Tape 132/Letter 12; & JMR Paris to NMR Lon. 6 April 1816, RAL xi/109/4/3/32, Tape 93.

149. JmD Paris, to H. Lon. 26 February 1816, *HP* BLAddMss. 57376, f. 36.

150. JMR Paris to NMR Lon. 9 March 1816, RAL xi/109/4/2/42, Tape 93.

151. At circa 24 French francs = £, this would amount to about £625,000 and £1.42 million, respectively. JmD Paris to JMR Paris 8 March 1816, "Agreement" between JmD & JMR Paris, 13 March 1816, RAL xi/38/59C & 60 & "Note," circa 13 March 1816, RAL xi/38/59C, respectively. See also TD Cambrai to H Lon. 19 April 1816, *HP* BLAddMss. 57417, f. 15; JmD Paris to GH Lon. 6 May 1816, *HP* BLAddMss 57372, ff. 133 & 135; GH Lon. to H Lon. 15–17 & 21 May 1816, *HP* BLAddMss 57372, ff. 127, 129, 131 & 136, respectively; & JMR Paris to NMR Lon. 2 & 9 March 1816, RAL xi/109/4/2/31 & 42, Tapes 92 & 93, respectively.

152. See JMR Paris to NMR Lon. 15–16, 18 & 22 April, 3 & 4 May 1816, RAL xi/109/4/3/44, 46, 53, 60 & 75, Tapes 94 & 95, respectively; & Orbell, p. 23. See also "French Reparation Loans: 1817–1818," The Baring Archive, ING-Baring Brothers & Co., 204228–204229.

153. NMR Lon. to H Lon. 22 February 1816 & "Statement of Sundry Treasury Bills discounted for Messrs. B J de Jonge [*sic*] on account of J C Herries Esq. Commissary-in-Chief London," 26 February 1816, *HP* BLAddMss. 57380, ff. 17 & 23, respectively.

154. H Lon. to NMR Lon. 20 & 22 February 1816, RAL xi/38/59C; H Lon. to et al. 24 October 1816, *HP* BLAddMss. 57417, f. 35; "Account of the Sale . . . of Exchequer bills by John Charles Herries Esq. part of £1,560,000 issued by him . . . to meet his bills on their Lordships from Francfort, [*sic*] Paris & Amsterdam," 26 February–22 October 1816, *HP* BLAddMss. 57399, ff. 27 et seq.; "An Account shewing the produce of certain Exchequer Bills for £1,560,000 imprested [*sic*] to the Commissary in Chief," 26 February–22 October 1816, *HP* BLAddMss. 57395, ff. 20 et seq.; "Account of bills on the Lords of the Treasury," 26 February–27 June 1816, *HP* BLAddMss. 57384, f. 3; GH Lon. to H Lon. 15 June 1816, *HP*. BLAddMss. 57372, ff. 150 & 152; NMR Lon. to H Lon. 5 & 14 March, 9–10 & 22 July 1816, *HP* BLAddMss. 57380, ff. 21, 26, 96, 99–101, 103–105, 107, 109, 121–122 et seq.; "J. C. Herries Esq., late Commissary in Chief in Account with N. M. Rothschild for Monies and Exchequer Bills rec'd from him in the Year 1816," *HP* BLAddMss. 57380, ff. 94–95, respectively; & JMR Paris to NMR Lon. 19, 21, 24 & 28 February 1816, RAL xi/109/2/1/35–37, 39, Tape 244/Letter 12–14, 16, respectively; & 3–4 & 8 May 1816, RAL xi/109/4/3/75 & 85, Tape 95, respectively.

155. GH Lon. to NMR Lon. 25 March 1816, RAL xi/38/59C. See JMR Paris to NMR Lon. 9 April 1816, RAL xi/109/3/36, Tape 94.

156. CMR Cassel to NMR Lon. to SMR & JMR Paris & to AMR Fft. 14, 20–23 & 28 December 1815, RAL xi/109/3/2/13, 23, 25–26, 30 & 37, Tapes 26–28, respectively, 10/11 & 14 January 1816, RAL xi/109/4, Tape 132/Letters 7–8, respectively; SMR Paris to NMR Lon. 4 & 16 December 1815 & 6 January 1816, RAL xi/109/2–3, Tape 176/Letters 10 & 13 & Tape 90 & RAL xi/109/4/1/12, Tape 177/Letter 3 & Tape 91, respectively; JMR Paris to NMR Lon. 17 January 1816, RAL xi/109/4/1/23; AMR Fft. to NMR Lon. 18 January 1816, RAL xi/109/4/1/30, Tape 205/Letter 4; & SMR

Fft. to NMR Lon. & JMR Paris 21 January & 2 February 1816, RAL xi/ 109/4/1/35 & 53, Tape 177/Letters 7 & 10 & Tape 245, respectively.

157. "Memorandum from Mr. Herries for Lord Liverpool & Mr. Vansittart 12 June 1816," *HP* BLAddMss. 57367, f. 23.

158. See "Statement of Cash received from J. C. Herries Esq. Commissary in Chief for Bullion delivered into the Mint and Subsidies paid by N. M. Rothschild," & "The Account of John Charles Herries Esq. with the Lords Commissioners of His Majesty's Treasury for the Sum of £9,789,778 . . . in his Account Current for the Year 1815 [etc]," *HP* BLAddMss. 57399, ff. 53–56, 69–71 & 91–92, respectively; "Statement of Cash received from J. C. Herries Esq Commissary in Chief, for Bullion delivered into the Mint and Subsidies paid by me," *HP* BLAddMss. 57383, ff. 108–110; "Cash charge against Mr Rothschild from 1815," *HP* BLAddMss. 57384, ff. 5–8; "John Charles Herries Esq. in Account Current with Mr. N M Rothschild for certain purchases of Specie and other Payments for the British Service in the Years 1815 & 1816 [*sic*]," *HP* BLAddMss. 57388; "Statement of Sums Paid to N. M. Rothschild by the Commissary in Chief," *HP* BLAddMss. 57390, ff. 2–7; & "General Statement of N M Rothschild Esq. Accounts for Foreign Transactions—1814, 1815, 1816," Nos.1 & 2, RAL xi/38/59C.

159. "Articles of Partnership," 1815, RAL C/1 [0000089].

160. See NMR Lon. to TD Paris 30 January 1816, RAL xi/38/59C.

161. See SMR Paris to NMR Lon. 23 & 29–30 October, 29 November, 5 & 16 December 1815, RAL xi/109/2–3, Tape 175/Letters 12, 14 & Tape 176/Letters 1, 9, 11 & 13, respectively.

162. I am indebted to Dr. John Orbell, archivist of The Baring Archive, ING Group NV, for the above-mentioned data. See also Orbell, pp. 22–23.

163. "Articles of Partnership," 1818, RAL C/1 [0000089].

164. MD Ams. to NMR Lon. 24 June 1814, RAL xi/109/0/2/11. My thanks to Mordichae Zucker for his translation of this letter.

By Way of a Conclusion

The story of Nathan Mayer Rothschild is a story of almost stunning success. Within one decade, he rose from the position of a failing commodities merchant in Manchester to become the creator of a financial dynasty, which for more than a century would hold the preeminent place in the international financial and commercial marketplace. In the view of David Kynaston, an authority on the history of the City of London, he became in the process "arguably the single most important figure in the entire history of the City of London."[1]

Nathan Rothschild achieved this eminence through a combination of personal force, ability, and fortuitous opportunity. When he moved to London, in 1808, the escalating market price of gold and silver caused by the Napoleonic War led him to believe that he could earn great sums of money by exporting foreign and English gold and silver, legally and illegally, from England to the Continent. Using funding from his father to make initial purchases, he employed experienced smuggler seamen to transport the cargoes across the Channel, and with his younger brother, James, organized a network of merchants, dealers, and bankers on the Continent to sell his specie and bullion.

To maximize his profits, he insisted that his clients sell his specie and bullion at the highest market price and use the proceeds to purchase bills of exchange on London at the lowest rate of exchange. He became, in Kynaston's words, "the consummate master" in the market of bills of exchange and foreign exchange, with a reputation as a tough and shrewd arbitrager.[2]

Nathan grossed millions of English pounds sterling from these transactions and, for as long as the war continued and the market price of gold and silver remained well above their Mint prices, he could have looked forward to a comfortable income. But the most significant opportunity for Nathan arose—and his importance in history became assured—when the desperate British government recognized that his skills and network were what it needed to supply large amounts of French specie to Wellington to pursue the war against Napoleon in France. He accomplished this commission by mobilizing his brothers and staff to fan out across Europe to purchase, collect, and deliver more than one million French coins to Wellington in the south of France. Given that Wellington had threatened not to pursue the war unless he received the money he demanded, it can be said that the efforts by the Rothschilds were as crucial to the defeat of Napoleon as any battle that was fought.

The relationship with the Rothschilds had a number of benefits for the British government. John Charles Herries, the commissary-in-chief, used Nathan to effect monetary transactions that the Bank of England either could not or would not undertake. Although Herries's authority reached into the Royal Mint, it was Nathan who collected and delivered the bullion to the Mint to strike the foreign gold coins which he and his brothers would later distribute to Wellington and to Great Britain's allies. During 1814–1816, millions of English pounds sterling passed through their hands, and the Rothschilds, in effect, functioned as Great Britain's unofficial bankers and paymasters.

But the relationship had equal benefits for the Rothschilds. Their success in carrying out that initial endeavor led Herries to award them additional commissions, the most important and remunerative of which was the payment of subsidies to Great Britain's allies for having fought against Napoleon. This assignment required the Rothschild brothers to reside temporarily in different money centers where they worked closely with merchant-bankers and financial representatives of European powers. It was this experience and the relationships that were created that formed the base for what would become the Rothschild financial dynasty, with houses in Paris, Naples, and Vienna as well as in London and Frankfurt. Of equal importance was the imprimatur of respectability that the patronage of the British government afforded the Rothschilds and the entrance it provided them to international financial circles and European officialdom. In this sense, Herries and the British government served as catalysts in the creation of the Rothschild financial dynasty.

When Herries departed from office and the British Commissariat was disbanded in October 1816, the Rothschilds lost their most powerful patron and confronted their greatest challenge. They had recently earned enormous income—greater it appears than any other merchant-bank—but that income had derived primarily from a multitude of arbitrage services during wartime on behalf of the Commissariat. With peace restored, the governments of Europe required other financial services which the Rothschilds had little or no experience in transacting.

Nathan Rothschild recognized that in the years to come he and his brothers would face strong competition from other banking houses, and that they would have to work even harder than before if they were to obtain a significant share of new business. They succeeded largely because Nathan's greatest strength was his commitment to his work.

Nathan may have provided the best insight into his nature in a letter he wrote to his brothers when he commented: "You can imagine that I have nothing to do after dinner, *since I do not read books or play cards or attend comedies and my sole entertainment is my business.*"[3]

That remark may have been written sarcastically but it speaks to the essential truth about the man. Nathan Mayer Rothschild was a man of business. That is the way he has to be seen to be understood.

Notes

1. David Kynaston, "The City of London in Nathan Rothschild's Time," *The Life and Times of N M Rothschild 1777–1836*, in Gray & Aspey, p. 42.

2. Ibid, p. 48.

3. NMR Lon. to AMR & his brothers 2 Jan 1816, RAL xi/109/4/1/5, Tape 263/Letter 13. Italics mine. My thanks to Dr. Rainer Liedke for this translation.

Bibliography

Archives

Great Britain

The Baring Archive, ING Group NV. London.
Northbrook Papers

The British Library Manuscript Collections. London.
Bathurst Papers. Loan 57.
Herries Papers
Liverpool Papers
Vansittart Papers

The Public Record Office at Kew.
Audit Office
Mint Papers
Treasury Papers

The Public Record Office, The Family Records Centre. London.
Will of Levy Barent Cohen

The Rothschild Archive, London.

University of Southampton Library, Southampton, UK. Archives and Manuscripts.
Wellington Papers

The Netherlands

Gemeentearchief, Amsterdam.
735. Hope & Co. Papers

Published Sources

Viscount Castlereagh. *Correspondence, Despatches, and Other Papers of Viscount Castlereagh, Second Marquess of Londonderry.* Edited by His Brother, Charles William Vane, Marquess of Londonderry. Third Series. Military and Diplomatic. London: John Murray, 1853. Vol. IX.

Earl Bathurst. *Report on the Manuscripts of Earl Bathurst, Preserved at Cirencester Park.* London: Historical Manuscripts Commission, 1923.

Buxton, Charles. Editor. *Memoirs of Sir Thomas Fowell Buxton, Baronet.* Philadelphia: Henry Longstreth, 1849.

Great Britain. *The Parliamentary Debates from the Year 1803 to the Present Time.* London: T. C. Hansard, 1814. Vol. XXVII (1813–1814). Great Britain. Parliament.

House of Commons. *Report together with Minutes of Evidence, and Accounts, from the Select Committee on the High Price of Gold Bullion.* Ordered, by The House of Commons, to be printed, 8 June 1810. Great Britain. Parliament.

House of Commons. *An ACCOUNT Of the Market Prices of Standard GOLD in Bars; Foreign (i. e., Portugal) GOLD in Coin; Standard SILVER in Bars; and Spanish DOLLARS; or Pillar Pieces of EIGHT: with The Courses of EXCHANGE with Hamburgh, Lisbon, and Paris:—From the 3d of January 1718, to the 3d of December 1736; and from the 3d of January 1746, to the 1st of March 1811 inclusive.* X, printed 30, penciled 227. Ordered, by The House of Commons, to be printed, 4 March 1811. Great Britain. Parliament.

House of Commons. *An ACCOUNT Of the MARKET PRICES of Standard GOLD in Bars, Portugal GOLD in Coin, Standard SILVER in Bars, and Spanish DOLLARS: with The Courses of Exchange with Hamburgh, Lisbon, and Paris; from the 1st of March 1811 to 1st of February 1813 inclusive.* XIII, 131–135. Ordered, by The House of Commons, to be printed, 6 April 1813. Great Britain. Parliament.

House of Commons. *An ACCOUNT of the MARKET PRICES of Standard GOLD in Bars, Portugal GOLD in Coin; Standard SILVER in Bars, and Spanish Dollars or Pillar Pieces-of-Eight:—with the COURSES of EXCHANGE with Hamburgh, Lisbon, and Paris:—From the 1st of February 1813, to the 1st of March 1814.* XII, 115–117. Ordered, by The House of Commons, to be printed, 5 April 1814. Great Britain. Parliament.

House of Commons. *An ACCOUNT of the MARKET PRICES of Standard GOLD in Bars, Portugal GOLD in Coin; Standard SILVER in Bars, and Spanish Dollars or Pillar Pieces-of-Eight; with the COURSES of EXCHANGE with Hamburgh, Lisbon, and Paris:—From the 1st of March 1814, to the 9th of February 1815.* X, 231–233. Ordered, by The House of Commons, to be Printed, 13 February 1815. Great Britain. Parliament.

House of Commons. *An ACCOUNT of the MARKET PRICES of Standard GOLD in Bars, Portugal GOLD in Coin; Standard SILVER in Bars, and Spanish Dollars or Pillar Pieces-of-Eight; with the COURSES of EXCHANGE with Hamburgh, Lisbon, and Paris:—From the 9th of February 1815 to the 26th of April 1816 inclusive.* XIII, 288. Ordered, by The House of Commons, to be Printed, 1 May 1816. Great Britain. Parliament.

House of Commons. *An ACCOUNT of the MARKET PRICES of Standard GOLD in Bars, Portugal GOLD in Coin; Standard SILVER in Bars, and Spanish Dollars or Pillar Pieces-of-Eight; with the COURSE of EXCHANGE with Hamburgh, Lisbon, and Paris:—From the 1st of January 1816 to the 1st of January 1817.* XVII, 71. Ordered, by The House of Commons, to be Printed, 25 February 1817. Great Britain. Parliament.

House of Commons. *An ACCOUNT of the MARKET PRICES of Standard GOLD in Bars, Portugal GOLD in Coin; Standard SILVER in Bars, and Spanish Dollars or Pillar Pieces-of-Eight; with the COURSE of EXCHANGE with Hamburgh, Lisbon, and Paris:—From the 1st of January 1817 to the 3rd of February 1818.* XIV, 30. Ordered, by The House of Commons, to be Printed, 13 February 1818.

Herries, Edward. Editor. *Memoir of The Public Life of the Right Hon. JOHN CHARLES HERRIES in the Reigns of George III, George IV, William IV, and Victoria.* 2 vols. London: John Murray, 1880.

Duke of Wellington. *The Dispatches of Field Marshal The Duke of Wellington, During His Various Campaigns in India, Denmark, Portugal, Spain, The Low Countries, and France, from 1799 to 1818.* Compiled from Official and Authentic Documents, by Lieut. Colonel Gurwood. London: John Murray, 1838. Vols. IX–XI.

Duke of Wellington. Wellington, 2nd. Duke of. Editor. *Supplementary Despatches, Correspondence, and Memoranda of Field Marshal Arthur, Duke of Wellington, K. G.* London: John Murray, 1858–1872. Vols. VII–VIII.

Secondary Works

Alexander, L. *Memoirs of the Life and Commercial Connections, Public and Private, of the late Benj. Goldsmid, Esq. of Reohampton.* London: Printed by and for the author. Entered at Stationers Hall, 1808.

Amburger, Erik. *Deutsche in Staat, Wirtschaft und Gesellschaft Russlands. Die Familie Amburger in St. Petersburg 1770–1920.* Wiesbaden: Otto Harrassowitz, 1986.

Anan'ich, Boris V. *Bankirskie doma v Rossii 1860–1914gg.* Leningrad: Nauka, 1991.

Anan'ich, Boris V., and Sergei K. Lebedev. "Russian Finance during the French Revolution and the Napoleonic Wars," in *Economic Effects of the French Revolutionary and Napoleonic Wars.* Edited by Erik Aerts and François Crouzet. Session B-1, Proceedings Tenth International Economic History Congress Leuven. August 1990. Leuven: Leuven University Press, 1990, pp. 38–47.

Aspey, Melanie. "Salomon's Archive," *The Rothschild Archive. Review of the Year April 2001–March 2002.* London: The Rothschild Archive, 2002, pp. 27–29.

Backhaus, Fritz. "The Jewish Ghetto in Frankfurt," in *The Life and Times of N M Rothschild 1777–1836.* Edited by Victor Gray and Melanie Aspey. London: N M Rothschild & Sons, 1998, pp. 22–33.

Buist, Marten G. "Russia's Entry on the Dutch Capital Market, 1770–1815," *Fifth International Conference of Economic History, Leningrad 1970.* Vols. IV–V. Edited by Herman Van der Wee, Vladimir A. Vinogradov, and Grigorii G. Kotovsky. The Hague: Mouton Publishers, 1970, pp. 151–164.

————. *At Spes Non Fracta. Hope & Co. 1770–1815. Merchant Bankers and Diplomats at Work.* The Hague: Bank Mees & Hope NV, 1974.

————. "The Sinews of War: The Role of Dutch Finance in European Politics (circa 1750–1815)," *Britain and the Netherlands*, vol. VI, *War and Society*, Papers delivered to the Sixth Anglo-Dutch Historical Conference. Edited by A. C. Duke and C. A. Tamse. The Hague: Martinus Nijhoff, 1977, pp. 124–140.

Challis, C. E. Editor. *A New History of The Royal Mint.* Cambridge: Cambridge University Press, 1992.

Chapman, S. D. "The Foundation of the English Rothschilds: N. M. Rothschild as a Textile Merchant 1799–1811," *Textile History.* Leeds: The Pasold Research Fund, Ltd., 1977. Vol. 8, pp. 99–115.

————. "The Establishment of the Rothschilds as Bankers," *Transactions. The Jewish Historical Society of England.* London, 1988. Vol. XXIX, pp. 177–193.

Clapham, John Harold. *The Bank of England.* Cambridge: Cambridge University Press, 1945. Vol. 1.

Cohen, Lord Justice. "Levi Barent Cohen and Some of His Descendants," *Transactions. The Jewish Historical Society of England.* London. XVI (1952) pp. 11–23.

Cope, S. R. "The Goldsmids and the Development of the London Money Market during the Napoleonic Wars," *Economica* IX: 33–36 (May 1942), 180–206.

Corti, Count Egon Caesar. *The Rise of the House of Rothschild.* Translated from the German by Brian and Beatrix Lunn. New York: Cosmopolitan Book Corporation, 1928.

Craig, Sir John. *The Mint. A History of the London Mint from A. D. 287 to 1948.* Cambridge: Cambridge University Press, 1953.

Crouzet, François. "Wars, Blockade, and Economic Change in Europe, 1792–1815," *The Journal of Economic History.* XXIV:4 (Dec. 1964), 567–88.

Cullen, Michael B. *The Cullen's Family Association with the de Rothschilds.* Copyrighted typescript. 1989. deposited in the Rothschild Archive: RAL T66.

Davis, Richard. *The English Rothschilds.* Chapel Hill: The University of North Carolina Press, 1983.

Dyer, G. P. "L'Atelier Royal de Londres et la Frappe de Louis d'Or en 1815," *Revue numismatique 6e série*, XVIII (1976), 136–141, Pl. XIII.

————. "The Royal Mint and the Striking of Louis d'Or, 1815," *Seaby. Coin & Medal Bulletin* (Dec. 1977), 419–422.

————. "Suspension and Restriction," 14 pages, unpublished. Great Britain, 2001.

————., and P. P. Gaspar. "Reform, The New Technology and Tower Hill, 1700–1966," in *A New History of The Royal Mint.* Edited by C. E. Challis. Cambridge: Cambridge University Press, 1992.

Emden, Paul H. "The Brothers Goldsmid and the Financing of the Napoleonic Wars," *Transactions. The Jewish Historical Society of England.* London, XIV (1940), 225–246.

Esdaile, Charles J. *The Duke of Wellington and the Command of the Spanish Army 1812–14.* New York: St. Martin's Press, 1990.

Ferguson, Niall. *The House of Rothschild. Money's Prophets 1798–1848*. New York: Viking Penguin, 1998.

―――. "The Fortunes of War," *Financial Times*, 24–25 October 1998.

Frey, Albert R. *Dictionary of Numismatic Names*. New York: Barnes & Noble, Inc., 1947.

Gash, Norman. Editor. *Wellington. Studies in the Military and Political Career of the First Duke of Wellington*. Manchester: Manchester University Press, 1990.

Gille, Bertrand. *Histoire de la Maison Rothschild*. Genève: Libraire Droz, 1965. Vol. I.

Gray, Denis. *Spencer Percival. The Evangelical Prime Minister 1762–1812*. Manchester: Manchester University Press, 1963.

Gray, Victor. "An Off-hand Man: The Character of Nathan Rothschild," in *The Life and Times of N M Rothschild 1777–1836*. Edited by Victor Gray and Melanie Aspey. London: N M Rothschild & Sons, 1998, pp. 14–21.

―――, and Melanie Aspey. Editors. *The Life and Times of N M Rothschild 1777–1836*. London: N M Rothschild & Sons, 1998.

Heckscher, Eli F. *The Continental System. An Economic Interpretation*. Oxford: Clarendon Press, 1922.

Helfand, William F. "James Morrison and His Pills: A Study of the Nineteenth Century Pharmaceutical Market," in *Transactions of the British Society for the History of Pharmacy*. I:3 (1974), pp. 101–135.

Hocking, William John. "Catalogue of the Coins, Tokens, Medals, Dies, and Seals in the Museum of the Royal Mint," *Dies, Medals and Seals*. London: His Majesty's Stationery Office, 1910, II, pp. 139–140.

Holtfrerich, Carl-Ludwig. *Frankfurt as a Financial Centre. From Medeival Trade Fair to European Banking Centre*. Munich: Verlag C. H. Beck, 1999.

Hughes, Robert. *Goya*. New York: Alfred A. Knopf, 2003.

Ingram, Edward. "Wellington and India," in *Wellington. Studies in the Military and Political Career of the First Duke of Wellington*. Edited by Norman Gash. Manchester: Manchester University Press, 1990, pp. 11–33.

Jonker, Joost. *Merchants, Bankers, Middlemen. The Amsterdam Money Market during the First Half of the 19th Century*. Amsterdam: NEHA, 1996.

―――, and Keetie Sluyterman. *At Home on the World Markets. Dutch International Trading Companies from the 16th Century until the Present*. The Hague: Sdu Uitgevers, 2000.

Kelly, E. M. *Spanish Dollars and Silver Tokens. An Account of the Issues of the Bank of England 1797–1816*. London: Spink & Son Ltd., 1976.

Kleeberg, John M. "The International Circulation of Spanish American Coinage and the Financing of the Napoleonic Wars," *XII. Internationaler Numismatischer Kongress Berlin 1997. Akten–Proceedings–Actes II*. Berlin: Herausgegeben von Bernd Kluge under Bernhard Weisser, 2000.

―――. "The Silver Dollar as an Element of International Trade: A Study in Failure," *Coinage of the Americas Conference at the American Numismatic Society, New York, Oct 30, 1993*. New York: The American Numismatic Society, 1995.

Kynaston, David. "The City of London in Nathan Rothschild's Time," in *The Life and Times of N M Rothschild 1777–1836*. Edited by Victor Gray and Melanie Aspey. London: N M Rothschild & Sons, 1998, pp. 42–49.

Landes, David S. "Research Is the Art of Encounter: The Sources of Business History," *The Rothschild Archive. Review of the Year April 1999–March 2000*. London: The Rothschild Archive Trust, pp. 7–12.

Lipman, Sonia, and V. D. Lipman. Editors. *The Century of Moses Montefiore*. Oxford: Oxford University Press for The Littman Library of Jewish Civilization in Association with the Jewish Historical Society of England, 1985.

Lowenstein, Steven. "The Shifting Boundary Between Eastern and Western Jewry," *Jewish Social Studies*. Bloomington: Indiana University Press. Vol. 4:1 (Fall, 1997), 60–78.

Michman, Jozeph. *The History of Dutch Jewry during the Emancipation Period 1787–1815*. Amsterdam: Amsterdam University Press, 1995.

Montefiore, Joshua. *A Commercial Dictionary: Containing the Present State of Mercantile Law, Practice, and Custom. Intended for the Use of the Cabinet, the Counting House, and the Library*. London: Printed by the Author, 1804.

Muir, Rory. *Britain and the Defeat of Napoleon, 1807–1815*. New Haven: Yale University Press, 1996.

Neal, Larry. *The Rise of Financial Capitalism. International Capital Markets in the Age of Reason*. Cambridge: Cambridge University Press, 1990.

———. "A Tale of Two Revolutions: International Capital Flows 1789–1819," *Bulletin of Economic Research* 43:1 (1991), 57–91.

Newman, Eric P., and Richard G. Doty. Editors. *Studies on Money in Early America*. New York: The American Numismatic Society, 1976.

Orbell, John. *Baring Brothers & Co., Limited. A History to 1939*. London: Baring Brothers & Co., Limited, 1985.

Rosten, Leo. *The Joys of Yiddish*. New York: McGraw-Hill Book Company, 1968.

Rothschild, Lord. *The Shadow of a Great Man*. London: New Court, St. Swithins's Lane, 1982.

Severn, John K. "The Wellesleys and Iberian Diplomacy, 1808–12," in *Wellington. Studies in the Military and Political Career of the First Duke of Wellington*. Edited by Norman Gash. Manchester: Manchester University Press, 1990, pp. 34–65.

Schilke, Oscar G., and Raphael E. Solomon. *America's Foreign Coins*. New York: The Coin and Currency Institute, Inc. Book Publishers, 1964.

Schroeder, Paul W. *The Transformation of European Politics 1763–1848*. Oxford: Clarendon Press, 1994.

Sherwig, John M. *Guineas and Gunpowder. British Foreign Aid in the Wars with France. 1793–1815*. Cambridge: Harvard University Press, 1969.

Solomon, Raphael E. "Foreign Specie Coins in the American Colonies," ch. 4 in *Studies on Money in Early America*. Edited by Eric P. Newman and Richard G. Doty. New York: The American Numismatic Society, 1976.

Thompson, Neville. *Earl Bathurst and the British Empire, 1762–1834*. Barnsley South Yorkshire: Leo Cooper, 1999.

————. "The Uses of Adversity," in *Wellington. Studies in the Military and Political Career of the First Duke of Wellington*. Edited by Norman Gash. Manchester: Manchester University Press, 1990, pp. 1–10.

Thomson, William. *Dictionary of Banking*. 6th ed. London: Pitman, 1926.

The Times. London. 14 Feb 1844, p. 8. col. d.

Ward, G. P. *Wellington's Headquarters. A Study of the Administrative Problems in the Peninsula 1813–1814*. Oxford: Oxford University Press, 1957.

Williams, Bill. "Nathan Rothschild in Manchester," in *The Life and Times of N M Rothschild 1777–1836*. Edited by Victor Gray and Melanie Aspey. London: N M Rothschild & Sons, 1998, pp. 34–41.

————. *The Making of Manchester Jewry, 1740–1875*. Manchester: Manchester University Press, 1976.

Wolf, Lucien. "(A) Early Business Letters of the Rothschilds," in Lucien Wolf, *Essays in Jewish History*. London: The Jewish Historical Society of England, 1934, pp. 261–268.

Yogev, Gedalia. *Diamonds and Coral. Anglo-Dutch Jews and Eighteenth-Century Trade*. Leicester: Leicester University Press, 1978.

Index